Inspiring Economics

Inspiring Economics

Human Motivation in Political Economy

Bruno S. Frey

Professor of Economics, University of Zurich, Switzerland

Edward Elgar
Cheltenham, UK • Northampton, MA, USA

Published by
Edward Elgar Publishing Limited
Glensanda House
Montpellier Parade
Cheltenham
Glos GL50 1UA
UK

Edward Elgar Publishing, Inc.
136 West Street
Suite 202
Northampton
Massachusetts 01060
USA

A catalogue record for this book
is available from the British Library

Library of Congress Cataloguing in Publication Data
Frey, Bruno S.
    Inspiring economics : human motivation in political economy / Bruno S. Frey.
    p. cm.
    Includes bibliographical references and index.
    ISBN 1-84064-205-X
    1. Economics–Psychological aspects. 2. Motivation (Psychology) 3. Human behavior–Economic aspects. 4. Economic man. 5. Economic policy. I. Title.

HB74.P8 F7 2001
330'.01–dc21
                                                                    00-069503
ISBN 1 84064205 X (cased)

Typeset by Manton Typesetters, Louth, Lincolnshire, UK.
Printed and bound in Great Britain by MPG Books Ltd, Bodmin, Cornwall.

Contents

v

Preface

Economics is inspiring – or rather, it *can* be inspiring. It is able to provide original and unexpected insights which differ from conventional views and general opinions. Economics is radical in the sense that many of its conclusions are not welcome in a streamlined world. It is also relevant and down to earth, as it squarely faces the trade-offs and conflicts rather than discussing them away. Its comparative approach makes it useful for politics: it suggests what can best be achieved from the feasible options.

This book wants to demonstrate that economics can fruitfully be applied to many different topics and questions.

Part I sets the stage. It discusses what I perceive to be the state of economics. While an inspiring economics exists, it is not the type of economics popular in many quarters of academic economics, and it certainly is not applied in graduate studies.

Part II introduces new insights from psychology into economics. Instead of economics imperializing other fields, I import findings from elsewhere. It is shown how behavioural anomalies initially detected in psychology can be dealt with in economics, without throwing reasonable (or rational) economic man overboard. The 'Crowding-Out Effect' discussed thereafter goes one step further. It identifies and empirically measures a relationship stating exactly the opposite of the relative price effect on which economics has so far been founded. The major consequence is that monetary rewards (often in the form of prices and wages) do not always bring about the desired behaviour. Thus, for example, pay for performance may result in poorer performance rather than better. Crowding theory therefore suggests the following, more balanced view: in general, pricing and regulating is less effective than is often claimed, and sometimes the best policy is not to intervene, but to leave it up to the persons concerned to find a solution on their own.

Part III integrates economics and politics. I argue for an improvement in democracy by involving the citizens directly via popular initiatives and referenda. This would be an innovation for many nations. It should be accompanied by a departure from the state being a territorial monopolist. Rather, FOCJ, or Functional, Overlapping, and Competing Jurisdictions are suggested. Finally, we turn to authoritarian nations and consider the way foreign aid affects politics and economics in developing countries. It is, moreover, empirically demonstrated how the aggressive warring acts of a particularly vile dictatorship, Nazi Germany, are reflected on the capital market.

This book covers many different topics, yet it has a common thread running through it. All of the chapters seek to embark on uncharted territory: they seek to illuminate a social issue; they focus on human behaviour, and especially on human motivation; and they are empirically oriented. Many of them provide econometric estimates.

The book conforms little to what today is considered 'economic science'. Many of my economics colleagues would argue that economics is the 'queen of the social sciences' for a quite different reason: because it is the most formal and rigorous of the social sciences. But this view comes at a price. Economics has not only become boring but also threatens to become irrelevant. Therefore I do not feel embarrassed about being unorthodox. In fact, I rather enjoy it!

Most chapters have been written in collaboration with co-workers. With one exception (Margit Osterloh, a colleague in business administration at my University), all of them are former or present scientific collaborators of my chair in economics at the University of Zurich. This reflects my understanding of what scientific research is. Joint work is not only fascinating, but it also invites younger scholars to reach the very frontiers of knowledge. Research centred around a chair thus provides a viable alternative to the less personal American type graduate education which, in my view, is too slavishly imitated today in Europe and elsewhere.

In the case of the co-workers included in this book, I am proud to say that in the short time since the underlying papers were originally written, they all have been appointed professors at reputable universities: Reiner Eichenberger is associate professor at the University of Fribourg, Felix Oberholzer-Gee is assistant professor at the Wharton School of the University of Pennsylvania, and Iris Bohnet is assistant professor at Harvard University. Marcel Kucher has just completed his doctorate and Alois Stutzer is presently working towards his doctorate. I am grateful to all of them for giving me permission to base the chapters on the jointly written papers.

To form a coherent whole, the underlying papers have been thoroughly revised. To improve readability, there are no footnotes and there are no references in the text (except for verbal citations). Explanatory notes on the references to the literature are given at the end of each chapter. The reader is informed about major contributions to the topic, as well as about the specific sources used in the text. Mostly, books are cited in order to provide a broader picture. The short comments are designed to help the reader to further pursue the topic without getting lost in the huge body of literature.

Special thanks are also due to Rosemary Brown for most carefully looking through the manuscript, for correcting mistakes and suggesting improvements, and to Reto Jegen and Stephan Meier for their great help in seeing the book through the press.

Bruno S. Frey
July 2000

Acknowledgements

Several chapters draw on material contained in, or are the thoroughly revised and updated versions of, articles published in various scientific journals, and are partly co-authored. I am grateful for permission to use this material.

Chapter 2 uses material contained in the article entitled 'From Economic Imperialism to Social Sciences Inspiration' and published in *Public Choice* **77** (1993): 95–105, used by permission of Kluwer Academic Publishers.

Chapter 3 is based on 'Economic Incentives Transform Psychological Anomalies' which was jointly written with Reiner Eichenberger and published in the *Journal of Economic Behavior and Organization* **23** (1994): 215–34, used by permission of Elsevier Science.

Chapter 4 draws on material which first appeared in an article written jointly with Reiner Eichenberger entitled 'Marriage Paradoxes', published in *Rationality & Society* **8** (1996): 187–206, used by permission of Sage Publications Ltd.

Chapter 5 is based on the paper 'From the Price to the Crowding Effect' originally published in the *Swiss Journal of Economics and Statistics* **133** (1997): 325–50, used by permission of Helbing Verlag.

Chapter 6 draws on an article jointly written with Felix Oberholzer-Gee and Reiner Eichenberger entitled 'The Old Lady Visits Your Backyard: A Tale of Morals and Markets' which appeared in the *Journal of Political Economy* **104** (1996): 1297–1313, used by permission of the University of Chicago Press.

Chapter 10 draws on material which was presented at the Third Kurt W. Rothschild Lecture at the Johannes Kepler University Linz.

Chapter 11 uses material contained in 'FOCJ: Competitive Governments for Europe' jointly written with Reiner Eichenberger and published in the *International Review of Law and Economics* **16** (1996): 315–27, used by permission of Elsevier Science.

Chapter 12 partly consists of 'The Political Economy of Stabilization Programmes in Developing Countries' written jointly with Reiner Eichenberger and originally published in the *European Journal of Political Economy*, **19** (1994): 169–90, used by permission of Elsevier Science.

PART I

On Economics

1. Inspiring, dismal or boring economics?

ECONOMICS TODAY

In the days of the classical economists, such as Malthus or Marx, economics was considered to be a dismal science. The future looked bleak; catastrophes, such as famines, or the destitution of the working class, were considered to be inevitable. Today, the situation is totally different. Economists are probably the most optimistic of all social scientists; they truly believe that the major problems of mankind can be solved by adequately using prices and markets.

The problem with economics today is that it has turned from a dismal science into a boring science. A long-time editor of the most prestigious professional journal in the field, the *American Economic Review,* has the following comment to make about his work:

> What was remarkable was the absolute dullness, the lack of any kind of new idea, that predominated in the selection of papers I got. Close to a thousand papers a year – and I swear that the profession would be better off if most of them hadn't been written, and certainly if most of them hadn't been published. (Clower, 1989, p. 27)

Present-day economics is concerned, to a considerable extent, with self-defined problems that few, if any, other persons are interested in. There is a well-known joke about economists, stating that: 'An economist is someone who cannot see something working in practice without asking whether it would work in theory'. This joke is only partly right. Unfortunately, most economists do *not* look at the real world at all. Rather, they live in a world of theory, which is their only reference. The analysis is characterized by a high degree of formalism and rigour. Relevance and originality matter little, if at all, mainly because these are considered to be non-scientific aspects escaping objective evaluation and measurement.

This sole emphasis on formalism and rigour distinguishes today's economics from earlier times. Especially, leading economists of the past studied their subject in order to better understand the ills they observed in the world, and to help overcome them. This motive was especially strong in the period of the great depression, with its huge number of unemployed. Today, some students

3

may still take up economics as their field because they are concerned about the state of the natural environment, and the possible responsibility of the economy. But once they experience today's economics education, particularly at leading graduate schools, most of them are utterly disappointed. And, unfortunately, they are not totally wrong. Indeed, a survey among American PhD students found that, according to their own judgement, only 3 per cent consider it to be important for success in their studies to have a thorough knowledge of the economy; but 57 per cent judged it necessary to have an excellent knowledge of mathematics, and 65 per cent to be good at solving formal problems.

Those students who stay in economics for graduate studies are arguably a specific selection of persons. They are mostly interested in formal structures, and are prepared to fulfil the demanding initiation rites in order to become 'competent' economists. Under the given conditions, for psychological and economic reasons, it makes no sense for them to raise questions about whether formalism and rigour are really so important for economics.

Those students who find out early enough that the current graduate education in economics is focused on formalism and rigour, but not on issues of content, either exit to practical professions, or enrol in business administration or some other field. As a result, the proportion of an age group studying economics is falling, and many economics departments run the risk of being closed down because of lack of students. Virtually all American graduate economics programmes, which are generally seen as leading the way, would have to close down if they relied only on American students. They survive solely because of the number of students coming from abroad.

HOW IMPORTANT IS ECONOMICS?

The evaluation of economics differs greatly, depending on whom one asks. Economists relish calling their field 'the queen of the social sciences', as it is the only one which successfully imitates the 'hard' natural sciences. It is true that many social scientists are impressed by the formalism of economics. At least some of them follow the logic of 'what is difficult to understand for the uninitiated, must be good and deep'. But many natural scientists, used to mathematical reasoning, are not so impressed, and would rather like to see what insights economics is able to come up with.

The course taken by orthodox economics in recent decades has contributed to severing the contact with other social sciences. An important reason for this is what many psychologists, political scientists, sociologists or lawyers consider to be an undue orientation towards formal structures instead of content. But another equally important reason is that they find the fundamental assumptions made in economics to be highly questionable, if not outlandish. Few are prepared to accept that people are purely selfish, that they constantly maximize their own utility, that they generally act rationally, or that they are able to predict the future using all the available information without systematic errors.

The policy relevance of contemporary economics is difficult to evaluate, as one cannot say how the development would have been without economic advice. Many economists, but even more impartial spectators, are convinced that the contribution of economics is substantial, though they hardly ever come up with convincing evidence. Others point out the declining importance of economists in policy advising, such as in the formation of NAFTA, and in the reform of the health system in the United States, or in the establishment of the Euro in the European Union. With respect to persons, few would deny the great importance on policy making of such extraordinary persons as John Maynard Keynes, or of Ludwig Erhard, who managed to introduce the social market economy in post-war Germany (against the will of the American occupation authority). But others may point out that even famous economists have been ineffective in economic policy, or have pressed for action that is considered disastrous from today's point of view. Pertinent examples are Arthur Lewis, James Meade or Maurice Allais – all later recipients of Nobel Prizes in economics – who, after World War II, pressed for the introduction of comprehensive state planning of economic activities.

It seems that an important part of economics devoted to real life issues has shifted away from academic economics. Much problem-oriented research is now being undertaken by profit-oriented consultancies, non-profit think tanks and also concerned individual writers. The latter sometimes are able to produce bestsellers, indicating that there is a demand for thinking about practical policy issues.

AN ALTERNATIVE: INSPIRING ECONOMICS

This book carries the title 'Inspiring Economics', because I am convinced that economics is able to contribute a great deal to analysing the real world, and to making relevant and novel suggestions for improvement. I believe that the economic way of thinking and analysing is extremely fruitful when dealing with the problems our societies are faced with. I even think that the economic approach to social problems may serve as a model for other social sciences.

Economics is:

- able to cover a broad set of issues ranging from the purely material to the artistic;

- adaptable to many circumstances; thus it enables the successful analysis of market as well as of more primitive barter economies;
- clear and internally consistent by providing a mode of analysis based on a few basic principles;
- realistic because it chooses the best feasible alternatives instead of comparing with an unreachable ideal; and
- empirically oriented, that is it comes up with propositions which withstand the test of reality.

The economics just sketched differs from the main current of economics as taught today at leading graduate schools. It is problem- and not model-driven. The problems addressed are not defined within the self-constructed theoretical world, but are informed by the world we live in. When it comes to the presumed trade-off between relevance and rigour, I diverge from many of my fellow economists. I am prepared to sacrifice some rigour for increased relevance, rather than the other way round. To state it in an extreme way: rigour often comes only after real insights have been gained; it is a sort of mop-up activity that may be useful for textbooks.

A second major difference from the main current of economics is my notion that a careful and reasoned application of the basic principles of economics yields a lot of, if not most, insights. The use of more advanced and complicated theoretical models may help us to better understand the world, but often the additional knowledge gained is small, if it exists at all. I thus believe that theoretical modelling is subject to strongly decreasing marginal returns. Sometimes, theoretical models even reduce insights, because they almost necessarily enforce tunnel vision.

DIRECTION OF THE BOOK

The following chapters seek to convey the flavour of what I consider to be 'Inspiring Economics'. They do not conform to the now established standards in economics – if they did, I would have had to formulate my first formal model by now! An economist embedded in orthodox economics – and for obvious career reasons these are often the younger ones – who by accident stumbles across this book and miraculously reads on to this point, will certainly lament the absence of rigour, and will probably classify it as sociology (which, in today's economic parlance, is about the worst thing one could say). Again, most often for career reasons, he or she will not be the least influenced by the arguments presented here.

Despite my rather fierce criticism of much of current economics, I am convinced that economics is still open. If one really tries hard to deviate from orthodoxy, this is possible without having to give up all hope of an academic career. Persons with new ideas are welcome – though only after some time. Scholars like Albert Hirschman, Gary Becker, Mancur Olson, James Buchanan, Gordon Tullock, Amartya Sen, or more recently Robert Frank and Timur Kuran, are examples among economists, and Elinor Ostrom and Richard Posner among other social scientists. Young academic economists, who are strong enough, may engage in this endeavour – provided they can escape the tunnel vision of orthodoxy.

Economics is a great science, full of fascination and relevance, and well able to link up with the other social sciences. The fact that much of economics today does not conform to this picture provides a challenge.

SUGGESTIONS ON THE LITERATURE AND SOURCES

The citation of the former editor of the *American Economic Review* is in
Clower, Robert W. (1989), 'The State of Economics: Hopeless But Not Serious?' in David Colander and A.W. Coats (eds), *The Spread of Economic Ideas*, Cambridge: Cambridge University Press.

An outstanding representative of the optimistic view of today's economics is
Simon, Julian L. (1998), *The Ultimate Resource*, 2nd edn. Princeton: Princeton University Press.

The emphasis on rigour rather than relevance has been castigated by
Mayer, Thomas (1993), *Truth versus Precision in Economics*, Aldershot, UK and Brookfield, US: Edward Elgar.
Blaug, Mark (1980), *The Methodology of Economics. Or How Economists Explain*, Cambridge: Cambridge University Press.

The survey of the evaluations on their graduate training by American graduate students in economics is due to
Colander, David and Arjo Klamer (1987), 'The Making of an Economist', *Journal of Economic Perspectives*, **1** (2), 95–111.

A respective study for graduate students in Europe (the Netherlands) is
Van Dalen, Harry J. and Arjo Klamer (1997), 'Blood is Thicker than Water: Economists and the Tinbergen Legacy', in Peter A.G. van Bergeijk et al. (eds), *Economic Science and Practice: The Roles of Academic Economists and Policy-makers*, Cheltenham, UK and Lyme, US: Edward Elgar, pp. 60–91.

The thesis on the unimportance of economists for practical policy is documented by
Reder, Melvin (1999), *Economics. The Culture of a Controversial Science*, Chicago and London: University of Chicago Press.

Cassidy, John (1996), 'The Decline of Economics', *New Yorker* (2 December), 50–60.

An attempt to collect theoretical approaches and statistical results on the policy influence of economists is made in
Frey, Bruno S. (2000), 'Was bewirkt die Volkswirtschaftslehre?' *Perspektiven der Wirtschaftspolitik*, **1** (1), 5–33.

A recent case for a concerned outsider writing a bestseller on an economic issue is
Forrester, Viviane (1997), *L'horreur économique*, Paris: Fayard.

A few references for books written by scholars whom I consider good examples for the openness and creativity of economics are
Hirschman, Albert O. (1970), *Exit, Voice and Loyalty*, Cambridge, MA: Harvard University Press.
Hirschman, Albert O. (1982a), *Shifting Involvements. Private Interests and Public Action*, Oxford: Martin Robertson.
Hirschman, Albert O. (1982b), 'Rival Interpretations of Market Society: Civilizing, Destructive, or Feeble?', *Journal of Economic Literature*, **20** (Dec.), 1463–84.
Becker, Gary S. (1971), *The Economics of Discrimination*, Chicago: Chicago University Press.
Becker, Gary S. (1981), *A Treatise on the Family*, Cambridge, MA: Harvard University Press.
Becker, Gary S. (1996), *Accounting for Tastes*, Cambridge, MA and London: Harvard University Press.
Olson, Mancur (1965), *The Logic of Collective Action*, Cambridge, MA: Harvard University Press.
Olson, Mancur (1982), *The Rise and Decline of Nations: Economic Growth, Stagflation, and Social Rigidities*, New Haven: Yale University Press.
Buchanan, James M. and Gordon Tullock (1962), *The Calculus of Consent. Logical Foundations of Constitutional Democracy*, Ann Arbor: University of Michigan Press.
Buchanan, James M., Robert N. Tollison and Gordon Tullock (eds) (1980), *Towards a Theory of the Rent-seeking Society*, College Station, Texas: Texas A&M University Press.
Tullock, Gordon (1965), *The Politics of Bureaucracy*, Washington DC: Public Affairs Press.
Tullock, Gordon (1994a), *New World of Economics: Explorations into the Human Experience*, New York: McGraw-Hill.
Tullock, Gordon (1994b), *On the Trail of Homo Economicus: Essays by Gordon Tullock*, Fairfax, VA: George Mason University Press.
Sen, Amartya K. (1970), *Collective Choice and Social Welfare*, republished (1979), Amsterdam: North Holland.
Sen, Amartya K. (1987), *On Ethics and Economics*, Oxford: Blackwell.
Frank, Robert H. (1985), *Choosing the Right Pond*, New York: Oxford University Press.

Frank, Robert H. (1999), *Luxury Fever. Why Money Fails to Satisfy in an Era of Excess*, New York: Free Press.

Frank, Robert H. and Philip J. Cook (1995), *The Winner-Take-All Society*, New York: Free Press.

Kuran, Timur (1995), *Private Truth, Public Lies: The Social Consequences of Preference Falsification*, Cambridge, MA: Harvard University Press.

Ostrom, Elinor (1990), *Governing the Commons: The Evolution of Institutions for Collective Action*, Cambridge: Cambridge University Press.

Posner, Richard A. (1988), *Law and Literature: A Misunderstood Relation*, Cambridge, MA: Harvard University Press.

Posner, Richard A. (1994), *Sex and Reason*, Cambridge, MA: Harvard University Press.

2. From economic imperialism to social science inspiration

ECONOMIC IMPERIALISM

It has become generally accepted within the economics profession to apply economic reasoning beyond the area of the economy. Such applications – known as Rational Choice Analysis – have, for instance, been made to education, health, the natural environment, the family, military conflict, ethics, history, sports, religion and the arts. At the same time, the rational choice analysis, on which economics is based, has been exported to several other disciplines, such as political science, international relations, sociology and law. In particular, the invasion of the rational choice paradigm into political science, called Public Choice, has proved to be a major success.

However, there are first signs that the easy gains in insights achieved when a paradigm is applied to a new area are diminishing. Economics, and in particular Public Choice, is no longer as exciting as it used to be. Normality in the form of orthodox neo-classical economics has taken over. Progress tends to be marginal; the subject becomes more and more standardized. Many contributions are rather mechanistic, while originality and innovation threaten to disappear altogether. Today, people fancy other areas, such as evolutionary or chaos theory, but it is, of course, an open question whether these new trends will ever reach a degree of popularity comparable to rational choice.

This rather sober evaluation of the present state of economics does not imply that there are no fascinating areas and topics in the field. Over the last few years, relevant new insights have been gained even in traditional subjects.

An example is the well-known problem of political organization, when the persons involved have an incentive to free ride. Based on theoretical and empirical research, we now know many of the conditions under which free riding can be overcome. Thus the normally proposed government intervention, or the assignment of private property rights, are not the only possible ways of solving the problem of overusing the commons. That situation is characterized by an access to a good, which is in principle open, but where there is rivalry in consumption. In many situations, voluntary self-organization has proved to be a good way of effectively administrating the commons.

Several new areas also provide interesting challenges. Up to now, a large part of political economy has been concerned with democratic politics. Non-democratic governments, which make up the largest number of all nations, have rarely been studied. Authoritarian governments will be the subject of the last part of this book.

As far as policy recommendations are concerned, economics still follows the traditional welfare view: a social welfare function is maximized, subject to the appropriate resource constraints. In public economics, for instance, this is the procedure followed by the Theory of Optimal Taxation and Optimal Public Pricing. On a macroeconomic level, the same approach has been used, for instance, to argue for the 'harmonizing', that is the equalizing, of taxes in the European Community. It seems that the fundamental message of constitutional economics applied to policy making has been totally neglected in many quarters of economics. A survey of professional economists undertaken some years ago revealed a surprisingly large share who agreed with the proposition that 'politicians endeavour to pursue an economic policy maximizing social welfare'. In the Federal Republic of Germany, 52 per cent of the respondents 'generally agreed' or 'agreed with provisions' to this statement, in Austria it was 50 per cent, and in Switzerland 49 per cent agreed.

Little is known about the impact of economics on practical politics. As was pointed out in the first chapter, the scarce evidence that exists seems to suggest that it is small. Almost no studies exist that seriously analyse the possible impact of economics on economic policy, and on society as a whole.

THE FUTURE: SOCIAL SCIENCE INSPIRATIONS

The diminishing marginal returns of the 'imperialist programme' of economics applied to many areas, as well as the limited impact on policy making, suggest that the time has come for a change in direction: in future, the main emphasis should not lie in exporting economics, but rather in *importing* aspects and insights from other academic fields. This book focuses on ideas from the social sciences which may improve economics. Inspiration from social (and literary) sciences is perfectly compatible with the basis of modern economics, which has proved to be so useful. Indeed, the economic model of human behaviour, properly understood, lends itself well to the integration of so far neglected aspects of people's actions. What is needed, however, is an effort to overcome the model of the 'homunculus oeconomicus', who is at all times in full control of his or her emotions, who does not know any cognitive limitations, who is not embedded in a personal network, who is but extrinsically motivated and whose preferences are not influenced by discussion processes.

There is already a considerable body of literature pointing the way in which this future development may go, and there are a great number of ideas from various social sciences which have been fruitfully introduced into economics. In order to illustrate how economics in general, and rational choice in particular, can profit from such 'social sciences inspirations', two areas are discussed here in which experimental cognitive social psychology has proved to enlighten economics: behavioural anomalies and human motivation. A third area borrows from sociology and philosophy, emphasizing the role of verbal discourse and personal relationships for human interaction.

Behavioural Anomalies

Experiments by psychologists, as well as by economists, have by now revealed overwhelming evidence that human beings do not act rationally in the sense of following the so-called von Neumann/Morgenstern axioms. These axioms state purely formal requirements on rationality, which define logically consistent behaviour. Individuals systematically deviate from expected utility maximization, which in rational choice analysis, and therewith in economics, is the generally used model to describe how persons decide on their future actions. Such *anomalies* of individual behaviour have been identified in real life, and even in a market which almost completely corresponds to perfect competition; that is, the stock exchange.

The reaction of economists to these empirical findings overwhelmingly has been to expand the classical subjective expected utility model, or to formulate a more general non-expected utility model of preferences. Maximizing these utility functions yields behavioural aspects which are consistent with the empirical observations; the former 'anomalies' therefore become integrated into formal theory.

Efforts at re-establishing logical consistency have been only partially successful. While many of the behavioural anomalies, such as certainty effect, preference reversals or probability biases, can be integrated into a more generalized utility theory, there are other anomalies, in particular framing effects, which have proved evasive.

It may, nevertheless, be argued that economists' efforts at integrating behavioural anomalies into the existing narrow notion of individual rationality are ill conceived. Individuals are in fact more rational than orthodox theory thinks them to be, in two respects:

1. Due to their cognitive limitations, individuals are not able to act consistently all the time and under all circumstances. But it is one of the defining characteristics of human beings that they are able to recognize their weaknesses and to overcome them (at least partly). A much-dis-

cussed way of circumventing anomalies, or reducing the cost incurred when falling prey to them, is to establish rules of self-commitment. Probably more importantly, individuals resort to social institutions in order to get help when struggling with their weaknesses. For example, individuals who know that they are unable to resist the temptation of consuming more and faster than they wish, have an incentive to support political actions forcing them to care more for their future, for example by introducing an obligatory old age pension scheme run by the state. This avenue of dealing with behavioural anomalies will be explored further in the following chapter.

2. Under some circumstances, individuals do not desire to act rationally in a narrow sense. Among close friends, but especially within the family, humans deviate from axioms of logical consistency on purpose, in order to acknowledge a particular relationship. A large share of the fine arts (literature and drama) deals with this kind of behaviour, the most prominent case being 'l'amour fou' or infatuation, where a lover rationally chooses to act irrationally in order to express his or her emotions and feelings. The reverse emotion of intense hatred, irrespective of the cost, has also been the subject of many novels and plays, a famous example being Heinrich von Kleist's *Michael Kohlhaas*. Maybe economists are not exactly the kind of people who experience this sort of sensation, but they should at least be prepared to acknowledge that it exists.

As in the case of cognitive limits to consistent behaviour, this does not mean that the rational choice approach has to be relinquished. Rather, we should look at rationality with a broader mind. Individuals are super-rational in the sense that, in general, they are able to guard themselves against self-destructive infatuation and hatred by resorting to appropriate rules and institutions. Thus, for example, in most countries of the world, political action has led to laws forcing individuals to let a certain period of time pass before getting married.

Analysing behavioural anomalies by accepting that human beings are either not able or not willing to act consistently – rationally in the orthodox sense – differs fundamentally from accounting for the same empirical observations by generalizing individuals' utility functions. The latter 'integrating' approach models human behaviour by adjusting individual utility functions; the former 'institutional' approach looks at the institutions arising as a reaction. The difference becomes particularly clear in an extreme case. If no behavioural anomalies are observed empirically, the individual's utility functions are, according to the 'integrating' approach, unchanged but, according to the institutional approach, there may well be individual rules and social institutions owing their existence to the anomalies; that is, if the institutions were removed, these anomalies would reappear.

Human Motivation

Economic analysis is based on the idea that individuals respond systematically to changes in relative prices. The incentives that are set from outside
motivate people to act in a predictable way. This (generalized) law of demand
has proved to be extremely successful in explaining the behaviour of voters,
politicians and bureaucrats. However, perceptive economists are well aware
that there must be other motivating forces. For example, the standard rational
choice calculus is not able to explain the level of vote participation (but it
serves quite well to account for the variations). There are a great many other
cases where individuals free ride far less than predicted by economists. For
instance, the expected punishment for tax evasion is so small that even risk-
averse citizens should cheat much more than they actually do. The reason for
the surprisingly high tax contributions has widely been attributed to tax
morale. Tax morale indeed provides a good explanation for the difference in
tax compliance in the case of Switzerland, where this factor can (indirectly)
be identified.

Psychologists and sociologists more generally distinguish between two
kinds of motivation: *extrinsic* motivation induced by manipulations of rewards or sanctions from the outside (the economist's relative prices), and
intrinsic motivation, where people perform an activity for its own sake because of reasons lying within their own person. Anybody looking at people's
behaviour must be aware that a phenomenon such as intrinsic motivation
does exist. Economists might nevertheless argue that they are only interested
in changes of behaviour (that is higher or lower vote participation or tax
evasion), but not in the level of those changes. As a consequence, important
aspects of the political and social life are left unexplained by rational choice
analysis. This position becomes fully untenable when intrinsic motivation is
not an (unexplained) constant, but is influenced by social factors. Experimental research in psychology has shown that, under identifiable conditions,
external interventions affect people's sense of self-determination, self-perception and their feeling of justice, which in turn influences intrinsic
motivation. Among psychologists, much attention has been paid to the 'hidden costs of reward', stating that introducing a reward into a situation, where
people already have a high interest in an activity, results in a decrease in their
intrinsic motivation. This so-called 'Crowding-Out Effect' will be more
thoroughly discussed in Chapter 5.

The damaging effect on intrinsic motivation, by changing external instruments, helps to explain why pricing (monetary rewards) and regulating (the
use of punishment) under identifiable conditions prove to have little or sometimes counterproductive effects. Thus, both the use of regulations and of
effluent charges may undermine intrinsic motivation in the form of, for exam-

ple, environmental ethics, because individuals perceive that the locus of control has shifted from internal to external forces, and that their own mental involvement has depreciated (see Chapter 5 for further discussion). Similar effects can be identified for crime deterrence by punishment, in social and in manpower policy.

The detrimental effect of external controls on intrinsic motivation is also directly relevant for the design of the basic institutions of the state (that is, for constitutional economics). David Hume and James Stuart Mill have already argued that a constitution should be designed so that it is able to check the behaviour of people with the worst of intentions, trying to free ride and to exploit the system. 'Average' behaviour is deemed to be of no concern, because the costs imposed on society by the most immoral members of it dominate. This argument overlooks that people's intrinsic motivation to act as good and responsible citizens is undermined when the constitutional provisions suggest that everyone acts as a knave anyway. It may well be that a constitution should give its citizens the feeling that they are trusted, and that they will not in general act as free riders. Such an approach bolsters citizens' self-determination, enhances positive self-perception and meets their sense of fairness. Such a constitutional policy is consistent with the empirical evidence collected on free riding behaviour and tax evasion.

Speechless Economics and Human Discourse

In economics, language and verbal exchange are attributed a minor role. More often than not, they are completely disregarded. Economists are particularly fond of models with no communication between the actors. Thus, the classical prisoner's dilemma game, which has shaped our thinking on free riding, artificially constructs a situation in which the prisoners are not able to speak to each other. Clearly, communication as such does not guarantee that no free riding occurs, but it definitely helps to form enforceable contracts to prevent it. While there may be some implicit agreements, the vast majority of contracts designed against free riding are in verbal, and often written, form.

A related aspect, disregarded by economists, is personal relationships, which again serve efficiently to prevent free riding. Economists tend to overlook that a large part of all activities within firms of all sizes, and between firms, is based on personal connections. The same holds for other institutions, in particular for interest groups, public bureaucracies, parties and government. Indeed, in small countries – such as Switzerland – virtually all important politicians know each other, and the situation is not much different in larger countries. The interaction has the character of a repeated game or, in sociological terms, 'embeddedness' matters, leading to quite different outcomes than if the personal relationship did not exist (see Chapter 8).

These considerations are relevant for many different areas in economics. Thus, in Public Choice, direct democracy is exclusively looked at as a particular form of making a social decision between known alternatives. The discourse among the citizens, which puts the issues on the individuals' agenda, raises their perception and exchanges the arguments in the media and among individual persons, is of crucial importance, and should therefore be studied. The choice between known alternatives is only one aspect of direct democracy; perhaps even more important is the process of verbal exchange which takes place before casting the vote in a referendum or initiative, that is, before an issue is well defined and put to the ballot. (This aspect will be more fully discussed in Chapter 9.) According to the philosophical and sociological theories of Habermas and others, such discourse not only improves citizens' perception and information, but may also shape the normative evaluation of the problem at stake.

THE MESSAGE

Economic imperialism has been a considerable success within the social sciences. While progress can certainly be made by further applying the economic approach, diminishing returns have set in. Economics has joined the ranks of normal science, where originality and innovation play a small role.

This is the message of this book: it is now time to embark on a new course and to switch from being an exporter to an importer of ideas. The social and literary sciences contain many ideas which can enrich future economics, without giving up its sound foundations. The areas of behavioural anomalies and human motivation are two fields where economics can benefit from insights from psychology; and discourse and personal embeddedness are aspects which economists can learn from philosophy and sociology. Many other concepts and ideas can fruitfully be borrowed from other social sciences.

SUGGESTIONS ON THE LITERATURE AND SOURCES

Economic imperialism is extensively demonstrated and critically discussed in
Becker, Gary S. (1976), *The Economic Approach to Human Behavior*, Chicago: Chicago University Press.
Kirchgässner, Gebhard (1991), *Homo Oeconomicus: Das ökonomische Modell individuellen Verhaltens und seine Anwendung in den Wirtschafts- und Sozialwissenschaften*, Tübingen: Mohr (Siebeck).

Frey, Bruno S. (1999), *Economics as a Science of Human Behaviour*, 2nd revised and extended edn, Boston and Dordrecht: Kluwer.
Lazear, Edward (2000), 'Economic Imperialism', *Quarterly Journal of Economics*, **115** (Feb.), 99–146.

The danger of running into diminishing returns by exporting economics to other areas has been pointed out by
Hirshleifer, Jack (1985), 'The Expanding Domain of Economics', *American Economic Review*, **75** (May), 53–68.

Aspects of free riding in the presence of public goods and commons have been analysed, using a large number of case studies and experiments by
Ostrom, Elinor (1990), *Governing the Commons: The Evolution of Institutions for Collective Action*, Cambridge: Cambridge University Press.
Ostrom, Elinor, Larry Schroeder and Susan Wynne (1993), *Institutional Incentives and Sustainable Development*, Boulder, CO: Westview Press.

An early economic study of non-democratic governments is due to
Tullock, Gordon (1987), *Autocracy*, Dordrecht: Kluwer.

A more recent analysis is
Wintrobe, Ronald (1998), *The Political Economy of Dictatorship*, Cambridge: Cambridge University Press.

Constitutional economics is developed and applied to policy issues in
Brennan, Geoffrey and James M. Buchanan (1985), *The Reason of Rules. Constitutional Political Economy*, Cambridge: Cambridge University Press.
Frey, Bruno S. (1983), *Democratic Economic Policy*, Oxford: Blackwell.
Mueller, Dennis C. (1995), *Constitutional Economics*, Cambridge: Cambridge University Press.

An empirical study of the position on the social welfare maximizing approach by economists is
Pommerehne, Werner W., Friedrich Schneider, Guy Gilbert and Bruno S. Frey (1984), 'Concordia Discors: Or: What do Economists Think?', *Theory and Decision*, **16**, 251–308.

Behavioural anomalies are extensively discussed in the following chapter of this book.

Sensations, such as love and hatred, have been introduced into economics in particular by
Hirschman, Albert O. (1982a), *Shifting Involvements. Private Interests and Public Action*, Oxford: Martin Robertson.
Frank, Robert H. (1988), *Passions with Reason. The Strategic Role of the Emotions*, New York: Norton.

The hidden costs of reward have been studied in psychology by
Lepper, Mark R. and David Greene (eds) (1978), *The Hidden Costs of Reward: New Perspectives on Psychology of Human Motivation*, Hillsdale, NY: Erlbaum.
Deci, Edward L. and Richard M. Ryan (1985), *Intrinsic Motivation and Self-determination in Human Behavior*, New York: Plenum Press.
Deci, Edward L. and Richard Flaste (1995), *Why We Do What We Do. The Dynamics of Personal Autonomy*, New York: Putnam.

The damaging effect on intrinsic motivation of external interventions has been introduced into economics as the 'Crowding-Out Effect' in
Frey, Bruno S. (1997), *Not Just for The Money. An Economic Theory of Personal Motivation*, Cheltenham, UK and Lyme, US: Edward Elgar.

The role of discourse has been emphasized in philosophy and sociology by
Habermas, Jürgen (1992), *Faktizität und Geltung: Beiträge zur Diskurstheorie des Rechts und des demokratischen Rechtsstaates*, Frankfurt: Suhrkamp.

PART II

Integrating Psychology

3. Economic incentives transform psychological anomalies

with Reiner Eichenberger

APPROACHES TO ANALYSING ANOMALIES

Over the last 20 years, characteristics of human behaviour have been identified which systematically deviate from the predictions of unbounded procedural rationality, and in particular from conventional neo-classical economics. These characteristics of human behaviour are often called 'anomalies', though viewed through non-neoclassical spectacles such behaviour may indeed look quite normal.

The best-known instances are:

- endowment effect: goods in a person's possession are valued more highly than those not held in the endowment;
- reference point effect: people do not evaluate final states of wealth, but mainly deviations from a specific reference point, which is most often the status quo;
- opportunity cost effect: out of pocket monetary cost is given greater weight in the decision calculus than opportunity cost of the same size;
- certainty and small probability effects: high and low chance events in particular are treated in a peculiar way by individuals; they consider certainty to be completely different from a very high probability and lend too much weight to small probabilities;
- anchoring effect: social states are evaluated from a particular starting point, the choice of which influences behavioural outcomes;
- availability and representativeness biases: recent, spectacular or personally experienced events are overweighted when individuals make decisions;
- overconfidence effect: people are convinced that they know observable facts better than is actually the case;
- framing effect: the way a decision problem is formulated, and the way the information is presented, affects individual decisions;

- preference reversal effect: individuals tend to choose high probability lotteries with low outcomes over low probability lotteries with high outcomes, but they are ready to pay more for the latter lottery.

It is generally unknown what factors cause such departures from standard neo-classical subjective expected utility maximization. A possible reason for the existence of anomalies is the cost of optimization, an explanation which relies on seemingly non-optimizing modes of human behaviour, such as experimenting, imitating, following authority and tradition, unmotivated search, and following habits or a hunch.

With respect to the questions posed, the procedures used, and the results reached, behavioural anomalies have been approached in two quite different ways, which may be called the 'psychological' and the 'axiomatic' approaches.

The '*psychological*' approach asks the question: 'What are the cognitive limitations of human beings?' The goal is to determine the nature of man, and to show that cognitive limits (and therewith anomalies) exist in important respects. This approach has mainly been pursued by social psychologists, but also by economists. The research has primarily been undertaken in the form of laboratory experiments. It has produced overwhelming evidence that anomalies do indeed exist at the level of individual behaviour, under a wide set of conditions.

The '*axiomatic*' approach accepts, and builds upon, the results found in the '*psychological*' approach, but from quite a different point of view. The question pursued here is, 'How must formal decision theory be adjusted in order to integrate anomalies into economic theory?' The goal is to transform 'anomalies' into 'regularities', in the sense that the maximization of individuals' objective function yields the behaviour observed. For that purpose, the von Neumann–Morgenstern axioms are changed mostly in the direction of generalizing subjective expected utility maximization. A case in point is prospect theory, which allows the integration of some of the (former) anomalies within the body of theory. It is difficult, however, to take several of them into account simultaneously. Moreover, some anomalies, like framing and availability effects, do not lend themselves in a satisfactory way to the axiomatic approach.

This chapter suggests a third approach, which has been neglected by both the psychological and the axiomatic approach, but which helps us to understand anomalies in the economic and social context. What can be called the '*incentive*' approach raises the question, 'How do individuals react when anomalies exist?' Individuals are taken to be able to cope with the problems and opportunities raised by anomalies. People are not logical machines, but rather human beings subject to cognitive limitations. Knowing this, they are able to respond systematically or 'rationally' (though not perfectly) to their 'irrationalities'. Two kinds of incentives induced by anomalies are considered.

1. When individuals are prone to anomalies, other actors have an incentive to exploit this 'irrationality'. Such activities are not without cost, and the potential 'exploiters' have to consider net (marginal) benefits.
2. Individuals subject to anomalies suffer utility (or profit) losses and therefore benefit from avoiding them. To reduce anomalies also entails cost, and the extent of the reduction undertaken depends on the (marginal) net benefits of doing so.

It will be shown that:

- The extent of anomalies depends on identifiable determinants influencing the marginal benefits and cost of exploiting and reducing anomalies, respectively.
- Anomalies will not, in general, be eliminated, as the benefits of reducing or exploiting them cannot always be expected sufficiently to outweigh the cost. Thus, the standard argument within economics that a competitive (economic) environment will eliminate 'irrationalities' is ill founded.
- The anomalies observed in real life are, in general, different from those observed in a laboratory setting, because they are transformed in response to the incentives to exploit and reduce them. While the influence of incentives on anomalies has sometimes been studied in a laboratory setting, the incentives were taken as given. One exception is the so-called 'market experiments', where incentives are created by mimicking a price system. These works are of great importance in understanding the relevance of anomalies. But they are restricted to one particular decision-making system, namely the market; they disregard other decision-making systems, such as democracy or bureaucracy. Moreover, market experiments usually only study the incentives to reduce, but not to exploit, anomalies and consider only a limited set of anomalies in a laboratory setting.

By contrast, our approach starts with human motivation and inquires what the determinants of the incentives are for both exploiting and reducing anomalies. The next section differentiates between various types of anomalies and discusses under what circumstances which type is observable. The third section identifies opportunities and incentives to exploit anomalies, concentrating on the real life evidence of how exploitation takes place. Following this, the incentives for reducing anomalies are considered. The propositions regarding the determinants of the marginal benefits and costs discussed are supported by a wealth of empirical evidence in the economic, psychological and behavioural science literature. The fifth section deals with the options available to influence anomalous behaviour, and the final section gives a summary.

WHEN ARE ANOMALIES OBSERVABLE AND WHERE?

Three aspects where anomalies can or cannot be empirically observed should be distinguished:

1. *Cognitive capacity of human beings.* If human beings were perfect, in the sense of not committing any logical error, no anomalies (in the sense of violations of assumed consistency axioms) would be observed. However, overwhelming evidence collected within the 'psychological' approach strongly suggests that individuals' cognitive capacities are severely limited, leading to anomalies. These experimentally found anomalies define the *capacity* for anomalies in an incentive-free setting.

2. *Exploitation of anomalies and setting of traps.* Anomalies, in the sense of limited human cognitive facilities, are not costly to individuals, as long as such 'irrationalities' are not taken advantage of by other actors. An obvious way of making profits (or of increasing one's utility) is to set up a 'money pump' where, after a succession of exchanges of goods and money, the exploiter contrives to hold on to the goods he or she started with and, in addition, gains a certain amount of money at the victim's expense. Normally, such exploitation of anomalous behaviour is undertaken by firms, and the victims are individuals, but this need not necessarily be the case. It may also happen that firms act in an anomalous way, and individuals exploit them.

   Firms not only have an incentive to exploit the given stock of anomalies, but also an interest in expanding the existing capacity of anomalies (which allows them to raise exploitation). New anomalies can be detected by investing resources in appropriate research, and known anomalies can be combined in such a way that they are magnified. The endowment and availability effects, for instance, can be called upon simultaneously, so that the victims are made to commit even larger errors, which can then be profitably exploited. An example is books that are sent to people who have not ordered them. The idea is that due to the endowment and availability effects, a larger proportion of people pay the bill accompanying the product instead of returning the whole package, compared with the proportion that would buy the same product for the same price in a shop.

3. *Reduction of anomalies resulting in trap failures.* Individuals do not necessarily fall prey to anomalies. At a given point in time, the traps set up by the firms may be empty for two different reasons: (i) individuals and activities that are anomaly-prone have been eliminated by a Darwinian process. People who have repeatedly been victims of anomalies have suffered financial losses and their weight in the economic process is thereby reduced or even fully eliminated by bankruptcy; (ii) individuals have expended resources in order not to fall into the anomaly traps, comparing the marginal benefit of not behaving anomalously and the marginal cost of reducing the probability of falling prey to an anomaly.

There are three basically different situations that can be identified in which it could be argued that 'no anomalies exist'.

1. Human beings have no cognitive limitation; that is, the set of psychological anomalies is empty and there is no capacity for anomalies.
2. Firms do not expend resources to set up traps, and no anomalies will be exploited, even though psychological anomalies exist.
3. No anomalies will be exploited, even though the firms have set up a large number of traps because, due to elimination and strong incentives to avoid them, nobody any longer falls into them. Under perfect competitive conditions and no transaction costs, the following outcome would be obtained: everybody subject to an anomaly would be immediately fully exploited, causing the anomaly to disappear.

The importance of anomalies is not necessarily reflected by the number of anomalies exploited, and therewith observable, but rather by the resources expended to set up traps, enlarge the capacity for anomalies and reduce anomalies, as well as by the rate of elimination of people and activities prone to anomalies. Empirical evidence suggests that anomalies are not, in general, completely eliminated. The same conclusion must be drawn on the basis of real-life observations: neither the reduction nor exploitation of anomalies is complete, and significant anomalies remain.

OPPORTUNITIES AND INCENTIVES TO EXPLOIT ANOMALIES

This section discusses how firms go about using anomalies to increase profits. By revealed behaviour, the anomalies exploited indicate opportunities where the expected return of employing resources to set traps is positive (larger than for competing purposes). By way of illustration, several prominent anomalies are discussed in turn.

Reference Point and Anchoring Effects

An actor who, in a bargaining situation, is able to set an anchor to his or her advantage, gains at the cost of the adversary. Setting an anchor is, of course, a time-honoured strategy in wage negotiations and similar situations. Surprisingly, it still seems to work when all negotiators should be aware of it. One reason seems to be purely psychological: anchors influence the decisions of negotiators, though they should not from the economic point of view. Other reasons are economic ones: it is difficult to predict what move is a strategically set anchor and which an unavoidable one. The latter is obtained if the other side can be convinced that the anchor set is beyond one's control, for instance that one is tied by rules or regulations, by orders from superiors, or by circumstances.

Endowment and Sunk Cost Effects

A widely-used strategy by firms is to induce people to acquire a product in order to establish an endowment effect: once people have a certain good in their endowment, they are much more likely to buy it; that is, they have a higher marginal willingness to pay than if they did not own the good. This strategy applies to a wide variety of goods, an example being that of a book club sending books at regular intervals to people which, after a certain period, either have to be returned or paid for. The same is often undertaken with journal or newspaper subscriptions. The anomaly-exploiting firms are careful to allow sufficient time before the decision to buy has to be made, in order to allow the endowment effect to sink in.

Firms also exploit the (related) sunk cost effect by defining a 'collection' of goods, for example stamps, coins or medals. The consumer tends to look at the first units bought in terms of sunk cost, inducing them to buy the whole series. To a certain extent, the film industry relies on the sunk cost effect when making follow-up films. In order to bring the investment made for seeing the first film (the price of the ticket and the time expended) to fruition, the audience feels forced to go and see the sequel.

The endowment effect is also exploited by other organizations, apart from profit-oriented firms, to further their own goals. Non-profit museums, that want to prevent a painting on loan leaving their institution, routinely resort to the endowment effect in order to convince the community either to prevent the sale by law, or to raise the money to buy it. Under these circumstances, virtually any painting is defined as belonging to the 'patrimoine national' simply because it is in a museum's and community's possession. The same people, who claim that parting with the painting would be a huge loss, would not even consider buying the painting if it was located elsewhere; for the same sum of money, they would generally prefer to buy another work of art. Such organizations rationally exploit the difference between the willingness to be compensated, and the willingness to pay found in many laboratory and real-life experiments.

Politicians are also skilful in exploiting the endowment effect. In order to win the 1983 election (which, up until then, had looked rather doubtful), Mrs Thatcher played on the Falklands being part of Britain's national endowment and, as a result of the national feelings aroused, was triumphantly re-elected. Clearly, few Britons would dream of wanting to acquire this island, even for free.

Framing

Instead of announcing a price increase to consumers, a firm does better to announce a price *decrease* relative to what the rise in price could have been. Here, framing seems to establish a new reference point, with the result that even a moderate rise, compared with what could have occurred, is taken to be a gain by the consumers affected. The question is, of course, whether the (potential) consumers can be made to accept the new reference point favourable to the firm. Consistent with the influence of reference points and frames, firms typically formulate labour contracts specifying a relatively low flat sum *plus* a per unit compensation and not a (financially equivalent, higher) flat sum *minus* a deduction for units below a given goal, because the incentives for work seem to be more favourable to the firm when workers are 'rewarded' for working towards a goal, than when they are 'punished' for not meeting it.

In the political sphere, framing is one of the most important devices used by the government to win the support of the population. In authoritarian systems, an official frame is imposed and everybody is forced to employ the corresponding language and concepts. In communist countries, for example, individuals were made to look at economic problems in terms of Marxist ideology, and not, for example, in terms of efficiency. If alternative information and points of view are lacking, the government is able to exploit its citizens to a certain extent, as the frames chosen will be to the politicians' benefit. A democratic system, on the other hand, can be defined as a system in which not only different frames are allowed to exist, but in which the incentives motivate the competing parties to present several different frames. In a democracy, in the absence of a coalition of parties against the voters, there is therefore little or no exploitation by framing.

Availability

In the economic sphere, there are many occasions when firms take advantage of the consumers' dependency on the recency or vividness of events. A large part of advertising relies on this bias. Availability is also particularly exploited when more expensive flight insurance is offered at airports to passengers who are already more than aware of the possibility of a plane crash. Stock market anomalies, such as the 'neglected firm effect' (the more intensely a firm is analysed by professional analysts, the lower the performance of its stock), can be exploited too. Thus, a Californian capital management firm outperformed the average stock market by buying (low-priced) stocks of firms not in the public eye and selling (high-priced) stocks of firms in the full public glare.

Firms may also take advantage of the heuristics which people employ in order to reduce anomalies, or to deal with difficult decisions. Thus, the strategy of 'eliminating by aspect' can be exploited via discount strategies, pricing items slightly below supposed thresholds (for example pricing at £6.99 instead of £7.00), or cleverly displaying information.

In politics, governments have always been eager to exploit taxpayers by relying on 'fiscal illusion'. Indirect taxes included in prices are less available and are therefore felt less than when they are added to the posted price, and direct taxes are less visible when income is paid out net than taxes which have to be paid after having received the gross income. In this respect, differences between countries are crass. In many European nations with representative democracies, direct and indirect taxes are included in price or income, while in the more direct democracies of Switzerland and the United States, the voters have forced their governments to tax more openly, thus reducing the governments' possibility of exploiting their availability bias.

Small Probabilities

Lotteries exploit people's attraction to the high sum to be won, especially the jackpot. Individuals tend to compare the low ticket price with the possible huge gain, both expressed in pounds (scale compatibility). They disregard the low probability of winning induced by the larger number of tickets sold. Lotteries also attract customers by giving them the option of choosing a 'lucky' number, thus capitalizing on the illusion of control.

INCENTIVES TO REDUCE ANOMALIES

How far individuals are able to reduce anomalies, and how much they are able to avoid traps, is determined by two major factors.

Perception

Individuals falling prey to an anomaly are often aware that they act in a non-rational way, and that they could improve their utility or profit by adjusting their behaviour. Perception is more likely, the less costly a comparison is with non-anomalous behaviour. If everyone in one's environment falls prey to an anomaly, it is difficult or impossible to overcome it. Some important anomalies, such as the endowment or sunk cost bias, affect only the persons directly involved, while other persons are not affected. One force working against comparison is overoptimism, or an 'ipsative' view of the world, where individuals refuse to consider themselves as part of the total set to which they actually belong.

Awareness of an anomaly also depends on the type of utility loss suffered. Out-of-pocket costs are clearly perceived, while monetary costs paid by cheque or credit card are less apparent. Individuals tend to be least aware of monetary costs when they take the form of automatic bank charges or of opportunity cost.

Formal education promotes perception. An abundance of experimental literature testifies that 'experts', that is people especially educated to perform a given task, are *less* likely to fall prey to anomalies. Experiments with real-estate agents and professional buyers and sellers of consumption durables showed, for example, that experts did better than non-experts (students) in the case of the anchoring effect, at least as long as general circumstances did not strongly change, but that the difference was not very large. In some cases, especially when the sunk cost effect applies, experts are as likely to fall prey to anomalies as other people.

Perception is also helped by experience. The more often individuals are confronted with a situation, the closer their behaviour corresponds to the rational choice model. This finding is supported by a large number of experiments, which allow for learning through repetition. Examples are the narrowing down of the difference between the willingness to pay and the compensation demanded, or the reduced bias in probability estimates. It has also been experimentally shown that, after a small number of arbitrage transactions (involving both incentive to act rationally and repetitions of the choice situation), all reversers converted to non-reversers after having suffered a financial loss caused by the reversal. In a real-life setting, medical doctors committed fewer errors in diagnosis than inexperienced medical students. Moreover, there is a stronger tendency to maximize objective expected utility when the subjects know that the game is going to be repeated several times.

However, in general, anomalies do not fully disappear with repetition. In experiments on preference reversals, it was shown that the frequency of behaving in an inconsistent manner only falls from about 60 to 40 per cent, and in another case is reduced by just half. Learning does not completely eliminate anomalies, because there is considerable cost attached to learning in unstable environments. In addition, under certain conditions, anomalies such as the availability, the hindsight or the outcome bias, may hinder the process of learning from experience.

Concerning the size of the utility gained by reducing anomalies, some scholars claim that there is little evidence that anomalies are reduced when monetary rewards for acting rationally are introduced. Not surprisingly, this view tends to be held mainly by psychologists, who concentrate on people's cognitive capacities, while some economists believe that only monetary incentives matter. Overwhelming evidence exists from laboratory studies that the incidence (frequency and size) of anomalous behaviour is reduced when the utility losses thereby brought about increase. Individuals act more rationally when faced with increasing incentives to act consistently, for a variety of problems involving choice. Moreover, for almost any type of anomaly, the same effect has been found. When the stakes are raised by undertaking experiments in a poor country (India), where a given sum of money to be won is of higher value to the participants in the experiment, the anomalies in question are smaller, but are not completely eliminated. Real-life observations also indicate that the bigger the stakes involved, the smaller the sunk cost effect.

The more important a decision is, the more utility is gained by reducing anomalies. Especially in financial markets, there is likely to be a larger effect on one's wealth if one succumbs to an anomaly, for instance if there is a sunk cost effect. Indeed, analyses of such markets show that, while anomalies exist, they are of relatively small size. On the other hand, when individuals fall prey to anomalies and experience only a small reduction in their utility, they do little about it. An example is the effect of framing on individual voting decisions. As an individual's vote has only a minute effect on the collective outcome, the utility loss suffered by being influenced by the frame is negligible. Suppliers of goods and services (producers) experience lower profit when they act in an anomalous manner. This loss is relatively easy to observe, as it is formulated in monetary units. Survival in a competitive environment (market) is threatened if the losses in profit are sizeable and happen over an extended period of time. In consumption activities, on the other hand, falling prey to an anomaly means that utility is lower than it would otherwise be, but the respective individual's survival is unlikely to be threatened. The incentive to reduce consumption anomalies is therefore smaller than in the case of production anomalies.

Finally, the stronger the competition, the greater are the incentives to reduce anomalies. This has been clearly shown in a great number of market experiments, for instance on preference reversals and on the certainty effect, as well as in other areas. In real-life financial markets, participants who consistently fall prey to an anomaly lose financial weight and tend to disappear. Under competitive conditions, there is therefore a stronger demand to reduce anomalies, for example by turning to experts for advice, by seeking more information, or by using appropriate rules.

Cost of Changing Behaviour

The marginal cost of acting differently in order to reduce anomalies is higher when complex tasks are involved. In these circumstances, individuals tend to resort to rule-guided behaviour. Under certain conditions, these routines lead to anomalies, such as the representativeness bias. The same applies when behaviour leading to anomalies is guided and sanctioned by tradition and norms.

Institutions and free riding also need to be considered. Institutions are behavioural regularities, which can be employed to reduce the frequency and size of anomalies. Individual institutions exist, with whose help anomalies can be reduced. An (already mentioned) important instance is self-commitment, which can be organized by oneself, and where no agreement with others is necessary. To establish collectively agreed institutions (for example a law or a constitutional provision) to reduce anomalies is more costly in anonymous situations compared with situations involving face-to-face interaction (for example within a small family firm). In an anonymous situation, the transaction cost of reaching an agreement is higher, partly owing to a stronger incentive to act strategically and to free ride.

POLICY ISSUES

Should the government intervene in order to reduce anomalies? From the welfare point of view, the issue is open: a reduction in the number of traps set (and the resources thereby expended) also reduces the incentives to avoid them (and thereby reduces the resources expended by the potential victims); however, such an efficiency-enhancing move also has distributional consequences, the potential victims gaining and the potential exploiters losing. The outcome will be determined by the political process, where the ability of the two groups to organize and put pressure on the government is crucial.

To influence the extent of anomalies exploited, the exploiters' and the exploitees' incentives and possibilities can be changed. The options are discussed in turn, with real-life examples provided for the purpose of illustration.

Influencing Resistance to Anomalies

The marginal benefits of avoiding traps are determined by the factors discussed in the previous section. Taking the example of books and newspapers being sent to consumers without having been requested, the perception of succumbing to the endowment effect may be raised by facilitating comparison. For this purpose, comparative advertising by competing suppliers (which would point out the higher price charged) or by consumer agencies, may be encouraged or mandated. Detection of the endowment effect may be facilitated by improving consumer education. The advantage of suppliers (who are experienced in setting up traps) over consumers (who, in the case of some goods and services, are only rare buyers) might be reduced, for example by legally requiring the consent of both adult members of a household for striking deals. The marginal cost to individuals of resisting an anomaly can, for instance, be lowered by facilitating self-commitment: if desired, one should have the right to have all unasked for goods and services automatically returned to the sender (at the sender's expense). In some cases, one should have the right to exclude oneself from being able to do business. The cost of resisting anomalies may also be lowered by admitting class action against suppliers who infringe on laws while exploiting anomalies. A further possibility is to make the right to withdraw from contracts mandatory for consumers.

Influencing the Rate of Elimination

In today's welfare-oriented societies, both the existing law, as well as a government in pursuit of votes, tend to work against the economic elimination of actors falling prey to anomalies. Actors, whether individuals or firms, who behave 'irrationally', are prevented from bankruptcy or even major losses, while 'rational' actors evading anomalies are 'punished' by being taxed. As a result, anomalous actions and actors increase in weight at the aggregate level (relative to no interaction); that is, public interference raises the number of anomalies.

Influencing Exploitation

The production function of setting traps, and therewith the return of using resources to exploit anomalies, can be affected in many different ways. In the example of books and journals used above, the marginal cost of trapping consumers by the endowment effect can be raised by restricting the frequency with which unsolicited goods may be sent, by barring these firms from using the public mail service, or by forcing them to compensate con-

sumers for the total transaction cost (including time) expended when returning the goods. The incentives of firms to exploit voters may also be reduced
by taxing the returns from exploitation.

To reduce the consequences of fiscal illusion, institutional provisions may
be taken, forbidding governments to increase indirect taxes, making automatic deductions from income, or including taxes in end prices. Without
referring to anomalies, one of the main thrusts of constitutional economics is
to decrease fiscal illusion by making sure that taxes of all kinds are equally
visible to citizens. It has been empirically shown that these measures reduce
the tax burden imposed on citizens, which may be interpreted as a decrease of
'exploitation' of the population by the politicians. Facilitating the formation
of new parties, and the competition with established ones, is an important
institutional mechanism to prevent the domination of 'official' frames of
defining political issues, thus increasing the cost of setting up traps.

Influencing Competition

A monopolistic firm engaged in exploiting anomalies does not set enough
traps to exploit all anomalies. This restrictive behaviour is due to the fact that
the firm is careful not to set so many traps that the potential victims are either
eliminated or are induced to muster sufficient resources to avoid the anomaly
traps. If, on the other hand, many firms are in strong competition with each
other, the pool of potential victims becomes a public good, which no firm has
an incentive to preserve. Free riding behaviour leads to a rush for exploitation. With perfect competition, all anomalies would be eliminated.

Competition can be restricted by granting a licence to only one supplier, by
forming a government-supported cartel (an approach regularly used in the
case of casinos and gambling halls), or by prohibiting activities which are
most likely to lead to anomalies (banks may, for example, be prevented from
offering all financial services to minors).

SUMMING UP

Anomalies lead to incentives for the different actors to adjust their behaviour.
People acting in an anomalous way can do better by reducing their anomalies, and clever people can profit by exploiting the anomalies of others. Due
to these reactions, anomalies and their frequency are not exogenously given,
but are endogenous and influenced by social processes. The 'incentive' approach proposed here differs basically from the prevalent 'psychological' and
'axiomatic' approaches used by other scholars. Our approach focuses on new
questions, in particular under which conditions are the incentives and the

possibilities large in order to exploit the anomalies of other people, and when are anomaly-prone people able to protect themselves against their own paradoxical behaviour?

Attention is directed towards the resources expended in handling/exploiting anomalies rather than on anomalies considered in isolation. Various anomalies have been discussed with examples from real life, and it has been shown that the conditions prevailing in the social environment (the institutions) determine which kinds of anomalies are observable and what their consequences are. Much of the behaviour in the everyday life of individuals and firms (and even of politicians) can be interpreted as attempts to exploit or reduce anomalies, or to set or avoid traps. The insights gained by our analysis are utilized to propose different measures, so that fewer resources are expended on anomalies.

SUGGESTIONS ON THE LITERATURE AND SOURCES

Surveys on behavioural anomalies by psychologists are

Kahneman, Daniel, Paul Slovic and Amos Tversky (eds) (1982), *Judgement under Uncertainty: Heuristics and Biases*, Cambridge: Cambridge University Press.

Arkes, Hal R. and Kenneth R. Hammond (eds) (1986), *Judgement and Decision Making: An Interdisciplinary Reader*, Cambridge: Cambridge University Press.

Dawes, Robyn M. (1988), *Rational Choice in an Uncertain World*, San Diego and New York: Harcourt Brace Jovanovich.

The following economists have prepared surveys on behavioural anomalies or paradoxes

Schoemaker, Paul J. (1982), 'The Expected Utility Model: Its Variants, Purposes, Evidence and Limitations', *Journal of Economic Literature*, **20** (June), 529–63.

Hogarth, Robin M. and Melvin W. Reder (eds) (1987), *Rational Choice*, Chicago: University of Chicago Press.

Thaler, Richard H. (1992), *The Winner's Curse. Paradoxes and Anomalies of Economic Life*, New York: Free Press.

Frey, Bruno S. and Reiner Eichenberger (1992), 'Behavioural Anomalies and Economics', in Bruno S. Frey, *Economics as a Science of Human Behaviour*, Boston and Dordrecht: Kluwer, pp. 171–95.

The axiomatic approach is represented by

Machina, Mark J. (1987), 'Choice Under Uncertainty: Problems Solved and Unsolved', *Journal of Economic Perspectives*, **1** (1), 121–54.

Prospect theory is due to

Kahneman, Daniel and Amos Tversky (1979), 'Prospect Theory: An Analysis of Decision Under Risk', *Econometrica*, **47** (2), 263–91.

That individuals are (sometimes) able to guard themselves against their own irrational future behaviour has been long argued by

Schelling, Thomas C. (1984), 'The Life You Save May Be Your Own', in Thomas C. Schelling, *Choice and Consequence. Perspectives of an Errant Economist*, Cambridge, MA and London: Harvard University Press, pp. 113–46.

Elster, Jon (1979), *Ulysses and the Sirens*, Cambridge: Cambridge University Press.

Market experiments relating to anomalies are extensively discussed in

Weber, Martin (1990), *Risikoentscheidungskalkül in der Finanzierungstheorie*, Stuttgart: C.E. Poeschel.

The concept of individuals' limited cognitive capacities is the basis of bounded rationality as developed by

Simon, Herbert A. (1982), *Models of Bounded Rationality*, Cambridge, MA: MIT Press.

That anomalies exist even on the most efficient market, the stock market, has been shown by

Shiller, Robert J. (1987), 'The Volatility of Stock Market Prices', *Science*, **235**, 33–7.

Real life observations of behavioural anomalies have been collected by

Samuelson, William and Richard Zeckhauser (1988), 'Status Quo Bias in Decision Making', *Journal of Risk and Uncertainty*, **1** (1), 1–53.

Russo, Edward and Paul J.H. Schoemaker (1990), *Decision Traps: Ten Barriers to Brilliant Decision-making and How to Overcome Them*, New York: Simon and Schuster.

The large difference between compensation demanded and willingness to pay has been empirically studied by

Knetsch, Jack L. and J.A. Sinden (1984), 'The Persistence of Evaluation Disparities', *Quarterly Journal of Economics*, **102**, 691–95.

Harless, David W. (1989), 'More Laboratory Evidence on the Disparity between Willingness to Pay and Compensation Demanded', *Journal of Economic Behavior and Organization*, **11** (3), 359–79.

Elimination by aspect, as a decision procedure, is due to

Tversky, Amos (1972), 'Elimination by Aspects: A Theory of Choice', *Psychological Review*, **79**, 281–99.

The systematic overestimation of one's capabilities and one's luck has been studied by

Weinstein, Neil D. (1980), 'Unrealistic Optimism About Future Life Events', *Journal of Personality and Social Psychology*, **39**, 806–20.

That framing systematically affects individuals' voting decisions has been analysed by

Quattrone, George A. and Amos Tversky (1988), 'Contrasting Rational and Psychological Analysis of Political Choice', *American Political Science Review*, **82** (3), 719–36.

4. Marriage paradoxes

with Reiner Eichenberger

THE NEO-CLASSICAL THEORY OF MARRIAGE AND BEYOND

This chapter discusses a particular application of anomalies to a family issue. The standard economic theory of the family has given us many valuable and novel insights into how individuals act within a family, and also how they choose to form a family. This constitutes a great step forward, compared with the previous notion in economic theory that households are a 'black box' and act as if they were individuals.

This economic theory of the family assumes that individuals act rationally and maximize their utility. This does not necessarily mean that their interests are selfish, as the theory explicitly allows for altruism among family members. They are taken to act according to the same principles within the family as in any other area. This unified theory is one of the main attractions of the economic approach. It compares favourably with other social sciences, in particular psychology, where explanations tend to rely on a set of isolated effects. There are particularly good reasons for applying the economic model of behaviour to the family, because the incentives to act rationally are particularly strong. For most individuals, family decisions are of central importance and the cost of wrong decisions may be extremely high. Thus, having a child, instead of remaining childless, binds the time and financial resources of the parents for about 20 years, perhaps even for the rest of their lives.

Much of the work on the economics of the family has been highly theoretical. The late-comers especially have often been more concerned with demonstrating the applicability of formal economic analysis to a new, unusual subject, than with providing new insights into how individuals act in the specific context of a family. Most importantly, empirical studies have been sadly neglected in favour of abstract formalisms. Among the many examples is the application of the theory of matching the supply of, and demand for, jobs to the marriage choice situation. While the analogy is well taken, no effort is made to seriously analyse the differences between job and marriage markets. Rather, economists' interest is to prove under what abstract conditions an equilibrium exists. There seems to be little interest in looking at real-world issues in the family, in relating their theories to empirical facts, or in subjecting them to an econometric analysis. Most economists in the field do not bother to look at the vast literature on the family produced by the other social sciences.

The existing economic literature disregards important aspects of the family. This chapter concentrates on four empirical observations with respect to marriage, which seem to contradict the economic theory of marriage. In this sense, they appear to be paradoxical:

1. people search surprisingly little for suitable marriage partners;
2. the characteristics of potential partners are evaluated in a very biased way;
3. individuals take astonishingly little advice on their marriage decision; and
4. the likelihood of one's own marriage ending in divorce is strongly under-estimated, and therefore too few precautions for the eventuality of a break-up are taken.

Our point of reference is the orthodox neo-classical theory just mentioned. The four observations would not have been predicted ex ante by that theory. We submit that the research on behavioural anomalies (see Chapter 3) helps to explain such paradoxical observations. It seems to be fruitful to integrate these new findings lying between economics and psychology. However, the rational choice view of human behaviour is not relinquished. Individuals to some extent fall prey to psychological anomalies in their marriage choice, and to that extent act 'irrationally'. But they are also rational enough to try to overcome these paradoxes. This view also provides us with an explanation of the emergence and functioning of several institutions related to marriage, which would otherwise be difficult to explain.

The next section discusses the four paradoxical observations concerning marriage. Possible standard neo-classical explanations are reviewed and rejected, and solutions are offered using elements of cognitive psychology. The third section identifies why, and in what respect, marriage decisions differ from other decisions in life. The institutional reactions to the marriage paradoxes observed are the subject of the fourth, and the final section summarizes the findings.

WHAT IS PARADOXICAL ABOUT MARRIAGE?

Little Search for Marriage Partners

Following the strict neo-classical economic model, one would expect to find that individuals undertake an extensive search before committing themselves to marriage, as the costs of choosing an unsuitable partner are normally high. Circumstantial evidence suggests, however, that surprisingly little time and few resources are devoted to finding the 'right' partner. Most importantly, a considerable number of men and women marry their first, reasonably serious, partner.

Table 4.1 shows the percentage of first unions that were formal marriages (in contrast to cohabitation) in the United States. For 84 per cent of the male and 93 per cent of the female Americans aged between 50 and 60, marriage was identical with the first union. While this percentage dropped for both sexes, the general observation still holds for more than one third of Americans aged between 20 and 30. Studies for Europe reveal the same pattern.

Table 4.1   Percentage of first unions that were formal marriages

Birth dates	Men (%)	Women (%)
1933–42	84	93
1943–52	70	78
1953–62	47	58
1963–74	34	36

Source: Laumann, Gagnon, Michael and Michaels (1994, p. 207).

There certainly is a 'marriage market' (social psychologists take this to be a matter of course). But the term is somewhat misleading if it is understood to mean that the participants have a large choice of partners they could marry. Rather, entry into the marriage market is characterized by considerable barriers, and the choice is strongly dominated by social and traditional factors. The marriage market is thus highly segmented and characterized not by vast choice possibilities but by high transaction costs shaping behaviour. The authoritative study on *Sex in America* aptly remarks that:

> The vast popularity of school and work as marketing places is part of the social game, whereby the firm hand of society inevitably guides us toward people that we and our stakeholders would view as acceptable sex (and marriage, *BSF*) partners. One reason why so many people met their partners at school or work is

that most people spend so much time there, going to school for years, then
working for decades. The total time spent in school and at work far overshadows
the time spent in such places as a bar or on vacation or in a health club. (Michael
et al., 1994, p. 74)

For similar reasons, marriages between persons living in the same neighbourhood are frequent. As a consequence, the marriage market is strongly
segmented and many participants have a very restricted choice:

> The myth is that each person has the whole world to choose from. The reality is
> that when we finish excluding everyone that we consider unsuitable or unobtain-
> able and when we finish dividing the market into sex for recreation or sex for
> possible marriage, there are very few people left for each of us to seriously
> consider. (Michael et al., 1994, p. 64)

This does not mean that no marriage market exists. What we want to emphasize is that the empirically interesting aspects of forming marriages are not
captured by an abstract analysis of the matching problem in analogy to any
other market but by the particular characteristics and forces that shape the
marriage process. To know that it is a 'market' (though delightful for an
economist to hear) explains little; what helps us to gain insights is a serious
analysis of the restrictions (or transaction costs) typical for this market.

A main characteristic of marriage decisions is that a more intensive search
does not necessarily improve marriage quality. Considerable empirical evidence reveals that more information, gained for example by cohabitation
before marriage, does not raise the subjective quality of marriage. Having
lived with the same partner before marriage is, according to many studies,
negatively correlated with the self-evaluated quality of marriage; the same is
true for experience acquired by having lived with previous partners, and also
for romantic involvements prior to commitment. More recent studies indicate
that these effects cannot fully be attributed to selection effects, according to
which those who cohabit prior to marriage may be less committed, or may be
poorer marriage prospects.

These observations are consistent with an economic explanation of our
claim that potential marriage partners engage in much less searching than
formal neo-classics predicts. There is little or no searching because the marginal benefits of information are low, and/or the costs are high. Such an
'explanation' is, however, purely ex post, and tends to become tautological if
no reasons are adduced why marginal benefits are low and costs are high.

The benefits of searching are reduced by asymmetric information, leading
to the undesired 'lemons' outcome. Individuals 'offering' themselves on the
'marriage market' may be interpreted by others as being 'lemons'. They are
taken to be people with hidden 'defects' and are therefore unattractive to

likely mates. In other markets, suppliers faced with such asymmetric information may overcome the problem by building up a good reputation – a
measure not available here, at least in the case of a first marriage.

Satisficing theory may also explain the limited amount of searching undertaken before marrying. The weighty decision of choosing a partner 'for life'
cannot be solved by explicit maximization, because it transcends the cognitive restrictions of human problem solving. The marriage decision opens up
new aspects not normally considered in standard neo-classical theory. In
particular, one's preferences about the type of partner and marriage may
markedly and unpredictably change during one's lifetime. Love may fade or,
more rarely, may increase during marriage. The quality of the chosen partner
may unpredictably change during the course of marriage, for instance as a
result of an illness or accident, or because of further education. Such uncertainties may always exist to some extent, but are much more pronounced in
the case of marriage. The information gathered during the search is therefore
of limited value. As a reaction, individuals cut the process short, thus con-
forming to the model of bounded rationality.

Additional, non-conventional reasons for the short duration of the search
can be deduced from experimentally-based decision theory:

1. *The search process itself creates special psychic costs.* Informing oneself
    on the marriage market before making a choice is problematic. The use
    of the market may, under identifiable conditions, undermine the intrinsic
    motivation needed for a successful partnership (see Chapter 5). Exploit-
    ing the opportunities presented by the marriage market tends to crowd
    out the internal values of trust and love on which modern marriages are
    based. Explicit exchange in a relationship may thus destroy the bonds on
    which marriage is built. Openly, or even furtively, evaluating the pros
    and cons of a prospective spouse in comparison to the alternatives avail-
    able on the marriage market is strongly condemned in a romantic
    relationship. The same holds for any attempt to openly offer material
    compensation in order to find an optimal match.

    This result, of course, is compatible with neo-classics – increasing
    search costs lead to a reduction of the intensity and time spent searching
    – but the point made here is that orthodox neo-classics does not take into
    consideration that searching tends to undermine the intrinsic motivation
    required for a successful partnership, and thus strongly increases the
    costs of searching.
2. *Endowment and sunk cost effects.* Once one has chosen a partner, one
    tends to get attached to him or her. In other words, a pronounced endow-
    ment effect emerges: once a partner has been chosen, he or she is valued
    more highly relative to other possible partners simply because the rela-

tionship exists. A wealth of empirical evidence reveals that partnership leads to an endowment effect. In particular, it has been observed that a separation generally leads to an intense feeling of loss. Moreover, even when the perceived quality of the relationship was low, both partners are subject to a sunk cost effect. There is a pronounced tendency to maintain a relationship, even when its continuation is considered costly by both partners because they do not want to give up the past investments in the relationship. An unwillingness to disengage oneself from a relationship, in which one has invested heavily, may even be considered a general human tendency. The investment of time and energy, as well as foregoing alternative relationships, commits one to remain in a relationship, even if it turns out to be painful.

   The endowment and sunk cost effects represent distortionary factors above and beyond the changed objective circumstances, that is, the accumulation of relationship-specific investments. Both effects are specific to the persons involved and are difficult, if not impossible, for outsiders to understand. Often, when friends observe the costs imposed on each other in a relationship, they advise separation. In many cases, the persons affected feel offended because they are subject to the endowment and sunk cost effects, and therefore have a psychological barrier to separating. Such behaviour clearly violates the standard neo-classical optimizing view that past costs should be irrelevant to current decisions relevant for the future.

The endowment effect produced by knowing each other results in breaking off the search earlier than if no such effect existed. The endowment effect is further strengthened by the fact that the costs of searching for an alternative partner are typically high in close relationships. The probability of divorce for a married couple is reduced. Consequently, the number of marriages is higher than if there was no endowment effect. More importantly, their average quality is lower, as more marriages are entered and fewer marriages dissolved than psychologically uncommitted outsiders would optimally advise.

Partial Evaluation of Marriage Partners

In today's western industrial countries, the great majority of young couples consider romantic love to be an absolute prerequisite for marriage. Someone who marries a person explicitly for material, or even 'practical' reasons (such as being a good cook), risks being chided by others. However, a partnership based on romantic love leads to a systematic overemphasis of a partner's characteristics related to love. Other characteristics important for marriage are underemphasized, or sometimes even completely ignored. Thus, few lovers are particularly concerned with whether their partner is well integrated into the family, ambitious with respect to their career, or able to run a joint household.

This systematic bias in decision-making for marriage based on romantic love, or autonomous marriage, is best visible when it is compared with arranged marriages. Predictably, love is more important, the more autonomous the marriage decision is, the more nuclear the family structure is, and the more freely the marriage partners can choose where they want to live. In arranged marriages, on the other hand, love is less important as a precondition for a successful and lasting relationship.

One rather sad fact found by empirical research on marriage is that, in general, love tends to fade over time. Why does romantic love nevertheless play such a dominant role in marriage decisions today? It may serve as a reliable signal for other characteristics, which are more relevant for the quality and stability of marriage. One would then be inclined to attribute corresponding importance to love in arranged marriages. However, parents and other persons arranging marriages obviously pay much less attention to love than the prospective partners themselves. Another explanation refers to the endowment effect. The great role love plays in (autonomous) marriage may be attributed to love yielding high utility in the first phases of a partnership. Over time, the partner is included in one's endowment. Indeed, according to empirical evidence, 'commitment to and satisfaction in adult romantic relationships increase as outcome levels increase' (Clark and Reis, 1988, p. 645). The choice of a marriage partner based on romantic aspects results in non-optimal outcomes.

Complementary traits, such as similar interests and viewpoints, are more important in the earlier phases of a relationship than substitutive traits, such as the capacity to perform certain chores of which the partner is not capable. Increased preferences for traits more important in an earlier phase, such as physical attractiveness, are negatively correlated with the subjective satisfaction from a partnership (marriage) in the long run. In arranged marriages, on the other hand, the complementary traits are not overstressed, because the parents, relatives or professionals arranging the marriage are not subject to the endowment effect. They are able to take all aspects into consideration deemed relevant for a particular marriage. Considerations such as these are not part of the standard neo-classical model of marriage.

Little Advice Sought

In marriage decisions based on romantic love, the (potential) partners seek little or no advice from professionals who are experts on the determinants of successful marriage. Nor do they seriously consult parents or other relatives who are experienced in marriage. This behaviour differs markedly from that regarding the choice of education and career, where one more often seeks advice on the suitability of a particular line of study or profession. Even more extensive advice is sought when buying durable goods, such as a car or a house, or when investing in financial markets. In a romantic marriage, the two individuals involved reject the advice of others because they believe that they are a special case which cannot be judged by outsiders. 'Average' experience is irrelevant to them.

Outside advice is incompatible with the notion of romantic love as a basic requirement for modern marriages. To seek advice from professionals, or even from parents, is interpreted as an obvious sign of mistrust towards the partner, and is therefore shunned. Standard neo-classical analysis, on the other hand, following the principle of the division of labour, would predict that the advice and help of professionals, or at least of relatives, is sought before making one of the most important decisions in life.

In reality, the direction of influence (advice) does not go so much from parents to offspring as in the reverse direction. Young people planning to get married make an effort to make their chosen partner attractive to their parents. The more agreeable the parents find the chosen partner, the more the new couple can hope to be materially supported by them. Due to the filtered information the parents receive from their offspring, they do not and cannot serve as objective advisers. The situation is different when the parents receive independent information from other sources, in particular within close-knit religious or social groups. The parents are enabled to advise, and the marriage decisions are more often arranged than autonomous. Conversely, in autonomous marriages based on romantic love, the individuals experiencing an endowment effect towards their partner tend to disregard, or outrightly reject, the advice proffered by their parents, who are unaffected by the endowment effect.

Underestimation of the Likelihood of One's Own Divorce

Empirical research testifies that a blatant discrepancy exists between the ipsative and the objective view of the expected success of marriage. Individuals strongly underrate the probability of their own marriage failing, that is the ipsative probability of divorce, even if they are fully aware of the high *average* divorce risk. An empirical analysis for the United States (Baker and Emery, 1993) finds a huge discrepancy between the two. The respondents of a survey accurately judged that in the United States in the 1980s roughly 50 per cent of the marriages ended in divorce. Despite this accurate estimate that 50 per cent of US couples who marry will divorce, applicants for a marriage licence assessed the likelihood that they personally would divorce to be 0 (zero) per cent! This large discrepancy is therefore not due to a lack of information, but is the result of a systematic cognitive bias.

Individuals thus tend to systematically underestimate their ipsative probability (that is the probability considered relevant for themselves) compared with the objective one, by placing themselves in a special category to which the average high divorce rate does not apply. Consider a white upper-class woman deciding to marry a black, working-class man. When it is pointed out to her that such marriages have a very high divorce risk, she will reply that this may well be true in general or on average, but not in her special case. She feels that the gloomy prediction does not apply to her. She is marrying a particular man who is outside the base on which the prediction is founded. This view cannot be faulted, because a happy marriage between any type of partners is indeed a logical possibility.

Another reason why the objective chance of divorce is rejected in the case of one's own marriage is that one falls prey to the illusion of control. People tend to think that they can influence the outcome of their marriage more strongly than is the case in actual fact.

The concept of ipsative probabilities for guiding one's choice in marriage creates a major problem for the standard neo-classical theory of marriage and divorce based on expected utility theory. According to that approach, individuals evaluate their future marriage outcome by using subjective probabilities of success and failure. As the ipsative probabilities of divorce tend to be systematically lower than objective assessments, too many marriages are concluded, and too few precautions are taken against failure than would be predicted on the basis of subjective expected utility theory. Despite the substantial commitment to one another (promised for a lifetime), usually no marriage contract is made specifying the duties and rights of each partner, which makes a dissolution costly. A major reason for not using marriage contracts is the systematic discounting of the riskiness of one's own marriage. In addition, a formal agreement is taken to be a sign of mistrust: one speaks about divorce even before the marriage is sealed. A formal contract constitutes an external intervention likely to crowd out intrinsic motivation. In particular, trust may be undermined. Due to the many uncertainties inherent in such a complex relationship, which cannot be fully regulated by formal contract, trust is, however, indispensable.

In the context of marriage, learning is severely limited or absent and, in some cases, may even be perverse. This may be called the 'Liz Taylor effect'. Whenever this actress gets married (and this has happened many times), she solemnly declares that this time it is for life, only to get divorced some months or years later. This outcome is easily predicted by even casual observers not burdened with her ipsative view. That learning with respect to issues of marriage and divorce is generally difficult, or does not happen at all, is supported by the observation that the probability of divorce increases sharply for persons previously divorced. Despite the failure of past marriages, roughly three-quarters of divorced people remarry at least once. Moreover, the probability of remarriage is higher for those who have been divorced than for widowed persons. The empirical observation that children from a divorced marriage tend to be more favourably inclined to romantic marriage can be interpreted as a case of perverse learning. The same interpretation may be applied (with some caution) to the observation that the time spent searching before a second marriage is shorter than before a first marriage.

WHY IS MARRIAGE DIFFERENT?

We have so far considered four specific aspects of marriage choice, where the decision-making process and outcome systematically deviate from what is predicted by the standard neo-classical economic theory of the family. In this sense, the findings are paradoxical. There are four reasons why the marriage decision is different from other decisions.

1. For many individuals, marriage is probably the single most important decision in their lives. At the same time, it is far more complex than most other decisions, because the consequences extend over an unknown period of time; one's own preferences with respect to the type of marriage, as well as the type of partner, may shift, and the character and behaviour of the partner, as well as the relevant social conditions, may change in unpredictable ways. Moreover, some kinds of rational behaviour are not chosen by the marriage partners, because the love and trust in the relationship would thereby be undermined. Such rational behaviour would be to search extensively for a marriage partner, to compensate for material or pecuniary differences in the value of the partners, or to seal marriage contracts with a finite period of validity.
2. The marriage decision is, for the vast majority of people, designed to be unique. Learning is therefore difficult, or impossible, as one cannot look back on one's own, but only at other people's experiences, which is quite a different thing. The necessary requirements for successful individual learning are absent. Even in the case of second and third marriages, it is difficult to learn from one's own experience. Moreover, no competitive processes exist forcing individuals to act rationally, at least not in the sense of a well-established economic market, in which irrational behaviour leads to bankruptcy and enforced exit from the market.

3. The decision-making process is accompanied by strong involvement on the part of the participants (the prospective marriage partners), which causes preference changes in the form of endowment and sunk cost effects, as well as illusions of control.

4. Elements of strategic interaction exist between the marriage partners themselves, and between the marriage partners and the outside world, most importantly the parents. The reactions of the prospective marriage partners, as well as those of the parents, are of a special nature, and are less known than the ones in other areas of decision making. Available information is deliberately distorted and thus often disregarded.

REACTIONS TO PARADOXES

Individuals are often aware that they are subject to paradoxical behaviour. They know that, under certain circumstances, their decisions concerning marriage deviate, to a greater or lesser degree, from what rational persons would choose. As this lapse from rationality imposes costs, individuals therefore make an effort to devise strategies to avoid such paradoxes, or at least to reduce their costs. This idea has already been used in the previous chapter to analyse how people endeavour to overcome various other behavioural anomalies. These strategies may take place both on the individual and collective, or institutional, level.

Individual Level

Marriage paradoxes can be completely eliminated, or at least their cost can be reduced, by committing oneself in advance to appropriate types of behaviour. One can, for example, prearrange a stay abroad in order to prevent the endowment effect from prevailing. One can also build up human capital in order to reduce the cost of a paradoxical marriage choice. Thus, overstressing complementary traits can partly be avoided by investing more in substitutive traits. Men may, for instance, learn to cook, so that choosing a wife who can't cook does not affect the marriage quality to the same extent.

Institutional Level

On a collective level, the number of norms and laws may be interpreted as an effort by rational individuals to overcome the pervasive existence of paradoxical behaviour with respect to marriage. Some important instances are:

1. *Arranged marriages.* In many societies, men and women of marriageable age subject themselves voluntarily, and by custom, to the will of their parents or relatives, whom they believe to be capable of selecting a suitable partner for them. The utility from an arranged marriage is therefore expected to be satisfactory to both partners, on average and in the long run. Parents indirectly arrange marriages when they steer their offspring's choice of a spouse by sending them to 'appropriate' schools and universities, or by getting them to join the 'right' social clubs. From the parents' point of view, they are likely to meet suitable partners there. In most marriages, the wife's status, income and opportunities in life are far more dependent on her husband's than vice versa. Parents in almost all societies are thus observed to be more concerned with finding appropriate mates for their daughters than for their sons.

2. *Alternatives to marriage.* Apart from marriage, other institutional forms of men and women living together have evolved. They are more flexible, not necessarily designed to last a lifetime, and the cost of separation is therefore reduced. It is no accident that the rise of romantic love is correlated with the search for new institutional forms of partnership, in particular cohabitation. Another institutional change is that the presumption of marriage being for life is effectively relinquished by allowing and facilitating divorce. Indeed, in most western industrial countries today, divorce by mutual consent is comparatively easy, and often sought.

3. *Marriage contracts.* Romantic feelings and the endowment effect curb the opportunity of the (potential) partners to talk openly about the possibility of divorce prior to marriage and, owing to this, many do not conclude a formal marriage contract. As a substitute, the law steps in and provides basic rules for separation. Some of the rights and obligations of the parties are defined by law and cannot be waived even by mutual consent. Among other things, marriage laws determine how the wealth brought into, and accumulated during marriage, as well as future income earned, is to be distributed upon divorce. Another institution which interferes in individual marriage decisions is the Catholic Church. In many countries, it requires couples who intend entering a Christian marriage, to attend a course before marriage, in which the partners have to discuss their relationship and its prospects.

4. *Minimum age.* As romantic love is, on average, strongest in the young, a minimum age limit for marriage may help to eliminate some of the paradoxes discussed. Empirical evidence indeed suggests that a higher marrying age has a positive effect both on the quality and stability of the marriage. In Switzerland, a related purpose is served by a law forbidding widows to remarry within a year of their husband's death.

SUMMARY

Neo-classical economics has greatly improved our insights into decisions taken in the family and with respect to marriage. Nevertheless, the rational view of marriage is, in important respects, not obviously compatible and is, in some cases, even in outright conflict with what is empirically observable. We have identified four aspects where today's real-life marriage decisions in western industrial countries systematically deviate from what is predicted by conventional neo-classical theory. Romantic love tends to lead to the following paradoxical aspects of marriage decisions:

- little searching for marriage partners;
- biased evaluation of the characteristics of potential partners;
- little advice in marriage decision; and
- underestimation of the likelihood of one's own marriage ending in a divorce.

To accept that such paradoxes, or underlying behavioural anomalies, exist does not mean that the rational choice approach is dropped. Rather, individuals are considered to be rational enough to react to the possibility of succumbing to paradoxical behaviour when making marriage decisions. Precautions may be taken at the individual level – mainly by precommitting oneself – or at the collective level. Various institutional devices existing in the context of marriage decisions can be interpreted as a response to the existence of marriage paradoxes. Our approach thus stays within rational choice, but is applied at a higher level, recognizing that romance alone is not the best basis for making a rational marriage choice.

In an ideal world, where the individual and collective level reactions were complete, one would no longer observe any marriage paradoxes. Information and transaction costs of such individual and institutional responses prohibit paradoxes from being completely eliminated. We thus empirically observe the simultaneous existence of both marriage paradoxes and reactions to overcome them.

SUGGESTIONS ON THE LITERATURE AND SOURCES

The economics of the family is due to
Becker, Gary S. (1991), *A Treatise on the Family*, enlarged edn, Cambridge, MA: Harvard University Press.

Matching theory has been applied by
Mortensen, Dale T. (1988), 'Matching: Finding a Partner for Life or Otherwise', *American Journal of Sociology*, **94**, 215–40.

An example of a strictly theoretical and non-empirical neo-classical approach is
Cigno, Alessandro (1991), *Economics in the Family*, Oxford: Oxford University Press.

The economics of the family is critically discussed in
Ferber, Marianne A. and Bonnie G. Birnbaum (1977), 'The New Home Economics: Retrospect and Prospects', *Journal of Consumer Research*, **4** (June), 19–29.
Hannan, Michael T. (1982), 'Families, Markets and Social Structures: An Essay on Becker's *A Treatise on the Family*', *Journal of Economic Literature*, **20** (March), 65–72.

Analyses of the family in the other social sciences are for example
England, Paula and George Farkas (1986), *Households, Employment and Gender: A Social, Economic and Demographic View*, New York: Aldine de Gruyter,

as well as many articles in the *Journal of Marriage and the Family*, the *American Sociological Review* and the *American Journal of Sociology*.

The empirical findings on courtship and marriage used in the chapter have partly been drawn from
Hill, Charles T., Zick Rubin and Letitia Anne Peplau (1976), 'Breakups Before Marriage: The End of 103 Affairs', *Journal of Social Issues*, **32**, 257–68.
Levinger, George and O. Moles (eds) (1979), *Divorce and Separation: Context, Causes and Consequences*, New York: Basic Books.
Cate, Rodney M. and Sally A. Lloyd (1992), *Courtship*, London: Sage.
Michael, Robert T., John H. Gagnon, Edward O. Laumann and Gina Kolata (1994), *Sex in America. A Definitive Survey*, Boston: Little, Brown.

The theory of asymmetric information and 'lemons' is due to
Akerlof, George A. (1970), 'The Market for "Lemons": Quality Uncertainty and the Market Mechanism', *Quarterly Journal of Economics*, **84**, 488–500.

Satisficing theory has been developed by
Simon, Herbert A. (1982), *Models of Bounded Rationality*, Cambridge, MA: MIT Press.

For the concept of romantic love see
Hendrick, Susan S., Clyde Hendrick and Nancy L. Adler (1988), 'Romantic Relationships: Love, Satisfaction and Staying Together', *Journal of Personality and Social Psychology*, **54** (6), 980–8.

Differences between arranged vs. autonomous marriage and rational vs. romantic marriage are discussed in
Kurian, George (ed.) (1979), *Cross Cultural Perspectives of Mate-selection and Marriage*, Westport, CT and London: Greenwood Press.

Evidence that love tends to fade over time has been collected by
Cimbalo, Richard S., Virginia Faling and Patricia Mousaw (1976), 'The Course of Love: A Cross-sectional Design', *Psychological Reports*, **38**, 1292–4.

Ipsative, subjective and objective views of the world are discussed in
Frey, Bruno S. and Beat Heggli (1999), 'An Ipsative Theory of Human Behaviour', in Bruno S. Frey, *Economics as a Science of Human Behaviour*, 2nd revised and extended edn, Boston and Dordrecht: Kluwer, pp. 195–211.

The empirical application to the case of marriage and divorce is due to
Baker, Lynn A. and Robert E. Emery (1993), 'When Every Relationship Is Above Average. Perceptions and Expectations of Divorce at the Time of Marriage', *Law and Human Behavior*, **17**, 439–50.

The illusion of control has been analysed by
Langer, Ellen J. (1975), 'The Illusion of Control', *Journal of Personality and Social Psychology*, **32**, 311–28.

The cost of marriage dissolution and pecuniary compensation for the differences in 'value' of prospective marriage partners are discussed in
Cohen, Lloyd (1987), 'Marriage, Divorce and Quasi Rents; or, "I gave him the best years of my life"', *Journal of Legal Studies*, **16** (June), 267–303.

5.　From the price to the Crowding Effect

ECONOMICS AND PSYCHOLOGY

Over the last few years, considerable work has been undertaken to bring economics and psychology closer together. Two different approaches may be distinguished. The first approach is to break completely with existing (neo-classical) economics and construct a 'psychological economics', where human beings are analysed according to the ideas and concepts of psychology. While such attempts are courageous, they have little or no effect on economics. Modern economics as the self-proclaimed 'queen of the social sciences' has achieved a well-defined core of assumptions and models, which are vigor-ously protected by academic economists against outside criticism.

The second approach is to introduce specific psychological effects into economics and to thereby improve the rational choice view of man. Promi-nent examples are:

- Scitovsky, who builds on Wundt's Law of the optimal degree of arousal, and refers to it as the 'desire for excitement'.
- Hirschman, who inquires into the conditions under which artistic activ-ity, entrepreneurship and innovation can be awakened. He thus does not take the effort expended as given. One possibility of activating people is to consciously create imbalances; they induce and even force people to become active in order to survive, or to at least maintain their standard of living.
- Simon, Selten and Tietz, and Williamson, who propagate that individ-uals are incapable of maximizing in any strict sense, and propose the concept of 'bounded rationality' as a more realistic, and psychologi-cally adequate alternative, which takes cognitive and motivational limitations of human thinking into account.
- Schelling, Thaler and Shefrin, and several other scholars such as Sen, develop the concept of 'self-commitment'. Persons, who are aware that, under certain conditions, they fall prey to temptation, can try to avoid the trap by binding themselves. An example is Ulysses, who had himself fastened to the mast of his ship in order not to succumb to the sirens' chant. Such theoretical ideas establish a relationship to psycho-

logical theories on how to master one's life. Variants of this approach have been used in Chapters 3 and 4, dealing with the attempt to overcome anomalies and marriage paradoxes.

- Leibenstein develops the notion of an 'inert area', from where individuals have no incentive to depart, even when utility increasing opportunities arise. A related idea, already introduced in the last chapter, has been coined 'ipsative behaviour' by Frey and Foppa.
- Schlicht employs Gestalt theory to explain the movement toward labour management, and employs various psychological theories to account for norms.
- Akerlof and Dickens, and various other economists, use the psychological notion of 'cognitive dissonance' to account for beliefs and consequent behaviour, which are otherwise difficult to explain in the economic framework. They show, in particular, that rational workers discount the risk they are exposed to in their job, and that they therefore use less safety equipment than would be optimal.
- Frank attributes an important role to emotions, which are trustworthy, as they are difficult to imitate. Signals, such as blushing, which are firmly based in psychological thinking, are given a role in economic models of human behaviour.
- In surveys and experiments, the notion of 'fairness', as applied to economic issues, has been explored for a large number of conditions. Fairness, in terms of 'reciprocity', draws directly on the notions of equity developed in psychology.

Some of these efforts to integrate psychological effects into economics have been noted by mainstream economists, in the sense that they are (often almost ritually) quoted at the appropriate moments, but they have had precious little effect on economic theory as a whole. The classical 'Homo Oeconomicus' is still used as a matter of course. The reason might be that these extended versions do not yield empirically testable implications that would differ greatly from the simple model of wealth maximization. The special features highlighted in the psychological effects are felt to be irrelevant under most circumstances. This position may well be tenable in some fields of economics in which abstract markets dominate, but it is most doubtful as soon as one goes beyond and looks at human behaviour in more general circumstances.

This chapter follows the second tradition: it seeks to improve the model of Homo Oeconomicus by introducing a particular, psychologically based effect. It thus amends the '(Relative) Price Effect' basic to economics.

The price effect applied to supply states that a higher price (other things being equal) induces an increase in supply, that is price and quantity are positively related. The 'Crowding-Out Effect' advanced here predicts the exact opposite supply response: a higher price induces a *decrease* in supply. This contrasting effect may be illustrated by two examples:

> A boy on good terms with his parents willingly mows the lawn of the family home. His father then offers to pay him money each time he cuts the lawn.

The crowding-out effect suggests that the boy will lose his intrinsic motivation to cut the lawn (he may go on doing so, but now he does it because he is paid), but he will not be prepared to do any type of housework for free.

> You have been invited to your friend's home for dinner, and he has prepared a wonderful meal. Before you leave, you take out your purse and give your friend an appropriate sum of money.

Probably nobody in their right mind would behave in this way, because virtually everyone knows that this would be the end of the friendship. By paying, the relationship based on benevolence is fundamentally transformed; if it survives at all, it becomes a commercial one. Yet there is one person who would not hesitate to pay a friend for dinner: classical Homo Oeconomicus would do so, following the price effect – and ends up without friends, to his or her own chagrin.

The two examples indicate that the price effect, on which economics is founded, is not valid under all conditions and circumstances, and that the relationship between a monetary reward offered and supply must be analysed in a wider perspective. The 'holy cow' of modern economics needs to be reconsidered. External and, in particular, monetary incentives do not mechanically induce human beings to act in the desired way, because they crowd out intrinsic motivation under identifiable conditions. Thus, external and internal incentives are not cumulative, as has been assumed as a matter of course in economics. A more refined model of humans is needed, a *Homo Oeconomicus Maturus*, whose behaviour to some extent relies on purely internal considerations, in particular on self-esteem and self-determination.

The next section develops the Crowding Theory, discussing its basis in social psychology, integrating it into economics, and analysing the conditions under which the crowding-out effect takes place. The following section presents empirical evidence on Crowding Theory in various domains. The fourth section econometrically analyses crowding effects in taxation. The next section considers spill-over effects to related areas. Conclusions are drawn in the final section: both economic theory and policy are strongly affected by the existence of crowding effects. More care should be taken when applying incentive payments in firms, or in the public sector (for example when following new public management ideas), or when using incentive instruments in economic policy (for example with respect to the environment).

CROWDING THEORY

Psychological Background

Social psychologists have empirically identified that external intervention, in the form of a reward, reduces individuals' intrinsic incentives. This relationship has been variously termed 'undermining effect', 'overjustification effect', 'the hidden cost of reward', 'corruption effect' or 'cognitive evaluation theory' by the psychological scholars involved.

The hidden costs of reward rest on the distinction between internal and external motivation: 'One is said to be intrinsically motivated to perform an activity when one receives no apparent reward except the activity itself' (Deci, 1971, p. 105). The distinction between intrinsic and extrinsic motivation is not clear cut. Indeed, it might be claimed that, in the last instance, all motivation comes from outside. On the other hand, what matters, after all, is the inner satisfaction one derives from one's behaviour. While the precise distinction might be important for psychology, for the purpose of explaining economically and socially relevant behaviour it suffices to distinguish between those activities which people mainly do just because they like them and other activities which they mainly do because of monetary payment, or because they are ordered to do them. In many cases, the two motivations go together. What matters in our context is that an identifiable relationship exists between intrinsic and extrinsic motivation.

Three psychological processes have been identified to account for the 'hidden cost of rewards':

1. When individuals perceive the external intervention to be controlling, in the sense of reducing the extent to which they can determine actions by themselves, intrinsic motivation is substituted by extrinsic control. This loss of self-determination shifts the locus of control from the inside to the outside of the person affected. Individuals who are forced to behave in a specific way by outside intervention, would feel 'overjustified' if they maintained their intrinsic motivation. They then behave rationally when reducing the motivational factor under their control; that is, intrinsic motivation.

2. Outside intervention undermines the actor's intrinsic motivation, if it carries the notion that the actor's intrinsic motivation is not acknowledged. The person affected feels that his or her competence is not

appreciated, which leads to impaired self-esteem, resulting in reduced effort. Self-esteem is of central importance for human beings.

3.   A person acting on the basis of his or her intrinsic motivation is deprived of the chance to exhibit this intrinsic motivation to other persons. Thus, when a host is paid by his or her guests, the host no longer has the possibility of showing them that he or she values their company as such. As a reaction, the persons affected exhibit 'altruistic anger', and will in turn relinquish the inner motivation and behave according to external motives.

Social psychology itself knows a theory competing with the hidden cost of reward. Equity literature has repeatedly found that increasing pay increases productivity and, presumably, intrinsic motivation. In contrast, cognitive evaluation literature has found that increasing pay decreases intrinsic motivation and hence, presumably, productivity. It follows, and has been empirically supported that, depending on the conditions, increased rewards raise or lower intrinsic motivation and productivity accordingly. The reverse also holds: when inadequate rewards are provided, intrinsic motivation may sometimes decrease, and at other times increase.

Conditions

The following conditions determine which rewards negatively or positively affect intrinsic motivation:

1.   External intervention *crowds out* intrinsic motivation if the individuals affected perceive the individuals to be *controlling*. Self-determination, self-esteem and the possibility for expression suffer, and the individuals react by reducing their intrinsic motivation in the activity controlled.
2.   External intervention *crowds in* intrinsic motivation if the individuals concerned perceive it as *supportive* (or informative in a positive way). Self-esteem is fostered and individuals feel that their self-determination is enlarged which, in turn, raises intrinsic motivation.

Both conditions are formulated in terms of subjective perceptions. Psychologists, however, have gone further, and have identified conditions which apply more generally. Thus, the undermining effect is found to be the stronger,

- the more the rewards are expected. Unexpected rewards do not, or only weakly, crowd out intrinsic motivation;
- the more salient the reward is;
- the more contingent the reward is on the task or on performance;

- the more deadlines and threats are used;
- the more intensive surveillance is;
- the more routine the rewarded work is.

Obviously, the hidden costs of reward are only relevant if the persons concerned have some amount of intrinsic motivation. Indeed, intrinsic motivation has been observed to be undermined particularly strongly for those who previously felt highly committed.

With respect to external intervention, psychologists have found that monetary rewards are more corrupting than other material rewards. Praise and social approval are more likely to be interpreted as supportive than as controlling.

Integration Into Economics

Crowding effects generalize the 'hidden costs of reward' in three important ways:

- Intrinsic motivation is potentially affected by all kinds of intervention coming from outside the person considered. Thus, not only rewards, but also commands, may crowd out intrinsic motivation;
- Intrinsic motivation may be reduced or raised (crowding-*out* and crowding-*in*). Thus there may not only be hidden 'costs' but also hidden 'gains';
- External intervention affects the internally held values of individuals. Hence, it not only affects narrowly defined intrinsic motivation, but also norms internalized by individuals. Moreover, external intervention may induce a shift from other regarding or group-regarding to more selfish preferences and behaviour.

These three generalizations greatly enlarge the scope and applicability of crowding theory. To apply crowding theory to issues dealt with in economics, it is necessary to simultaneously take into account the price effect normally considered in economics. Here, attention is focused on crowding-out, because it affects behaviour contrary to the price effect.

Supply falls

Consider a normal, positively inclined, supply function (S in Figure 5.1) for an activity. At zero price, the individuals considered are prepared to supply the quantity q^{IM}, that is to some extent they are assumed to undertake the activity for its own sake, or be intrinsically motivated. Such behaviour is perfectly consistent with economic theory. Following the price effect, con-

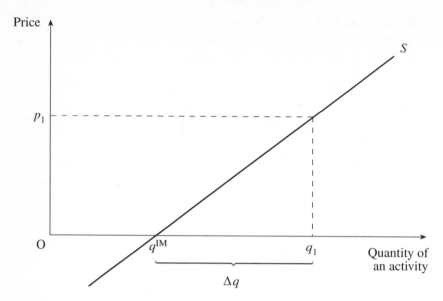

Figure 5.1   Conventional supply theory

ventional economic theory predicts that a price rise (from O to p_1) raises
supply from q^{IM} to q_1, moving along the supply curve.

The extrinsically induced supply increase Δq is perfectly *additive* to the
intrinsically supplied quantity q^{IM}, thus $q_1 = q^{IM} + \Delta q$.

In contrast, the crowding-out effect induces a shift in the supply curve to
the left (Figure 5.2). With a positive price offered, the supply curve moves to
the left (from S to S'), until intrinsic motivation is completely crowded out (at
S''). More precisely, each supply curve is associated with a given stock of
capital of intrinsic motivation. Once this capital stock is exhausted, or at least
constant, supply only moves along S'' as the price effect exists.

The supply response moves quite differently than suggested by conventional economic theory. In Figure 5.2, it is assumed at first that the
crowding-out effect prevails over the price effect, and supply falls: the
individuals concerned reduce the extent of their activity. Beginning at point
C, the price effect dominates. Only when point E is reached does the
quantity supplied exceed the amount previously intrinsically supplied. At
point D on supply curve S'', the stock of intrinsic capital is constant (and
possibly exhausted), so that the price effect exclusively determines supply
behaviour.

In stark contrast to the additivity assumption held in conventional economics, intrinsic and extrinsic motivation are non-additive. The figures serve

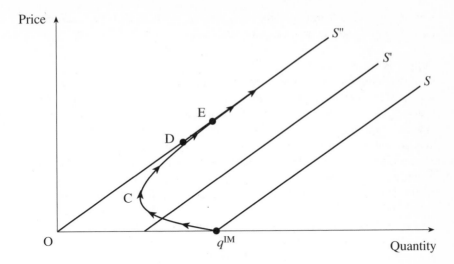

Figure 5.2   Supply including crowding-out effect

merely as illustrations. They refer to only part of the crowding theory. What they do show is that crowding-out is not presented as an alternative to conventional economics, but rather as an *extension*. Moreover, it should be kept in mind that the crowding-out effect depends on particular conditions. The following propositions on the size of the crowding effect can be formulated, based on insights gained by psychologists.

The crowding-out effect is the more pronounced,

- the more personal the relationship between a principal and his or her agent is;
- the larger the agent's participation possibilities are;
- the more uniform the external intervention is; that is, the less individual differences in intrinsic motivation are acknowledged by the principal; and
- the more the external intervention (in particular the rewards extended) are contingent on specific performance, instead of being directed at general behaviour.

Obviously, the crowding effect also has important consequences on policy. Thus, many seemingly 'modern' compensation systems have to be reconsidered. As will be argued in Chapter 7, pay-for-performance schemes negatively affect performance in so far as they reduce work morale, a specific kind of intrinsic motivation. Under certain conditions, for example with volunteers who are essentially intrinsically motivated to work, it may be a mistake to introduce monetary compensation at all.

Supply is transformed

External intervention, in the form of a monetary reward, affects the nature and quality, and not only the quantity, of the supply forthcoming. Quite generally, laboratory research indicates that quality tends to be substituted by quantity. Equally well established is the negative effect on incidental learning that people acquire in complex tasks, because attention is focused on the central task that is rewarded. For tasks that are not well understood, monetary incentives can be dysfunctional; that is, lead to lower performance. Finally, external rewards have been found to decrease artistic and verbal creativity. These results, gained by psychologists, must be seen in perspective. They only refer to how intrinsic motivation is affected and do not, or insufficiently, consider the more direct incentive effects of monetary compensation on performance. Thus it has been well established in the Economics of Culture that artists are able to create masterpieces even when they are doing so for monetary gain.

In important cases, external intervention via money transforms the nature of a good or relationship even more fundamentally. Sometimes, the offer of a monetary reward completely destroys the existing commodity in question. At the beginning of this chapter, the example of paying a friend for a dinner invitation was given. Romantic love is an equally striking case: it simply cannot be bought, and if an attempt were made to buy it, the good is no longer unselfish love but, taken to the extreme, prostitution. The same is true for trust, admiration or friendliness, which change their intrinsic nature when they are bought. This is the problem of the millionaire girl, who never knows whether her suitors love her, admire her and are friendly to her because of herself or because of her money. As long as money is involved, the suitors have no means of revealing 'sincere', that is intrinsic, love and admiration. Rulers essentially face the same problem. The literature is full of accounts of how such 'unfortunate' persons undertake experiments to try to differentiate between the two, usually by faking to be poor and powerless – sometimes even with success, but revealingly so, mostly in fables.

The transformative effect of money on human relationships has been discussed under the term 'Commercialization Effect'. It can vary greatly between historical periods. Thus, for example, from the 16th to the 19th century, the prevailing view in Europe was that the use of prices improves or, in other words, crowds in intrinsic motivation. Montesquieu, for example, believed 'commerce ... polishes and softens ways of behaviour, as we can see every day'. Thus, the crowding effects have a considerably long history.

EMPIRICAL EVIDENCE ON CROWDING THEORY

Experiments

Social psychologists have extensively studied the hidden costs of reward in the laboratory. There are such a large number of laboratory experiments on the crowding effect that it is impossible to summarize the results. Fortunately, there have already been not less than five formal meta-analytical studies of crowding theory. The first meta-analyses undertaken essentially support the findings that intrinsic motivation is undermined if the externally applied rewards are perceived to be controlling by the recipients. This view was challenged on the basis of a meta-analytical study referring to the period 1971–91. It concluded that the undermining effect is largely 'a myth'(Cameron and Pierce, 1994). This study attracted a great deal of attention, and many scholars, on that basis, seem to have concluded that no such thing as a crowding-out effect exists.

The most extensive and recent study by Deci, Koestner and Ryan (1999) shows that these conclusions are unwarranted: the crowding-out effect is indeed a robust phenomenon of significant size under the specified conditions. It identifies a number of significant shortcomings and misinterpretations. One is that Cameron and Pierce omitted nearly 20 per cent of the relevant studies as outliers, used mistaken control groups, and misclassified some of the studies. Another is that they included dull and boring tasks, for which a crowding-out effect cannot occur, as the participants had no intrinsic motivation to begin with. In order to correct these failures, an extensive meta-analysis including all the previous studies, as well as several studies which have appeared since then, was undertaken. The 128 studies analysed span the period 1971–97. It turns out that tangible rewards undermine intrinsic motivation for interesting tasks (that is tasks for which the experimental subjects show an intrinsic interest) in a highly significant and very reliable way, and that the effect is moderately large. This holds in particular for monetary compensation, which is perceived to be controlling by the experimental subjects, and therefore tends to crowd out intrinsic motivation. The crowding-out effect is stronger with monetary than with symbolic rewards. It is also larger with expected than with unexpected rewards. When the problems at issue are complicated, the negative relationship between reward and performance is stronger than when the problems are simple. In all these cases, it is a requirement that the behaviour was initially perceived to be interesting, and therefore intrinsically rewarding. As a consequence, a bonus system usually, but not always, makes employees lose intrinsic interest in the immediate goal, such as serving the customers.

Experimental economic research has also identified various crowding effects on motivation in the economic setting. There have been an increasing number of studies done on the subject. Several experiments demonstrate the existence of a crowding-out effect on intrinsic motivation in the form of a reduced tendency for reciprocity, that is towards more narrowly conceived selfish behaviour.

Some experiments have been able to find the exact relationship between pay and performance, as displayed in Figure 5.1 above. Whenever money was offered, the standard price effect was observed; that is, a larger amount of money results in higher performance. The mere incidence of payment, however, even lowered performance in many cases. In these experiments, with all performing the same task, only those groups which received a considerable amount of pay did as well as the groups that worked for nothing. The evidence suggests that the type of contract and the (monetary vs. non-monetary) work environment evoke different responses from the agents.

The crowding effects have also been studied in contract enforcement, with respect to the trustworthiness of the participants. In an evolutionary game experiment, a first mover relies, to a certain degree, on the trustworthiness of a second mover, because the legal system allows only incomplete contracts. The first mover can either offer a contract, or not play at all, while the second mover has the choice of performing or breaching the contract. The level of contract enforcement is given by the probability of bearing the resulting costs of non-compliance. It was found that low levels of legal enforcement tend to crowd in trustworthiness: the first movers must make careful decisions on whom to enter a contract with, as they cannot rely on the legal system. As a consequence, the second mover is motivated to behave in a trustworthy way. In contrast, when contracts are near-perfectly enforced, there is no observable crowding effect taking place, as first movers enter the contracts because they know that the second movers are deterred from breaching the contract. Personal trust is replaced by institutional trust. With intermediate levels of law enforcement, however, trust is crowded out, as the first movers can neither rely on the second movers' reciprocal behaviour nor on the legal system, resulting in a non-monotonic relation between trust and the degree of contract enforcement.

Crowding effects have not only been identified in experiments, but also are of great importance for practical, real-world problems.

Case Studies

Day-care centres provide a striking case of monetary intervention achieving the opposite of what would be expected on the basis of the price effect. Such institutions are confronted with the problem that parents sometimes arrive late to pick up their children, which forces the employees to stay after the official closing time. To remedy the situation, economists would typically suggest imposing a monetary fine for collecting children late. Such punishment is expected to induce parents to be on time. A study on a day-care centre in Israel revealed a completely different outcome. After the introduction of a rather hefty fine, the number of parents arriving late *increased* substantially, which is in line with the crowding-out effect. Introducing a monetary fine transforms the relationship between parents and day-care employees from a mostly personal to a more monetary relationship. As a result, the parents' intrinsic motivation to keep to the time schedule was reduced or crowded out altogether, the perception being that the employees were now 'paid' for the disamenity of having to stay longer. Being late for picking up children was no longer associated with any feeling of guilt.

Another case study documents that the crowding-out effect can also be induced by commands or regulations. Several little villages in Colombia were threatened by the lack of clean water because of uncontrolled deforestation by the villagers gathering wood. This is a typical common property resource problem in which purely selfish individuals disregarded the unfortunate effects on the environment of collecting wood. In an experiment undertaken with these villagers, and closely mimicking this situation, it turned out that the members of the village did take the negative external effects into account to a considerable extent, partly because they were in close contact with each other and discussed the common property issue among themselves. However, when regulatory controls were suggested to (further) improve the situation in order to reach an efficient outcome, the villagers responded in an unexpected way. Instead of coming closer to an efficient solution, the opposite occurred. Regulatory control induced the villagers to substitute group-regarding with more selfish preferences. They then collected as much wood as they found beneficial for themselves, and disregarded the negative effects on the water supply. This case demonstrates that regulatory control may supplant self-motivation.

A crowding effect was also identified with respect to performance measurement in the airline industry. The specific issue was how airline carriers deal with delays and the responsible factors or persons. Attributing a single delay as exactly as possible to its source (as suggested by the principal agent theory) turned out to be negatively correlated with the achieved end, namely the airline's on-time flight performance. The most successful company was the one that used the general term 'team delay' to indicate the source of a delay caused by the personnel. It thereby crowded in the intrinsic motivation to help out other units and groups, instead of provoking disagreements, finger-pointing and cover-up activities.

Econometric Studies

Work motivation is an area where crowding theory is particularly relevant. One econometric study looks at firms where the intensity of the personal relationship between the principals and the agents depends on the form of supervision. In the case of managers as agents of a certain firm, three major types can be distinguished:

1. The managers are controlled by the parent company. This corresponds to a rather impersonal relationship so that, following our proposition above, a positive influence of monitoring on managers' performance is expected, because intrinsic motivation is little affected or not at all.
2. The managers are controlled by their firm's chief executive officer, which represents a personalized relationship. According to our proposition, monitoring in this case tends to reduce the agents' effort, as external intervention shifts the locus of control towards external preferences, and the agents perceive that their competence is not acknowledged by their superior.
3. The managers' behaviour is regulated by the board of directors. The crowding-out effect is, according to crowding theory, expected to be greater than in case 1 but smaller than in case 2.

The data set refers to 116 managers in medium-sized Dutch firms in 1985 (Barkema, 1995). They range from between fewer than 100 to more than 30 000 employees and cover a wide variety of industries. The managers' individual effort is operationalized as the number of hours invested. Three aspects capture the intensity of supervision: the regularity with which their performance is evaluated; the degree of formality of the evaluation procedure; and the degree to which the managers are evaluated by well-defined criteria. The results are consistent with the proposition advanced. The econometrically estimated parameters, capturing the effect of external intervention on work performance, turn out to be positive and statistically significant in case 1 of impersonal control. In case 2 of personalized control, on the other hand, the corresponding parameter is statistically significant and negative; regulating strongly crowds out intrinsic motivation, so that the net effect of control on performance is counterproductive. In the intermediate case 3 of somewhat personalized control, the estimated parameter does not deviate from zero in a statistically significant way.

Another econometric study looks at the voluntary sector, which is of substantial size in developed economies. Several studies have established that intrinsic motivation is important when it comes to volunteering. A unique data set from Switzerland is used to evaluate how financial rewards for volunteers affect their intrinsic motivation. The incidence of rewards is found to reduce volunteering. While the size of the rewards induces individuals to provide more voluntary work, the mere fact that they receive a payment significantly reduces their work efforts by approximately four hours. The magnitude of these effects is considerable. Evaluated at the median reward paid, volunteers indeed work *less*. These findings have important implications for policy towards voluntary work. Direct incentives may backfire, leading to less volunteering. Even individuals reacting to changes in relative prices, as they are in our data set, may be subject to motivational crowding-out.

We now consider in more depth another important social and economic issue – tax evasion. It will be shown that more intensive political participation possibilities, in the form of popular referenda and initiatives, result in lower tax evasion in the respective political units as intrinsic motivation, in the form of tax morale, is crowded in.

CROWDING EFFECTS IN TAXATION

The intrinsic motivation to pay one's taxes – or tax morale – depends strongly on the extent of trust the citizens have in the political system. When individuals are alienated from government, and do not think that they are treated fairly by the political process, they are more inclined to pursue their selfish interests, that is to evade taxes, only taking into account the expected probability of being punished. A crucial factor increasing trust in government is the extent to which the citizens can actively participate in the political process.

Switzerland presents a suitable test case because the various cantons have different degrees of political participation possibilities. It is hypothesized that the more extended political participation possibilities in the form of citizens' meetings, obligatory and optional referenda and initiatives there are, and the broader the respective competencies are, the higher is tax morale and (ceteris paribus) tax compliance. In an empirical analysis, a crowding-in effect is hypothesized.

On the basis of these characteristics, about one-third of the 26 Swiss cantons are classified as pure direct democracy (D), another third as pure representative democracies (R), and the rest satisfy only some of the characteristics. A cross section/time series (for the years 1965, 1970, 1978, that is 78 observations) multiple regression, explaining the part of income not declared Y_{nd}, yields the following results (t-values in parentheses):

$$Y_{nd} = 7.17 - 3.52p - 2.42f + 0.79*t - 0.36*d - 2.72Y(\ln) + 0.57**NY - 1.09*A - 7.70**D$$
$$\phantom{Y_{nd} =} (-1.98)\ (-0.62)\ (2.10)\ (-2.51)\ (-0.30)\qquad (2.98)\qquad (-2.53)\quad (3.80)$$

R^2(adj.) = 0.69, d.f. = 41, F = 11.08; *,** indicate statistical significance at the 95 per cent and 99 per cent levels, respectively.

$$Y_{nd} = 8.98 - 3.22p - 2.32f + 0.59t - 0.42**d + 1.03Y(\ln) + 0.60**NY - 0.82A + 4.02*R$$
$$\phantom{Y_{nd} =} (-1.72)\ (-0.36)\ (1.70)\ (-3.47)\qquad (0.29)\qquad (3.07)\qquad (-1.93)\ (2.23)$$

R^2(adj.) = 0.65, d.f. = 41, F = 9.43

The explanatory variables are:

p = probability of detection (the number of individual income tax audits per 1000 taxpayers);
f = penalty tax rate;
t = mean marginal tax rate;
d = income deduction possibilities;
$Y(\ln)$ = per capita income (in natural log.);
NY = non-wage income;
A = old-age taxpayers' share (reflecting experience in tax matters).

The coefficients of the variables indicating the type of democracy (D, R) – the other variables being used to control for other influences – have the theoretically expected signs. In cantons with a high degree of direct political control (D), tax morale is (ceteris paribus) higher. The share of income concealed falls short of the mean of the other cantons by 7.7 percentage points or, in absolute terms, the average amount of income concealed is about SFr 1600 (per taxpayer) less than the mean income concealed in the other cantons. In contrast, in cantons with a low degree of political control typical for more representative cantons (R), tax morale is (ceteris paribus) lower. The part of concealed income is four percentage points higher than the average income gap, and the mean income undeclared exceeds the mean of the other cantons by about SFr 1500. The estimation results are consistent with the hypothesis that greater democratic participation possibilities lead to higher civic virtue, as reflected in taxpayer behaviour.

The empirical evidence collected for Switzerland suggests the existence of two (extreme) kinds of democratic tax institutions: one is based on the premise that the citizens are responsible persons and that, in principle, they are prepared to contribute to the provision of public goods and the redistribution of income by the state, provided this process is reasonably efficient and fair. The corresponding tax laws allow the citizens to declare their own income and to make generalized deductions. The tax statements are, in principle, accepted as trustworthy, and the tax authority bears the burden of the proof if it doubts the declarations. Such a tax system supports a citizen's intrinsic motivations and strengthens his or her normative sense that everyone should carry a fair share of taxation. Tax morale is bolstered and tax evasion is reduced.

The second type of tax institution starts with the assumption that all citizens want to exploit the tax laws to the fullest, and cheat whenever they can. The corresponding tax laws deduct the taxes directly from gross income, and the citizens then reclaim from the government any deductions granted by the tax authorities. In the whole process, the burden of proof always lies with the individual citizen. Such a tax system crowds out intrinsic motivation and the normative notion that all citizens should help in carrying the tax burden. Tax morale is undermined and the citizens make an effort to evade taxes.

MOTIVATIONAL TRANSFER EFFECT

Remember the example of the boy willingly mowing the lawn presented at the beginning of this chapter? A contingent pay by his father does not only crowd out his intrinsic motivation to cut the grass, but also to do any other housework.

External intervention may thus have an indirect damaging effect on intrinsic motivation. The crowding-out effect may spread to further areas, even into those areas where the external intervention has not been applied. If intrinsic motivation is crowded out in areas where it is a major (or even the only) behavioural incentive, the overall outcome of an external intervention tends to be even more strongly against the principal's interest. There may thus be an indirect 'Motivational Transfer Effect', which has to be added to the direct crowding-out effect. A further example is provided by policy instruments, such as effluent charges or tradable permits. They work efficiently where they are applied, but an induced substitution of environmental ethics by monetary incentives may well lead people to protect the environment less in areas where no external incentives exist. This undesired motivational transfer effect not only takes place with monetary incentives, but also with rules and regulations.

That intrinsic motivation (in the broadest sense) may be linked across the board has been observed in several instances. Thus norms may spread by analogy. If a similarity is perceived between an area in which a norm is valid and another area where the norm is not yet applied, its validity can expand to the latter area too. The concept of 'attitudinal spillover' and 'reputational spillovers' has been employed in economic contexts. Neurological research suggests that the molecular construction of the brain limits the power to differentiate between varying circumstances, in our case between those areas where external interventions produce overjustification, and areas where a similar type of intrinsic motivation applies, but no external intervention takes place. This is known as the 'spread effect'.

Psychologists have collected considerable direct and indirect empirical evidence for the motivational transfer effect. Intrinsic motivation is taken to transcend areas where the following conditions are met:

- individuals strive to be consistent with their commitment to a moral principle;
- people are used to returning a favour with a favour; that is, to acting according to the principle of reciprocity. When this attitude is destroyed by a monetary reward, the resulting fall in intrinsic motivation tends to spread to related areas;
- individuals frequently use the beliefs, attitudes and actions of others, in particular that of 'similar others', as a standard of comparison. The loss of intrinsic motivation, due to monetary intervention, tends to crowd out the respective intrinsic motivation of 'similar others'. With tax evasion, for example, 'there is a clear, positive relationship between self-reported evasion and the tax evasion of friends and relatives – that is, "similar others"' (Cialdini, 1989, p. 215).

CONCLUSIONS

Crowding theory introduces a so far disregarded but crucial, and empirically well supported, psychological effect into economics. Its integration into economics shows that it certainly does not substitute for the conventional price effect, but that it amends it.

Crowding theory has important implications for economic theory. In particular, a systematic relationship between intrinsic and extrinsic motivation is established; a negative relationship designates the crowding-out effect, a positive relationship the crowding-in effect. Both effects are well supported by laboratory experiments under carefully controlled conditions. In order to show the relevance for actual social issues, crowding theory has also been applied to pressing policy problems. Crowding-out has been empirically analysed to take place when monetary compensations are offered, to find sites for locally unwanted government projects, as well as in other circumstances pertaining to social and environmental policy. Crowding-in has been identified for the effect of direct citizen participation on tax morale and, more generally, different constitutional settings on citizens' behaviour.

It is important to interpret the crowding theory developed here correctly. Three crucial aspects should be taken into account when considering the relevance of this concept.

1. The crowding-out effect works in the opposite direction to the price effect. The net effect depends on relative size. When crowding-out is small, the qualitative effects predicted by conventional economics hold. If, on the other hand, crowding-out is strong, the price effect may be dominated, and the unconventional effect of an external intervention is to be expected.

    As far as I am aware, the crowding-out effect is the only effect systematically working in the opposite direction to the price effect. The many anomalies and paradoxes borrowed from social psychology certainly tend to weaken the effect of any given price change, but they do not reverse it. Thus, crowding theory makes a more far-reaching claim.

    The policy consequence is straightforward: *take care not to intervene too much with what individuals want to achieve by themselves. Leave them as they are as much as possible, and give them the chance to follow their intrinsic motivation more fully.* This policy conclusion does not mean that one should exclusively rely on intrinsic motivation and disregard institutional conditions shaping external incentives. Nor should it be assumed that intrinsic motivation is always 'good' and 'socially beneficial'. Historical experience shows that many of the worst crimes in mankind were performed by people who followed inner motives and ideologies. Robespierre and Himmler provide vivid examples that intrinsically motivated people may create great evil. Passions are often uncontrolled and hazardous.

2. Crowding effects depend on particular conditions. They do not always take place, and can sometimes be ignored. In particular, when economic relationships are abstract and when personal contacts are irrelevant, as is the case for the model of a perfectly competitive market, there is no crowding effect. Behaviour is fully determined by relative prices, that is by extrinsic motivation. As traditional economics has focused on such markets (or on markets close to it) to a large extent, it was correct to exclusively consider the relative price effect. However, as soon as one leaves such abstract, impersonal markets, the conditions identified may obtain, and intrinsic motivation may be important. Then it is necessary to consider carefully how far intrinsic motivation is affected by external intervention.

3. Crowding-out effects are due to people's perceptions of being controlled by external intervention. The resulting marginal shift in the locus of control from inside to outside the person tends to undermine intrinsic

motivation. External intervention can come from a variety of sources, including government. Government intervention, however, need not be connected with a feeling of being controlled. There are certainly programmes which have the opposite effect; that is, which support intrinsic motivation. In so far as this is the case, morality is crowded in, and civic virtue, tax morale and other manifestations of intrinsic motivation are strengthened.

In contrast, the price system and, in particular, monetary rewards are often perceived to be a controlling external intervention by individuals, and can therefore lead to crowding effects. In particular, the price system is often looked at in this light. Thus, not only government programmes and intervention have the potential to negatively affect morality. The same holds, for instance, for pay-for-performance schemes. As they are defined to be contingent on a particular performance (output), they serve to strengthen external motivation and tend to crowd out work morale.

The social sciences and, in particular, economics should pay more attention to intrinsic motivation as an incentive, and as a viable possibility for policy making. This applies to current policy, as well as to policy at the level of the constitution. It is an essential task to establish institutions, that is to take constitutional choices, which support individuals' own initiatives.

SUGGESTIONS ON THE LITERATURE AND SOURCES

An effort to develop a 'psychological economics' independent of neo-classical economics has, for example, been undertaken by

Furnham, Adrian and Alan Lewis (1986), *The Economic Mind. The Social Psychology of Economic Behaviour*, Baltimore and Brighton: Wheatsheaf Books, Harvester Press.
Lea, Stephen E.G., Roger M. Tarpy and Paul Webley (1987), *The Individual in the Economy. A Survey of Economic Psychology*, Cambridge: Cambridge University Press.

More specific psychological effects have been integrated into economics by various scholars, most importantly by

Scitovsky, Tibor (1976), *The Joyless Economy: An Inquiry into Human Satisfaction and Dissatisfaction*, Oxford: Oxford University Press.
Hirschman, Albert O. (1970), *Exit, Voice and Loyalty*, Cambridge, MA: Harvard University Press.
Simon, Herbert A. (1982), *Models of Bounded Rationality*, Cambridge, MA: MIT Press.
Schelling, Thomas C. (1980), 'The Intimate Contest for Self-command', *Public Interest*, **60** (Summer), 64–118.

Sen, Amartya K. (1977), 'Rational Fools: A Critique of the Behavioral Foundations of Economic Theory', *Philosophy and Public Affairs*, **6**, 317–344.

Leibenstein, Harvey (1976), *Beyond Economic Man. A New Foundation for Micro-economics*, Cambridge, MA: Harvard University Press.

Frey, Bruno S. and Klaus Foppa (1986), 'Human Behavior: Possibilities Explain Action', *Journal of Economic Psychology*, **7**, 137–60.

Schlicht, Ekkehart (1998), *On Custom in the Economy*, Oxford: Clarendon Press.

Thaler, Richard H. and H.M. Shefrin (1981), 'An Economic Theory of Self-control', *Journal of Political Economy*, **89** (April), 392–406.

Tietz, Reinhard, Wulf Albers and Reinhard Selten (1986), 'Bounded Rational Behavior in Experimental Games and Markets', Proceedings of the Fourth Conference on Experimental Economics, Bielefeld, 21–25 September, New York: Springer.

Akerlof, George A. (1984), *An Economic Theorist's Book of Tales*, Cambridge: Cambridge University Press.

Frank, Robert H. (1988), *Passions with Reason. The Strategic Role of the Emotions*, New York: Norton.

Williamson, Oliver E. (1985), *The Economic Institutions of Capitalism. Firms, Markets, Relational Contradicting*, New York: Free Press.

The psychological background to crowding theory is due to
Deci, Edward L. (1971), 'Effects of Externally Mediated Rewards on Intrinsic Motivation', *Journal of Personality and Social Psychology*, **18** (1), 105–15.

Lepper, Mark R. and David Greene (eds) (1978), *The Hidden Costs of Reward: New Perspectives on Psychology of Human Motivation*, Hillsdale, NY: Erlbaum.

Deci, Edward L. and Richard M. Ryan (1985), *Intrinsic Motivation and Self-determination in Human Behavior*, New York: Plenum Press.

Deci, Edward L. and Richard Flaste (1995), *Why We Do What We Do. The Dynamics of Personal Autonomy*, New York: Putnam.

An excellent survey of the psychological background, with applications to economics, is provided by
Lane, Robert E. (1991), *The Market Experience*, Cambridge: Cambridge University Press.

Crowding theory is more fully developed in
Frey, Bruno S. (1997), *Not Just for the Money. An Economic Theory of Personal Motivation*, Cheltenham, UK and Lyme, US: Edward Elgar.

An overview of the experimental and field evidence on crowding-out and crowding-in is given in
Frey, Bruno S. and Reto Jegen (2001), 'Motivation Crowding Theory: A Survey of Empirical Evidence', *Journal of Economic Surveys*, forthcoming.

This study provides all the references to the results mentioned in the text.

The econometric study on the effect of supervision on the work morale of managers is due to

Barkema, Harry G. (1995), 'Do Job Executives Work Harder When They Are Moni-
    tored?', *Kyklos*, **48**, 19–42.

An attempt to place crowding effects in the framework of evolutionary game
theory is undertaken in
Bohnet, Iris, Bruno S. Frey and Steffen Huck (2001), 'More Order with Less Law:
    On Contract Enforcement, Trust and Crowding', *American Political Science Review*.

The role of tax morale to explain tax evasion has been analysed by
Pommerehne, Werner W. and Hannelore Weck-Hannemann (1996), 'Tax Rates, Tax
    Administration and Income Tax Evasion in Switzerland', *Public Choice*, **88** (1–2),
    161–70.

6. The Old Lady visits your backyard: a tale of morals and markets

with Felix Oberholzer-Gee and Reiner Eichenberger

THE NIMBY PROBLEM AND COMPENSATION

Political decision-makers in all industrialized, democratic countries are confronted with strong local opposition to major capital investments. Cries of NIMBY (Not In My Backyard) greet the developers of nuclear power plants, waste incinerators, airports, prisons, and clinics for the handicapped. NIMBY projects are defined as all undertakings that increase overall welfare, but impose net costs on the individuals living in the host community. Although citizens readily acknowledge that these collective enterprises are socially desirable, they are not prepared to have them carried out in their immediate neighbourhood. This is not surprising, as the prospective host community has to bear the negative externalities associated with these projects. Supporting NIMBY projects is a public good.

Economists have devised handy tools to deal with NIMBY problems. As the aggregate net benefits of undertaking these projects are positive, one must simply redistribute them in an appropriate way. Host communities must be compensated to make their net benefits positive, while everyone else is taxed to raise the sum of compensation. Incentive-compatible auctions prevent prospective host communities from misrepresenting their preferences. Although it may be argued that these auctions are questionable for reasons of fairness, they remain ingenious because the trade is voluntary. All participants are better off, and the outcome is Pareto superior to the project not being executed at all.

In reality, however, siting procedures based on price incentives have rarely proved to be successful. The search for hazardous waste landfills and nuclear waste repositories in the United States provides a good example: despite the use of hefty compensation, only one small radioactive waste disposal facility and a single hazardous waste landfill (located in – *nomen est omen* – Last Chance, Colorado) have been sited since the mid-1970s. States that rely on compensation-based siting have experienced no greater success than those using other methods.

This chapter analyses why compensation schemes frequently fail. The traditional economic theory of compensation is incomplete in important re-spects because it neglects the influence of moral principles. In the sphere of politics, where NIMBY battles are typically fought, such moral considera-tions dampen the effects of price incentives. In the next section of this chapter, we develop a more complete theory of compensation: if offered in a political context, monetary compensation initially reduces the support for a facility due to the effect of bribery and the crowding-out of public spirit. In the following two sections, these counterproductive effects of financial incen-tives are empirically tested in the case of siting a nuclear waste repository. The fifth section discusses the interplay between market forces and moral considerations, which may produce a compensation cycle. The final section offers policy conclusions and extends the analysis to the public support for the development of new technologies.

Our work has been stimulated by an idea in the tragicomedy *Besuch der alten Dame* – literally *The Visit of the Old Lady* – written by the Swiss dramatist, Friedrich Dürrenmatt. Friedrich Dürrenmatt (1921–91) is consid-ered to be one of the foremost modern dramatic writers in the German language. *The Visit* is generally acclaimed to be his masterpiece. The 20th Century Fox movie *The Visit*, directed by Bernhard Wicki, and starring Ingrid Bergmann and Anthony Quinn, brought the story to the attention of an international audience. The *Times* critic, Irving Wardle, called *The Visit* a piece that 'sets no limits to human corruptibility'.

Claire Zachanassian, the incredibly rich widow of an Armenian oil tycoon, returns to her home town and demands justice for the wrong done to her in her youth. At that time, she became pregnant by her lover, a young man named Alfred Ill. After he repudiated fatherhood, she brought a paternity suit against him. He won the case by bribing two members of the community to bear false witness. Upon her return as an immensely rich widow, Claire Zachanassian offers a gift of one billion dollars to the community if Ill is put to death by the citizens of the community. This offer is at first rejected by the citizens as being deeply immoral. However, they subsequently raise their individual consumption and increasingly accumulate debts, which finally induces them to kill Ill. The Old Lady, having seen justice done, pays the sum of money and leaves. In this sense, Dürrenmatt's Old Lady relates to a situation in which an explicit monetary reward undermines morals.

A MORE GENERAL THEORY OF COMPENSATION

Conventional economic analysis assumes that offers of monetary compensation increase the willingness to accept otherwise unwanted projects. To win the support of a prospective host community, the compensation offered has to be large enough to offset the net disutility imposed by the facility. Such negative externalities include the risk posed by the project, as well as expected economic impacts such as loss of employment or declining property values. If the desired support does not materialize, the compensation needs to be increased. Thus it is taken for granted that it is possible to move on a supply curve for the acceptance of locally unwanted projects. How, then, can the frequent failure of compensation schemes be explained? It is proposed that the effect of bribery and the crowding out of intrinsic motivation are key factors in understanding this phenomenon.

The Effect of Bribery

Innumerable case studies, regarding siting disputes, show that compensation offers are commonly regarded as bribes. If individuals incur moral costs by publicly showing that their approval can be bought, the introduction of monetary incentives generates two countervailing effects: it increases the likelihood of acceptance by reducing the net disutility generated by the facility, and it reduces the willingness to accept the noxious facility by imposing moral costs.

Economists tend to overlook the moral costs of accepting price incentives, and most often rightly so: in a market setting, the effect of bribery does not dominate the relative price effect. However, most siting decisions are not taken in the market, but in the realm of politics, where moral principles play a much more important role. At the polls, expressing moral views is inexpensive because an individual citizen has practically no chance of deciding on an issue in a community of some size. Therefore, the opportunity costs of supporting or rejecting the siting proposal are neglected and moral views tend to dominate the voting decision.

The cost of moral behaviour is the most important determinant for the size of the effect of bribery. In addition, there are a number of other conditions, which account for its prevalence: first, not all public issues pose pertinent moral questions. Moral considerations loom larger if voters decide on subsidizing abortion clinics or cutting welfare programmes than if they consider raising a new building for government administration. Second, the effect of bribery will be smaller if compensation is paid in kind, and thus directly offsets the negative impacts of the facility. In the case of a number of siting projects, environmental groups refused monetary payments, but agreed to the disputed projects after an in-kind restoration of nature at some other place had been offered. In the case of noxious facilities, many compensation packages contain the extension of medical facilities or the supply of fire-fighting equipment. Compensation typically does not take the form of cash payments to individual residents living in the host community.

Crowding Out Public Spirit

Publicly-spirited citizens may vote in favour of hosting noxious facilities if they feel it is their duty to contribute to the well-being of their region. This behaviour need not be irrational. The formation of such preferences may be the result of selfish parents trying to rig their children's preferences towards altruistic behaviour. Individuals then raise their utility by living up to their civic duty. There is ample evidence that residents living in prospective host communities care about the social consequences of siting disputes, and are prepared to contribute to the public good. For example, holding private net costs constant, they are more willing to vote in favour of NIMBY projects if there is a perceived 'need' for the facility, if their own site is safer than other locations available, and if the site selection process allocates the burdens in a 'fair' manner.

Where public spirit prevails, monetary compensation may lower acceptance levels for NIMBY facilities because monetary rewards deprive individuals of the possibility of indulging in altruistic feelings. After all, no one can pretend to act out of civic duty if the compensation package in itself offsets the disutility generated by the facility. Moreover, experiments in social psychology show that compensation not only destroys the possibility of showing one's intrinsic motivation but, under specific conditions (discussed in Chapter 5), negatively affects this motivation itself. Extrinsic (price incentives) and intrinsic (public spirit) motivations must be regarded as scarce factors guiding human behaviour. Rational actors respond to increasing external financial incentives by reducing the scarce motivators that are under their control; that is, they lower their public spirit. Taking this crowding-out effect into account, compensation undermines public spirit and reduces the willingness to permit siting.

As has been pointed out in the last chapter, the crowding-out of civic duty prevails under specific conditions. First, as a prerequisite, the initial public spirit must be of considerable size. The willingness to contribute to the public good is positively correlated with the gain in overall welfare. Second, the crowding-out effect is stronger in political than in private decisions, because the opportunity costs of forgoing compensation are hardly accounted for at the polls. In the political realm, intrinsic motivation may initially (without compensation) dominate the rational voter's decision calculus, and thus lead to unexpectedly high levels of support for the siting of a noxious facility. When price incentives are introduced and civic duty is crowded out, intrinsically motivated support dwindles. Third, public spirit is crowded out to an even larger extent if regulations are used instead of price incentives. The fewer motivational adjustments an individual is allowed to make, the more intrinsic motivation is crowded out. While price incentives preserve the freedom to undertake an activity – although at a higher price – regulations are even more restrictive. Therefore, the latter more fully crowd out civic duty. Indeed, the majority of siting cases, where regional or central governments attempted to coerce communities into accepting facilities, have ended in violent protests.

Hypotheses

A more general theory of compensation, we contend, takes the effect of bribery and the effect of crowding out of public spirit into account. Moreover, it recognizes that both effects become larger as we move from private decision-making, where opportunity costs are fully accounted for, to voting decisions. The theory leads to three testable propositions for the case of siting locally unwanted projects:

1. Introducing monetary compensation decreases the existing willingness to host a noxious facility if bribery and crowding-out effects outweigh the standard relative price effect;
2. People partially support siting proposals out of consideration for the public good. Once price incentives are introduced, the acceptance-enhancing role of variables associated with civic duty will vanish;
3. When public spirit has been crowded out and the effect of bribery dominates the individual decision calculus, variations in compensatory offers leave the expressed willingness to accept a site unaffected.

TESTING FOR PUBLIC SPIRIT

These three propositions are tested using, as an example, Switzerland's search for a low- and medium-level radioactive nuclear waste repository. Due to strong local opposition, the Swiss developer experienced extreme difficulty in finding a site. In June 1993, it was proposed to build the repository in Wolfenschiessen, a small village with a population of 2100, including 640 families, located in central Switzerland. Half a year before this announcement was made, we conducted an hour long personal interview with 305 persons living in Wolfenschiessen. At that time, four communities were still under consideration as possible sites. Many respondents found it likely that Wolfenschiessen would be chosen. In order to test the theory, it seemed ideal to conduct a survey. As at the polls, moral behaviour is inexpensive in interviews. Individual respondents know that their answers are not binding, and that they are unlikely to influence the aggregate outcome. Carefully conducted personal surveys are thus generally thought to represent how people would vote in an actual referendum.

All respondents were asked whether they would vote in favour of building the radioactive waste repository in their community, if the developer and the federal parliament were to propose this. The procedure described was identical to the one actually employed in Switzerland. In order to build a repository, the developer, the federal parliament and the local town hall meeting all have to agree on the project. A bare majority (50.8 per cent) of the citizens living in the host community indicated they would support this siting decision.

Table 6.1 presents the results of a binary logit analysis, testing a model for the acceptance of noxious facilities (Column I, 'without compensation'). The model contains three classes of variables.

First, economic consequences influence the voting decision. As individual estimates of the risks posed by the repository get larger, and expected economic consequences become more negative, the level of support is expected to decrease. Homeowners are less likely to vote for the facility because there are no provisions to protect property values. Second, the model tests for the level of public spirit: if civic duty matters, supporters of nuclear energy may exhibit a greater willingness also to support the siting of the repository in their home town. Judged from a moral perspective, one cannot argue that it is desirable for Switzerland to generate nuclear energy and then not contribute to solving the waste problem. Likewise, respondents are expected to support the facility more strongly if the site selection rule is thought to be acceptable. A sensible site selection process identifies comparatively safe locations and thus minimizes social risks. Publicly-spirited citizens not only care about the private, but also about the social risks. The variable 'Importance of fair procedure' captures the individual concerns for procedural fairness. We expect it to be negatively correlated with the level of support: if a person sets very high standards in terms of fairness, it will become more difficult to find an appropriate siting rule and, thus, less likely that this person feels intrinsically motivated to support the project.

Following standard economic theory, none of the variables measuring public spirit should influence individual voting decisions. Enjoying the benefits of nuclear energy, or approving of the current siting procedure, in no way implies that homo oeconomicus is prepared to bear the costs of a noxious facility.

*Table 6.1   Determinants of acceptance to host a nuclear waste repository –
results of a binary logit analysis (N = 255)*

Independent variables	Willingness to accept facility without compensation (I)		Willingness to accept facility with compensation (II)	
	Estimate (S.E.)	Change in probability of acceptance (*t*-ratio)	Estimate (S.E.)	Change in probability of acceptance (*t*-ratio)
Constant	12.64		−1.59	
	(28.96)		(23.69)	
Individual risk estimate	−0.71	−7.1%**	−0.29	−4.4%**
(1=very low to 6=very high; effect of 1 point increase)	(0.13)	(−5.54)	(0.12)	(−2.51)
Negative economic impacts expected	−1.30	−12.9%**	−1.02	−15.4%*
DY, 1=yes, 0=otherwise	(0.45)	(−2.93)	(0.48)	(−2.12)
Home ownership	−1.23	−12.2%**	−0.55	−8.3%
DY, 1=yes, 0=otherwise	(0.45)	(−2.77)	(0.34)	(−1.63)
Support for nuclear energy	1.15	+11.4%**	−0.09	−1.3%
DY, 1=yes, 0=otherwise	(0.41)	(2.80)	(0.34)	(−0.27)
Acceptance of current procedure	0.63	+6.2%**	0.12	+1.8%
(1=not acceptable at all to 6=completely acceptable; effect of 1 point increase)	(0.13)	(4.95)	(0.11)	(1.07)
Importance of fair procedure	−0.09	−1.0%	−0.56	−8.4%**
(1=not important at all to 6=very important; effect of 1 point increase)	(0.19)	(−0.49)	(0.16)	(−3.47)
Political orientation	0.06	+1%	0.17	+2.5%
(1=left to 6=right)	(0.14)	(0.40)	(0.13)	(1.31)
Income	−0.01	0%	0.01	0%
SFr 1000 per month	(0.04)	(−0.32)	(0.03)	(0.25)
Age	−0.01	0%	0.00	0%
	(0.02)	(−0.32)	(0.01)	(0.25)
Sex (effect of being female)	−0.31	−3.1%	−0.22	−3.3%
	(0.39)	(−0.81)	(0.33)	(−0.68)
Effect of level of compensation	–	–	−0.16	−2.4%
US$ 2175 vs. 4350			(0.36)	(−0.44)
DY, 1=increase, 0=otherwise				
Effect of level of compensation	–	–	−0.11	−1.7%
US$ 2175 vs. 6525			(0.40)	(−0.28)
DY, 1=increase, 0=otherwise				

Notes:
* = significant at the 95%-level; ** = significant at the 99%-level.
The estimated coefficients can be interpreted as the log of odds ratios for a dichotomous independent variable. Since these coefficients are not an intuitively meaningful quantity, we provide derivatives indicating changes in the probability of voting for the repository. Holding all other independent variables at their mean value, these derivatives show the effect of point for point changes in a single independent variable. Thus, the derivative for the Individual risk variable −7.1%) is interpreted as follows: if A estimates the risk to be one point higher than B, A's probability of accepting the repository is on average 7.1% lower than B's, ceteris paribus.

Third, the model contains a number of personal characteristics as control variables. The dependent response of the estimates is supportive votes. Those who did not care about the construction of a nuclear waste repository were omitted from the analysis.

The results of the econometric analysis correspond to the theoretical expectations advanced. Higher perceived risks, negative economic impacts, and ownership of a home all significantly decreased the willingness to host a nuclear waste repository. Personal characteristics did not exercise any significant influence. The variables linked to civic duty point to a sizeable effect of this type of intrinsic motivation. Respondents, who support the Swiss nuclear programme, refrain from free riding when it comes to sharing the burden associated with this technology: they exhibit an 11.4 percentage points higher probability of accepting the waste repository. The acceptance of the current procedure is also an important predictor for the level of support. With every additional point on an acceptability scale from 1 to 6, chances of approval of the facility increase by 6.2 percentage points. As expected, the importance of taking fairness into consideration is negatively correlated with levels of support, pointing to some crowding out of civic duty due to perceived procedural unfairness. However, the effect is minimal and statistically not significant.

EFFECTS OF COMPENSATION

To test the hypotheses formulated above, we repeated the same question, asking our respondents whether they were willing to accept the construction of a nuclear waste repository if the Swiss parliament decided to compensate all residents of the host community. The amount offered for the life-time of the facility varied from \$2175 per individual and year (N=117) to \$4350 (N=102) and \$6525 (N=86). The compensation offered here is quite substantial. Median household income for our respondents is \$4565 per month.

Testing the Effect of Bribery and the Crowding-Out Effect

As a result of introducing financial incentives, the support for the facility *dropped* drastically, namely by more than one-half, to 24.6 per cent. This is consistent with our first proposition and is partially due to the effect of bribery. Many respondents expressed their dismay at the idea of monetary payments: when asked why they rejected the proposition, 83.2 per cent stated that they could not be bribed. Equation II in Table 6.1 summarizes the results of a binary logit analysis of the reactions to the offer of compensation. As proposed in hypothesis 3, increases in compensation ($2,175 vs. $4,350 and $2,175 vs. $6,525) did not significantly increase the willingness to accept the waste repository.

In order to corroborate this result, we offered increases in compensation (from $2175 to $3263, from $4350 to $6525, and from $6525 to $8700) to all those who had declined the initial proposal. Again, the rate of acceptance did not change significantly. Only one single person switched to the supporting camp. This outcome is consistent with the notion that, due to the low cost of answering in surveys, increased material incentives have no effect on survey statements.

The econometric analysis (Table 6.1, estimate II) also confirms that compensation crowds out public spirit: the support of nuclear energy and the acceptance of the current siting procedure, both indications for the willingness to contribute to the public good, ceased to muster support once financial incentives had been introduced. Moreover, those who found it important that the siting decision be fair had a strongly increased probability of rejecting the proposal. Thus, there is strong confirmation for the second hypothesis. In a situation where the display of public spirit is meaningless because material incentives offset the noxious character of the facility, the determinants of civic duty no longer positively influence the voting decision.

The effect of bribery and the crowding-out effect are not unique Swiss phenomena. Increased tax rebates failed to elicit increased support for a nuclear waste facility in Nevada. Similar results, consistent with the hypotheses advanced above, have been reported for Wisconsin, for Washington State, and for Nevada. In all these instances, monetary incentives failed to increase public support for the proposed nuclear waste facilities.

A Competing Hypothesis: Strategic Behaviour

One might argue that the observed price inelasticity is the result of strategic behaviour. According to this view, respondents hope to be compensated even more generously when rejecting initial offers of compensation. However, this argument fails to explain the high initial approval of the facility without compensation, and the fact that increases in monetary rewards had absolutely no influence on support. Moreover, when asked why they declined the compensation offered, only 4.9 per cent of all respondents indicated that the financial incentives provided were insufficient. These statements are incompatible with the hypothesis of strategic behaviour.

THE COMPENSATION CYCLE

As in Dürrenmatt's play, we are still far from the final curtain when observing the rejection of compensation. The money the Old Lady placed on someone's head raised the expected income of the citizens, changed their consumption patterns, and ultimately led to the death of treacherous Mr Ill. Although not as dramatic, we propose that, under specific conditions, material incentives will also come to dominate the morally laden statements made at the polls or in surveys.

A year after our survey, the Swiss developer formally offered compensation to the community of Wolfenschiessen amounting to over $3 million per year for the next 40 years ($4687 per family), or approximately 120 per cent of the community's annual tax revenue. In July 1994, the community decided in a town hall meeting, with a three-fifths majority, that it wished to host the site. This change had been brought about by the substitution of the moral principles that were responsible for the effect of bribery.

The Substitution of Moral Principles

Once compensation has been offered, citizens who think it probable that the noxious facility will be located in their home town experience an increase in expected lifetime income. In the play, Dürrenmatt has his once poor characters purchase and wear yellow shoes as a sign of the dramatic rise in expected income, and thus current consumption. While the opportunity costs of rejecting financial rewards and investment opportunities are at first largely ignored at the polls, they are decisive in subsequent private decisions. Circumstantial evidence for Wolfenschiessen confirms that expected compensation left its mark on private behaviour. When constructing new homes, for instance, the residents are reported to have added extra rooms because the 'employees of the waste repository will have to live somewhere'.

Facing the opportunity costs of the effect of bribery on private behaviour, citizens demand new moral arguments that are in line with their economic interests. Most individuals attach some value to inner-personal consistency. Claiming that one's approval cannot be bought and, at the same time, making use of investment opportunities brought about by the noxious facility, are seen as incompatible. On a social level, such hypocritical behaviour may provoke social sanctions, especially in small communities where the costs of observing hypocrisy are generally low (for example, in Swiss town hall meetings where voters decide by raising their hand). Interest groups respond to the demand for new moral arguments by pointing out the moral virtues of accepting the facility. In-kind compensation for socially beneficial projects (schools, fire stations) makes it easier to link the monetary rewards with positive values. In the end, price incentives alter the moral decision calculus by replacing the bribery aspects of compensation with new moral considerations.

The substitution of moral considerations by market forces can be observed in other contexts as well. Thus price increases are regarded as unfair in situations of excess demand. In laboratory posted-offer markets, producers initially hesitate to increase their prices when taking fairness into consideration. However, once the opportunity costs of profits forgone are felt, prices converge on the competitive surplus maximizing equilibrium.

Moving in Cycles

Under specific conditions, market forces create a compensation cycle, as shown in Figure 6.1. At the outset (A), the individual's decision is influenced by the expected negative consequences of the facility and by his or her public spirit. Support for the project is granted freely because it is perceived to be of no consequence. If feelings of civic duty are not strong enough to elicit the support deemed desirable, the developer introduces monetary compensation to offset the negative impacts of the facility. However, due to the effect of bribery and the crowding-out effect, financial rewards decrease support to level (B). In this situation, increasing the compensation is ineffective (C).

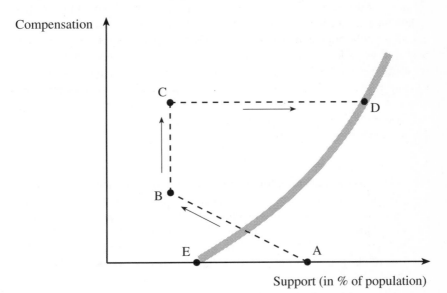

Figure 6.1   The compensation cycle

In the long run, social sanctions for hypocritical statements, and the need for inner-personal consistency, increase the demand for moral arguments that correspond to the economic interests of the agents. Ultimately, these considerations will come to dominate political decisions: while 75 per cent of the respondents in Wolfenschiessen rejected financial incentives when they were first offered (in the survey), two-thirds of the voters supported the siting in a town hall meeting one year later. Similar to the Swiss case, the town of Eagle, NY, also completed a full compensation cycle before it accepted a solid-waste landfill.

As may be seen from Figure 6.1, there is a notional, long-run supply curve connecting points D and E: higher compensation induces higher support, provided sufficient time has elapsed. However, a developer cannot choose a point on this supply curve. The compensation cycle is similar to the expectation-augmented Phillips-curve, and the distinction between the short-run and long-run Laffer curve. In all these cases, short-run outcomes are not stable equilibria, due to forces within the system.

POLICY IMPLICATIONS AND CONCLUSION

This provides a theory of compensation, which takes the effect of bribery and the crowding out of public spirit into account. More generally, a new interpretation of the relationship between political and market behaviour is offered. Individuals act more differently in the two spheres than is usually acknowledged in public choice theory and in market analysis. In politics, moral issues play a larger role than in the market. Expressing moral views is essentially without cost in political decisions, while in the market it is not. As has been shown, moral considerations are fragile; under identifiable conditions, they are crowded out or decisively adjusted when price incentives are introduced.

Our theory allows for the identification of various factors which influence the acceptability of compensation offers.

1. Conventional siting approaches are characterized by a decide–announce–defend (DAD) structure: following secret investigations into the (technical) suitability of a location, the prospective host community is confronted with the siting proposal and promises of compensation. As notions of civic duty are crowded out, and the effect of bribery dominates the political sphere, the project is most likely rejected. Here it is suggested that binding decisions at this early stage are responsible for the failure of many compensation schemes.
2. As long as the effect of bribery dominates individual expression, verbal opposition to noxious facilities is to be expected. In this situation, many

developers break off negotiations, hoping to find another host community more willing to take the project. However, compensation packages meeting the needs of the residents living in the prospective host community would show their effect only if sufficient time were allowed.

3. Developers are able to minimize the perceived moral cost of accepting compensation by clearly distinguishing the financial incentives from bribes. A compensation contingent on support for the project is lowering acceptance levels as it emphasizes the (morally questionable) role of compensation in bringing about a change of opinion. Despite the loss of efficiency, in-kind compensation benefiting the community as a whole weakens the effect of bribery.

The analysis presented here covers a large number of issues. Consider the development of new technologies, like gene technology. Many politicians are reluctant to express their support of gene technology because of the intricate moral questions involved. The rational voter will disregard the opportunity costs of not developing gene technology, and support the party whose moral judgements he or she shares. In Europe, there is a marked tendency to choke off, or at least slow down, developments in gene technology. The analysis presented here suggests that resistance can be overcome by allowing private decisions to play a part. If a patient is allowed to decide whether to forgo improved medical treatment because it is based on gene technology, or if the consumer may choose between a conventional tomato and the juicier and cheaper gene-technology equivalent, we can trust the relative price effect to show its effect. In the analysis undertaken here, moral considerations are considered to be endogenous. Thus the availability of superior medical techniques, or better quality and cheaper consumer goods, will lead to an adjustment in the moral judgements of the public at large. Interest groups will be quick to point out the benefits of gene technology for patients, and healthy nutrition for the poor, once such arguments are demanded. The theory also explains the politicians' fondness for trial periods and limited tests. These produce the type of private behaviour that creates the moral standards compatible with economic interests.

Siting decisions, and the frequent rejection of compensation for locally unwanted projects, are thus but one example of decisions taken in the political sphere, which tend to be dominated by moral evaluations. If moral principles are decisive for voting behaviour, further research will have to take the emergence of moral views into account. Economists improve their understanding of social choices if economics once again becomes a science studying moral principles.

SUGGESTIONS ON THE LITERATURE AND SOURCES

There is a large literature dealing with the Not In My Backyard problem. See, for instance,

Rabe, Barry G. (1994), *Beyond NIMBY: Hazardous Waste Siting in Canada and the United States*, Washington, DC: Brookings Institution.
Gerrard, Michael B. (1994), *Whose Backyard, Whose Risk: Fear and Fairness in Toxic and Nuclear Waste Siting*, Cambridge, MA: MIT Press.
Easterling, Douglas H. and Howard Kunreuter (1995), *The Dilemma of Siting a High-level Nuclear Waste Repository*, Boston: Kluwer.

Overcoming the NIMBY problem by offering compensation, in particular in the context of incentive-compatible public auctions, has been suggested by

Kunreuter, Howard and Paul R. Kleindorfer (1986), 'A Sealed-bid Auction Mechanism for Siting Noxious Facilities', *American Economic Review*, **76** (May), 295–9.
O'Sullivan, Arthur (1993), 'Voluntary Auctions for Noxious Facilities: Incentives to Participate and the Efficiency of Siting Decisions', *Journal of Environmental Economics and Management*, **25**, 12–26.

That compensation may be perceived as bribes has also been noted by

O'Hare, Michael, Laurence Bacow and Debra Sanderson (1983), *Facility Siting and Public Opposition*, New York: Van Nostrand Reinhold.
Portney, Kent E. (1991), *Siting Hazardous Waste Treatment Facilities: The NIMBY Syndrome*, New York: Auburn House.

The usefulness of a referendum format in surveys on individual evaluations of social issues has been discussed by

Arrow, Kenneth J., Robert S. Solow, Edward Leamer, Paul Portney, Ray Radner and Howard Schuman (1993), 'Report of the NOAA-Panel on Contingent Valuation', *Federal Register*, **58** (10), 4601–14.

The effect of bribery and the crowding-out effect in the context of nuclear waste facilities have also been observed by

Kunreuter, Howard and Douglas Easterling (1990), 'Are Risk Benefit Tradeoffs Possible in Siting Hazardous Facilities?', *American Economic Review*, **68** (May), 64–9.
Carnes, S.A. et al. (1983), 'Incentives and Nuclear Waste Siting', *Energy Systems and Policy*, **7** (4), 324–51.
Dunlap, Riley E. and Rodney K. Baxter (1988), *Public Reaction to Siting a High-level Nuclear Waste Repository at Hanford: A Survey of Local Area Residents*, Pullman: Washington State University.
Herzik, Eric (1993), *Nevada Statewide Telephone Poll Survey Data*, Reno: University of Nevada.

7. Motivation, knowledge transfer and organizational forms

with Margit Osterloh

KNOWLEDGE AS A SOURCE OF COMPETITIVE ADVANTAGE

Knowledge generation and transfer is an essential source of a firm's sustainable competitive advantage. The question is, which organizational form is most conducive to knowledge generation and transfer? The most prominent suggestion for organizing firms is to introduce market elements and prices through such methods as profit centres, spin-offs, or holdings. We intend to show that such organizational forms are suitable only under special circumstances defined by specific aspects of knowledge and motivation. In line with the knowledge-based view of the firm, we distinguish explicit knowledge from tacit knowledge. We ask what kinds of motivation are needed to generate and transfer tacit knowledge, as opposed to explicit knowledge. To explore this question, we resort to the well-established and widely empirically supported social psychological theory of the interaction between intrinsic and extrinsic motivation, extensively drawn upon in Chapters 5 and 6.

Intrinsic motivation is not simply additive to the motivation induced by prices (extrinsic incentives). Rather, under certain conditions, the use of the price system undermines intrinsic motivation (crowding-out effect), making motivation endogenous to organizational forms. We argue that knowledge transfer is intimately connected to motivation, and that sustainable competitive advantage requires corresponding motivation management. We will demonstrate which organizational forms are suitable for generating and transferring tacit knowledge, as well as explicit knowledge. In addition, we will show the type of motivation, whether intrinsic or extrinsic, these organizational forms should engender for effective knowledge transfer and sustainable competitive advantage to take place.

Over the last few decades, firms have increasingly been restructured by introducing market elements, such as profit centres, divisional units, or holdings. The purpose is to exploit the advantages of the price mechanism by making the exchanges between the actors or departments more explicit and by rewarding employees according to their contribution to the firm's profit. This strategy corresponds to a view of firms as the governance structure 'of last resort, to be employed when all else fails' (Williamson, 1991, p. 279).

But this view, espoused by many economists, has recently been challenged. It has been argued that firms take the place of markets when they are superior with respect to non-market coordination and commitment of the persons involved. However, what 'non-market' organization means is left unexplored. The resource-based theory of the firm as the leading alternative approach to economic theory is also vague with respect to organizational forms. Most adherents of the resource-based view consider knowledge to be the most strategically important resource.

Knowledge is created by the flow of information and is the product of human behaviour. It thus fundamentally differs from information, which is composed of a string of messages not connected as such to individuals.

It is also important to distinguish between two types of knowledge. *Explicit* knowledge can be coded in writing or symbols, while *tacit* knowledge cannot. But only a small part of our knowledge is explicit. Tacit knowledge is acquired by, and stored within, individuals and cannot be transferred or traded as a separate entity. In contrast, explicit knowledge has the character of a public good (except when such knowledge is patented or copyrighted). The transferability and appropriability of explicit knowledge thus differs from tacit knowledge. There are two important consequences:

1. Tacit knowledge is a crucial source of sustainable competitive advantage, because it is difficult for competitors to imitate it.
2. The contribution of a particular employee's tacit knowledge to team output cannot be measured and paid accordingly. This has important motivational ramifications.

EXTRINSIC AND INTRINSIC MOTIVATION

Following economists' advice to 'run a firm as if it were a set of markets' means rewarding employees according to their marginal productivity, and relying on *extrinsic* rather than *intrinsic* motivation.

A Comparison

Employees are *extrinsically* motivated if they are able to satisfy their needs indirectly, especially through monetary compensation. Extrinsically motivated coordination in firms is achieved by linking employees' monetary motives to the goals of the firm. The ideal incentive is offered by a strict pay-for-performance system.

Although many economists admit the existence of intrinsic motivation, they tend to leave it aside because it is difficult to analyse and control. Even if the assumption of opportunism is accepted as an 'extreme caricature' (Milgrom and Roberts, 1992, p. 42), opportunism is taken as a prudent worst-case assumption when designing institutional structures. Opportunism is a strong form of extrinsic motivation where individuals are not constrained by any rules. In the transaction cost view, the task is to establish institutional settings that mitigate the hazards and costs of opportunistic behaviour.

Motivation is *intrinsic* if an activity is undertaken for one's immediate need satisfaction. A corresponding activity is valued for its own sake. Intrinsic motivation can be directed to the activity's flow, to a self-defined goal, such as climbing a mountain, or to the obligations of personal and social identities. The ideal incentive system is in the content of the work itself, which must be satisfactory and fulfilling for the employees.

The behavioural view of organization emphasizes intrinsic motivation. This approach has a long tradition in motivation-based organization theory. Intrinsic motivation is also drawn upon by critics of transaction cost theory, as is the literature on psychological contracts. They emphasize intrinsic motivation in the form of identification with the firm's strategic goals, shared purpose, and the fulfilment of norms for their own sake.

Proponents of the behavioural point of view tend to consider intrinsic motivation as an undisputed organizational advantage because it lowers transaction cost and raises trust and social capital. However, intrinsically motivated employees do not always work to the benefit of their employers. Thus, intrinsic motivation has both advantages and disadvantages.

Disadvantages of Intrinsic Motivation

Motivation is not a goal in itself, but should serve to support a firm's goals. Enterprises are not interested in producing some kind of intrinsic motivation with their employees, say the joy of stamp collecting. Rather, employees must be motivated to perform in a coordinated and goal-oriented way. For this purpose, managers must compare the benefits and costs related to motivating employees intrinsically and extrinsically. Two specific problems arise in connection with relying on intrinsic motivation in an organization:

1. Changing intrinsic motivation is more difficult, and the outcome more uncertain, than relying on extrinsic motivation, or carrots and sticks. For this reason, economists, as well as managers, traditionally prefer a reward and command policy.

2.   Intrinsic motivation can have undesirable content. As history shows,
      some of the most terrible crimes have been motivated intrinsically, at
      least in part. Envy, vengeance and the desire to dominate are not less
      intrinsically motivated than altruism, conscientiousness and love.

To discipline the effects of undesirable intrinsic motivation, external intervention via carrots and sticks is needed. Management makes unwanted
outcomes of intrinsic motivation in co-workers, superiors and customers
costly and therefore less attractive.

Advantages of Intrinsic Motivation

Under specific conditions relevant for organizations, intrinsic motivation is
superior to extrinsic motivation.

1.   Intrinsic motivation is needed for tasks that require creativity. In con-
      trast, extrinsically motivated persons tend to produce stereotyped repetition
      of what already works. Experimental research also shows that the speed
      of learning and conceptual understanding are reduced when people are
      monitored. With extrinsically motivated employees, the pressure of sanc-
      tions leads to lower learning levels, and the work performed is more
      superficial than with intrinsically motivated employees.
2.   Intrinsic motivation also helps overcome the so-called 'multiple task'
      problem. Contracts cannot completely specify all relevant aspects of
      employee behaviour and its desired outcome. Moreover, the goals to be
      set are often not clear to the principals. Financial goals cannot always be
      broken down into operational goals for employees. Accordingly, con-
      tracts offering incentives to reach given goals can give rise to dysfunctional
      behavioural responses. Agents focus only on the rewarded aspects of the
      job and disregard the unrewarded ones. Nor do they have sufficient
      incentives to reflect on the adequacy of the goals they should achieve for
      the overall success of the firm. Multiple task problems are the subject of
      incomplete contracts, which are characteristic of employment contracts.
      Empirical evidence suggests that the outcome of incomplete contracts
      will not normally be evaluated by variable pay for performance. Rather,
      firms rely considerably on intrinsic motivation.
3.   Most importantly, intrinsic motivation enables the generation and trans-
      fer of tacit knowledge under conditions in which extrinsic motivation
      fails. In these cases, the multiple task problem is combined with the
      problem of 'free riding' in teams.

ORGANIZATIONAL CONSEQUENCES OF MOTIVATION CROWDING EFFECTS

If the two types of motivation were independent and additive, intrinsic and extrinsic motivation could be managed by firms according to their relative advantages and disadvantages. The separation of intrinsic and extrinsic motivation would also correspond to a useful division of labour between psychology focusing on intrinsic motivation and economics focusing on extrinsic incentives. However, as has been extensively discussed in the previous two chapters, under certain conditions there is a trade-off between the two types of motivation.

Social psychologists, as well as some unorthodox economists, suggest that contracts may involve strong emotional ties and loyalties. These socio-emotional relations establish a psychological contract that goes beyond transactional exchanges but includes a reciprocal appreciation of intrinsic motivation. If such a contract is breached, the reciprocal good faith is put into question. In this case, the parties to the contract perceive that the employment arrangement is transformed into an extrinsically motivated (transactional) contract. For example, when guests express their appreciation of a host's efforts with a symbolic gift (such as a bunch of flowers), the host's intrinsic motivation tends to be raised. However, when guests try to present money as a gift, the host's intrinsic motivation is destroyed.

An important part of psychological contracts involves the perception of fairness. Experiments and field studies show that fairness increases the willingness to perform and decreases shirking.

Although general crowding effects have not been fully explored, we can still surmise the consequences of specific organizational designs on motivation. We focus on three aspects of crowding effects that should be taken into consideration when integrating market elements (such as profit centres or variable pay for performance) into the firm.

1. *Participation* is an alternative to markets as a coordination mechanism. Participation signifies agreement on common goals. Participation raises the perceived self-determination of employees and therewith strengthens intrinsic motivation. As experiments show, the strengthening of self-determination and intrinsic motivation takes place only when agreements about the goals serve primarily as self-control and self-obligation. In contrast, perceived external control inhibits creativity in the pursuit of goals.

2. *Personal relationship* in lieu of the anonymous market is a precondition for establishing psychological contracts based on emotional loyalties, often called team spirit. Team-based structures enable such a personal

relationship. Personal relationship strongly raises the intrinsic motivation to cooperate. Linking-pin organization as a network of interlocking teams raises intrinsic motivation based on psychological contracts. In contrast, neither perfect markets nor the price system rely on psychological contracts. An example is the anonymous relationship between buyers and sellers on financial markets.

3. *Contingency of reward* for performance can crowd out intrinsic motivation. This holds provided the perceived controlling effect of reward is stronger than the perceived informing effect, and the price effect is overruled. The crowding-out effect provides a possible interpretation for the overwhelming empirical evidence that there is generally no valid connection between pay and performance. Instead, the 'literature on incentive plans is full of vivid descriptions of the counter-productive behaviours that piece-rate incentive plans produce' (Lawler, 1990, p. 58). The same holds for managerial compensation, a fact admitted even by the proponents of principal-agent theory, who favour time-based compensation and oppose strict forms of variable pay for performance in situations that need high intrinsic motivation.

COMBINING MOTIVATIONAL AND KNOWLEDGE REQUIREMENTS

Managing motivation, especially balancing intrinsic and extrinsic motivation, is an important and hard-to-imitate competitive advantage. This capability is crucial for all tasks in which the goals are difficult to formulate and where it is difficult to attribute task completion to particular employees. As pointed out, the generation and transfer of knowledge often constitutes such a task. At the same time, the generation and transfer of knowledge is the most crucial resource of firms. Employees who are extrinsically motivated could resort to free riding. This situation cannot be alleviated by strengthening the carrot-and-stick policy when the conditions for crowding out apply. In such conditions, external intervention undermines the necessary intrinsic motivation of employees.

Managing intrinsic motivation is difficult and often risky. Situations that require intrinsic motivation must be distinguished from those that do not. Markets rely systematically on price effects and therefore can crowd out the intrinsic motivation needed for specific forms of knowledge generation and transfer. In what follows, organizational forms that integrate market elements into firms are contrasted with those not using market elements.

When the transfer of tacit knowledge is at stake, introducing market mechanisms is bad advice. With the launch of its first personal computer in 1981,

IBM chose to outsource all the major components. The microprocessor was bought from Intel, while the operating system was licensed from Microsoft. Moreover, the distribution channels were outsourced to a large number of retailers, such as ComputerLand, Sears, BusinessLand, and MicroAge. The strong extrinsic incentives produced by the market enabled IBM to get its first PC on to the market in only 15 months and to launch an attack against Apple, the market pioneer. However, with the passage of time, IBM learned a hard lesson. Because outsourcing necessitates making knowledge explicit to allow production and service level agreements, the competitors in the markets for PCs had an open door to imitate IBM. They could buy the same operating system from Microsoft, the same software from Lotus, WordPerfect and Microsoft, and use the same distribution channels. As a result, IBM lost much of its competitive advantage, as well as its ability to direct the evolution of the PC architecture.

The right balance between insourcing and outsourcing is crucial, because no company is able to develop all the technology necessary internally for a product to be successful in the future. Motorola, a leader in wireless communication technology, seems to be a firm that has chosen the right balance. To retain its competitive advantage in the long run, battery technology is critical for Motorola. It therefore develops the critical parts of its value chain (fuel cells and solid-state energy sources) internally, and buys the less critical battery technologies, such as nickel cadmium, on the market.

Figure 7.1 presents a typology of organizational forms. It discusses which organizational forms can best enable the transfer of explicit or tacit knowledge with respect to the required extrinsic or intrinsic motivation. The four types of organization occur only rarely in pure form. For the sake of clarity, hybrid forms of organization, like strategic alliances and interfirm networks, are not taken into consideration.

Cell 1 in Figure 7.1 describes the situation commonly considered by economists when they suggest running a firm 'as if it were a set of markets'. Prominent examples of this advice are profit centres, spin-offs, or holdings. An effort is made to replace commands by contracts and transfer prices. This advice is well taken if the necessary knowledge to be transferred between the decentralized units is either encapsulated in a marketable product, or is otherwise explicit. Only explicit tasks are communicable by means of contracts. In situations of a marketable product or a contract, monetary rewards and extrinsic motivation fulfil their task. In the case of profit centres, transfer prices referring to comparable market prices serve to calculate the contribution of each unit to the corporate outcome. Transfer prices help to remunerate leaders of profit centres according to their performance.

As the example of IBM shows, a problem arises when the resources become imitable. The very idea of extrinsically motivated competition between

Knowledge generation and transfer

	Tacit	Explicit
Intrinsic	2 Knowledge-based production teams	3 Knowledge-producing teams, for example quality circles
Extrinsic	4 Independent knowledge workers	1 Profit centres, spin-offs, holdings

Motivation (left of the rows)

Figure 7.1   Combining motivational and knowledge requirements in organizational forms

decentralized units hinders the flow of tacit knowledge to where it is needed. Therefore, the critical parts of the value chain should not be outsourced or separated into different profit centres.

Cell 2 considers the case of 'knowledge-based production teams'. The exchange of tacit knowledge is concentrated within an organizational unit. In addition, knowledge remains tacit and cannot be translated into action subject to commands. Examples are the construction of complex facilities, or the development of an outstanding product design, like Benetton's fashion design. The tacit knowledge is embodied in the product itself, or in the firm-specific routinized processes leading to the product. Because of the tacitness of this knowledge, it can neither be made explicit via reverse engineering nor can it be encapsulated in an expert-system software. In the case of Benetton, fashion design moreover has to be integrated with garment knowledge, Benetton's own market knowledge, and its manufacturing expertise. As in the cases of IBM and Motorola mentioned above, such activities are the basis for a long-running competitive advantage in the form of core competencies that are difficult to imitate. To keep this advantage, these activities have to remain inside a working team and should not be dissected into profit centres or outsourced.

There are reasons for containing tacit knowledge at both the team and the individual level. At the team level, competition between firms, as well as between profit centres, hinders the transfer of tacit knowledge. The members of a unit have no incentive to give up their individual competitive knowledge advantage, as long as they are compensated according to the unit's profitability. Because of the uncodifiable nature of tacit knowledge as part of the multiple task problem, the transfer of tacit knowledge cannot be assured by a complete contract.

At the individual level, employees cannot be identified and sanctioned if they hold back their tacit knowledge. Peer pressure, often presumed to be a solution to the free riding problem, does not work at the individual level. Agents cannot monitor one another, or mete out punishments to those who do not process tacit knowledge. An example (particularly relevant here) is the joint production of this chapter. Each author is unable to determine the share of his or her contribution to the joint output.

The well-known solution to the team production problem of appointing a person to receive the difference between revenues and costs (residual claimant) does not apply to tacit knowledge. With physical activities, such as jointly lifting cargo into a truck, each team member would realize if another one was shirking. The team member acting as a residual claimant is able to assess the contribution of the other team members and can prevent shirking. Such assessment becomes more difficult if the product of team work does not consist in physical activities, but in processing explicit knowledge, which is harder to measure. Preventing shirking is impossible when tacit knowledge has to merge within the team. The joint output can be evaluated solely on the market. Tacit knowledge can be efficiently marketed only if it is encapsulated in goods or services. It follows that, in the absence of intrinsic motivation, free riding will take place.

So far, it has been argued to what extent intrinsic motivation is required in knowledge-based production teams. But how can this required motivation be achieved?

1. Participation and personal relationship foster employees' intrinsic motivation, because their perceived self-determination is raised.
2. Crowding-out effects are to be avoided, by refraining from individual variable pay for performance and the resulting competition. In teams, efforts to help are reduced by individual incentives. For this reason, time-pay according to the qualifications of the team members is often the practice. In team-based compensation, a crowding-in effect is produced if pay is accompanied by non-financial social recognition strengthening perceived competence.
3. Effort can be put into selecting intrinsically motivated persons for the tasks on hand. In any case, an intrinsic motivation to generate and transfer tacit knowledge cannot be forced, but can only be enabled under

suitable conditions. By its very nature, intrinsic motivation is always voluntary.

The generation and transfer of explicit knowledge is not only associated with extrinsic motivation, nor does the transfer of tacit knowledge always require intrinsic motivation. Cell 3 in Figure 7.1 deals with those cases where parts of tacit knowledge are made explicit. The conversion of tacit knowledge into explicit knowledge at the individual level is an important part of the process of creating firm-specific tacit knowledge. During this process, individual tacit knowledge is amplified and crystallized in the form of routines. According to the resource-based view of the firm, organizational routines, embodied in the individual's as well as in the firm's tacit knowledge, are the most sustainable source of hard-to-imitate competitive advantages.

Organizational knowledge creation can be characterized as a 'knowledge spiral' in which tacit and explicit knowledge interact during four modes of knowledge conversion. In the socialization mode, tacit knowledge is mainly shared between individuals as learning by doing. In the externalization mode, parts of tacit knowledge are translated into explicit knowledge. Externalization is supported by metaphors, analogies, narratives, or visuals. In the combination mode, different explicit knowledge is bundled together, mainly by the exchange of documents, computerized communication, or formal education. Thus, the body of explicit knowledge becomes enriched and systemized. In the internalization mode, the new body of explicit knowledge is converted into rules of action and practice, that is the 'firm's memory' in the form of routines. Routines serve to enable the firm to deal with bounded rationality, while at the same time acting as a repository of firm-specific knowledge. To a high degree, routines are applied habitually and therefore become integrated into the body of tacit knowledge stored within individuals. At the same time, the habitually stored and practised routines become integrated into the shared organizational tacit knowledge. The 'knowledge spiral' leads to a higher and richer level of shared knowledge.

Thus, both socialization and externalization are required to create an ever growing body of organizational routines. Externalization is the dominant mode of knowledge conversion in cell 3, while socialization is prevalent in the activities of cell 2. Externalization, as part of the process of creating firm-specific routines, takes place in 'knowledge-producing teams'. Examples are quality circles or task forces. Both are widely used to enhance total quality and continuous improvement in many industries, for example in car manufacturing. Participants contribute their mostly tacit knowledge about the production process by using, for example, narratives. The aim is to implement improved routines, which become part of the firm's repository of knowledge.

As in cell 2, the knowledge transfer itself cannot be observed and measured. However, its outcome can be both observed and measured. This outcome cannot be attributed to an individual working in a team. Hence, the conversion from tacit knowledge to explicit knowledge requires intrinsically motivated group members committed to the group. For this reason, these teams are, in most cases, formed voluntarily, and their tasks are defined by themselves to support self-determination.

Cell 4 deals with independent knowledge workers in a firm. They are independent in the sense that they are not working in a team with co-specialized workers with whom they share tacit knowledge. Examples are lawyers or experts in computing or finance. These workers rely strongly on their specific tacit knowledge. The application of tacit knowledge itself cannot be measured, but its output can be compensated according to its value to the organization. In contrast to cells 2 and 3, this output can be attributed to the independent knowledge worker. In this particular case, no intrinsic motivation is needed. However, the performance of such independent knowledge workers does not contribute to a sustainable competitive advantage; other firms can easily woo them away and profit from their tacit knowledge.

CONCLUSIONS

The analysis suggests four conclusions:

1. Intrinsic motivation is important for firms. It has great advantages in areas where prices and markets play a minor role. The decision to rely on, and enable, intrinsic motivation depends strongly on the need to generate and transfer tacit knowledge. This knowledge is an important source for sustaining competitive advantage, as demonstrated by the resource-based view of the firm. The transfer of tacit knowledge, within teams and between teams, cannot be directly observed and the output cannot be attributed to a particular employee. At best, managers can observe the result of knowledge generation and transfer in terms of output. Explicit knowledge, on the other hand, is tradable. Managers are more capable of observing how well workers with individual knowledge have performed in this respect, and can reward them accordingly.
2. The crowding effects make both intrinsic and extrinsic motivation endogenous variables. Intrinsic motivation is not simply additive to extrinsic motivation induced by rewards. Crowding effects thus restrict the applicability of standard transactions cost and agency theory for organization design. Assuming that people act in an opportunistic way promotes exactly

those worst-case conditions whose consequences standard organization theory is designed to overcome.

3. The conditions can be identified under which market elements, such as profit centres or holdings, are beneficial. Markets systematically use extrinsic incentives for motivational purposes. No problem arises insofar as explicit knowledge is to be transferred, or tacit knowledge is encapsulated in a product, or service attributable to a residual claimant. In contrast, if the tacit knowledge of several team members is crucial for a joint output (either in the form of a product or in the form of explicit knowledge), the use of market elements may lead to withholding knowledge that is needed to establish and preserve the competitive advantage of a firm. When the transfer of tacit knowledge within or between teams is crucial, (transfer) prices as well as commands are unsuitable for motivation. Instead, organizational forms that emphasize participation and personal relationship, such as linking pins or overlapping teams, are needed.

4. Firms may be interpreted in a new light. Firms are able to manage motivation better than the market. According to the relative advantages and disadvantages of intrinsic motivation, firm managers can choose an optimal combination, and can obtain it by taking motivational crowding effects into account.

SUGGESTIONS ON THE LITERATURE AND SOURCES

The main exponent of transaction cost theory is
Williamson, Oliver E. (1985), *The Economic Institutions of Capitalism. Firms, Markets, Relational Contradicting*, New York: Free Press.
Williamson, Oliver E. (1996), 'Economic Organization: The Case for Candor', *Academy of Management Review*, **21**, 48–57.

Surveys of the neo-classical theory of the firm are provided in book form by
Milgrom, Paul and John Roberts (1992), *Economics, Organization and Management*, Englewood Cliffs, NJ: Prentice-Hall,

and in the form of articles by
Gibbons, Robert (1998), 'Incentives in Organizations', *The Journal of Economic Perspectives*, **12** (4), 115–32.
Prendergast, Canice (1999), 'The Provision of Incentives in Firms', *Journal of Economic Literature*, **37**, 7–63.

The motivation-based organization theory has been put forward by
McGregor, Douglas (1960), *The Human Side of Enterprise*, New York: McGraw-Hill.
Argyris, Chris (1964), *Integrating the Individual and the Organization*, New York: Wiley,

and, more recently, by

Donaldson, Lex (1995), *American Anti-management Theories of Organization. A Critique of Paradigm Proliferation*, Cambridge, UK: Cambridge University Press.
Davis, James H., F. David Schoorman and Lex Donaldson (1997), 'Towards a Stewardship Theory of Management', *Academy of Management Review*, **22** (1), 20–47.

Important contributions to the knowledge-based theory of the firm are, for instance,

Conner, Kathleen R. and Coimbatore K. Prahalad (1996), 'A Resource-based Theory of the Firm: Knowledge versus Opportunism', *Organization Science*, **7** (5), 477–501.
Kogut, Bruce and Udo Zahnder (1996), 'What Do Firms Do? Coordination, Identity, and Learning', *Organization Science*, **7**, 502–18.
Foss, Nicholas J. (1996), 'Knowledge-based Approaches to the Theory of the Firm: Some Critical Comments', *Organization Science*, **7** (5), 470–6.
Grant, Robert M. (1996), 'Toward a Knowledge-based Theory of the Firm', *Strategic Management Journal*, **17** (Winter Special Issue), 109–22.

The difference between explicit and tacit knowledge has been emphasized by

Polanyi, Michael (1966), *The Tacit Dimension*, London: Routledge and Kegan Paul.

It has been made fruitful for the theory of the firm by

Nonaka, Ikujiro and Hirotaka Takeuchi (1995), *The Knowledge-creating Company*, New York and Oxford: Oxford University Press.

The concept of psychological contracts has been developed by

Rousseau, Denise M. (1995), *Psychological Contracts in Organizations*, Thousand Oaks, CA: Sage.
Morrison, Elizabeth Wolf and Sandra L. Robinson (1997), 'When Employees feel Betrayed: A Model of How Psychological Contract Violation Develops', *Academy of Management Review*, **22** (1), 226–56.

The flow interpretation of intrinsic motivation is due to

Csikszentmihalyi, Mihaly (1975), *Beyond Boredom and Anxiety*, San Francisco: Jossey-Bass.

The example of IBM in the discussion of cell 1 (Figure 7.1) has been provided by

Chesbrough, Henry W. and David J. Teece (1996), 'When is Virtual Virtuous? Organizing for Innovation', *Harvard Business Review*, **74** (Jan./Feb.), 65–73,

and the example of Benetton in the discussion of cell 2 by

Richardson, James (1996), 'Vertical Integration and Rapid Response in Fashion Apparel', *Organization Science*, **7** (4), 400–12.

PART III

Political Economy

8.   Identification in democratic society

with Iris Bohnet

TOWARDS A BROADER VIEW OF DEMOCRACY

In *economic theory*, individual actions are taken to be coordinated by the market; that is, by anonymous price signals. In the *economy*, on the other hand, individuals are not isolated, but interact by many other means, notably by talking to one another. Communication is even more important in areas where the market does not produce efficient results. While the competition of parties for government, and the competition of pressure groups and citizens for subsidies, describes many parts of democracy well, the direct interaction of the citizens in the form of communication accounts for one specific feature of a viable democracy: it increases 'other-regarding behaviour'.

Many non-economists therefore stress the crucial role of discussion in democracy and reject the notion of 'teledemocracy', or 'instant electronic voting', which lack a 'face-to-face' interaction. The discourse between citizens is an essential element of a lawful state and, under suitable conditions, allows a consensus to be reached among individuals based on insight. While the notion that discourse always motivates people to transcend their own interests to seek the public good is certainly extreme, discussion has been shown to systematically influence individuals' behaviour in instances where economists would not expect any effect. Experimental evidence demonstrates that individuals contribute much more to public goods if only they can talk to one another. However, the discussion envisaged by experimentalists, and also by philosophers, is a face-to-face interaction between individual persons, and is thus necessarily restricted to small groups. Democratic decisions are normally taken in large number settings, where face-to-face discussion among the citizens is impossible. Two surrogates for the missing interpersonal discussion may be considered.

1.   The discourse between the citizens is substituted by discussions in representative bodies, that is parliaments. This solution faces a fundamental principal agent problem, which relates both to the representativeness of the members of parliament and their incentives to pursue the will of the

citizens. Moreover, the discussion among the members of parliament, many of which are professional politicians, may be quite different from the talk between ordinary citizens.

2. The discussion between citizens may be substituted by non-verbal communication or identification. This type of interaction is less demanding than face-to-face discussion and may take place between a much larger number of citizens.

This chapter is devoted to an analysis of the second option. It is asked how far, and in what respects, the outcomes of verbal interactions deviate from non-verbal interactions. For that purpose, the results of experiments are reported. They consider the behaviour of individuals in the same decision situations but with differing interaction possibilities, namely discussion or identification. The next section summarizes the knowledge about the effects of discussion on the outcome of conflictual decisions in experiments. The following section analyses the effect of substituting discussion by mere identification in a variety of experiments undertaken by us. The fourth section considers in what sense discussion and identification might be relevant in real life democracies, and the final section concludes that, in important conflictual situations, verbal communication may to some extent be substituted by non-verbal communication (identification) among the citizens. Conditions are identified in which discussion is more effective than identification, but also in which non-verbal types of communication are preferable to discussion.

EXPERIMENTAL EFFECTS OF DISCUSSION

When individuals communicate with each other, situations of conflict are mitigated because the extent of 'other-regarding' behaviour increases. The persons involved tend to act less egoistically and to take the interests of the other discussants more into account. In a Prisoner's Dilemma situation, individuals are prepared to contribute to the common good by acting more cooperatively, that is they behave less like free-riders. According to game theory, however, pre-play communication is irrelevant ('cheap talk') as no binding contracts can be closed, and rational players should choose to act non-cooperatively in the Prisoner's Dilemma game, and to share nothing in the Dictator Game. (These games are explained in the Appendix to this chapter.)

Laboratory experiments have unequivocally shown that when the players are able to talk to each other in a Prisoner's Dilemma situation *before* the decision is taken, they are significantly more 'other-regarding'. In one of the first public good experiments with communication, cooperation increases from 31 per cent to 72 per cent as soon as the subjects do not have to take the decision anonymously but are allowed to talk to each other (Dawes, McTavish and Shaklee, 1977). These results were further substantiated by later experiments with one-shot communication and decisions, and with repeated communication and decisions. Interestingly, repetition in a communication setting leads to the opposite result of repetition in anonymous games: cooperation increases to 90 per cent for ten or more periods (Isaac and Walker, 1988).

A meta-study (Sally, 1995) comparing over 100 articles in the principal (Anglo-American) journals of political science, social psychology, economics and sociology, supports the increased cooperation effect of communication. Here 130 different treatment conditions are distinguished, of which one-third involved communication among the participants. Allowing for all possible variables inducing cooperation to rise, the study finds that the presence of discussion in one-shot games is highly significant and increases the cooperation rate by more than 45 percentage points on average. In a repeated game, the frequency of discussion is important: subjects who may talk to each other before each round are 40 percentage points more likely to contribute to the public good than they would be in an anonymous setting.

It may be hypothesized that, in the structurally equivalent Dictator Game, discussion also leads to more other-regarding behaviour, inducing the allocator (the one who gets a fixed sum of money) to share more with the recipient. This game is chosen as it offers the purest indicator for altruism. The utility of the other person directly depends on the behaviour of the allocator, without being mitigated by the uncertainty of the provision of a public good.

A replication of the Prisoner's Dilemma experiments with economics students at the University of Zurich, undertaken in the winter semester 1993/94, confirms the increasing cooperation effect of communication. A cross-game comparison indicates that discussion evokes the same effect in the Dictator Game – people become more 'other-regarding' after having talked to one another. All subjects participated in both games, the Prisoner's Dilemma and the Dictator Game, in a random order. In our Prisoner's Dilemma framework, students were confronted with a dichotomous decision between a cooperative ('other-regarding') and a defective (egoistic) strategy. In the Dictator Game, half of the subjects had to decide how they wanted to allocate a previously received sum (SFr. 13.00) between themselves and a randomly chosen counterpart. The more they passed on to the second person, the more 'other-regarding' was their behaviour. Table 8.1 exhibits the results of our experiments.

In this experiment, the situation of 'no discussion' is not equivalent to strict 'anonymity'. The players knew that all participants belonged to the body of economics students at the University of Zurich (the relevant set, however, the

*Table 8.1   Effects of discussion on 'other-regarding' behaviour
            (Experiments at the University of Zurich, November 1993)*

	No discussion	Discussion
Prisoner's Dilemma: percentage of subjects choosing the cooperative strategy	12% (N=172)	78% (N=100)
Dictator Game: share of sum of money allocated to the recipient	26% (N=78)	48% (N=34)

first semester students, consisted of more than 500 persons). This explains why, in a situation where no discussion takes place, the players showed a non-negligible amount of other-regardedness. However, what matters in our context is that, in both decision situations, other-regardedness rises significantly ($p < 0.001$) when the players engage in pre-play discussion.

EXPERIMENTAL EFFECTS OF IDENTIFICATION

In democracies, face-to-face discussion between the citizens, and even among politicians, is usually impossible, or at least rare. The set of persons one is aware of, without ever having talked to them, is much larger. Non-verbal communication, or *identification* is therefore more relevant for democracy, even if only two-way interaction is considered. Identification has several meanings, one of which is the identification with a person, in the sense of taking another person as a role model. We use a different meaning: it is not the identification *with* somebody, but the identification *of* somebody which is relevant here. While students may well identify with the student body when they play the games anonymously, seeing the other group member(s) has an additional effect. Social sanctioning becomes possible. Thus it is not only unselfish behaviour which is costly, but also amoral actions. Not observing some standards of 'other-regardedness' to which others relate may be sanctioned by social approval or disapproval.

The question is how far non-verbal communication may be a substitute for discussion; that is, how far the prospect of social sanctions may account for the same effects exhibited by communication. The effects of identification on 'other-regarding' behaviour are thus compared with the anonymous situation on the one hand (Table 8.2), and with discussion on the other (Table 8.1).

In our one-shot Prisoner's Dilemma game, identification nearly doubles the share of participants cooperating (p=0.033). Discussion has, however, an additional feature, as it is able to increase cooperation to much higher levels

*Table 8.2   Effects of identification on 'other-regarding' behaviour
(Experiments at the University of Zurich, November 1993)*

	No identification	Identification
Prisoner's Dilemma: percentage of subjects choosing the cooperative strategy	12% (*N*=172)	23% (*N*= 64)
Dictator Game: share of sum of money allocated to the recipient	26% (*N*=78)	50% (*N*=56)

(78 per cent, see Table 8.1). Talk allows the participants to exchange prom-ises for cooperative behaviour which, though not being enforceable contracts, have a psychologically binding effect: the participants' behaviour is coordi-nated towards mutually advantageous cooperation. When the participants in the Prisoner's Dilemma game are only able to identify each other, such a 'psychological contract' based on promises is unfeasible, which explains the lower rate of cooperative behaviour.

In the Dictator Game, identification (Table 8.2) results in an equal sharing of the amount between the allocator and the recipient; that is, the share of the sum of money passed on rises from 26 per cent to 50 per cent ($p < 0.001$), and thus reaches a similar level as with discussion (Table 8.1). The expected standard of 'other-regardedness' seems clear: allocators restore equity. The additional feature attributed to talk, namely the formation of a psychological contract, is of no importance here because no behaviour needs to be coordi-nated.

The experimental results presented accord well with previous research, as far as it exists. No Dictator Game experiments with the effect of identifica-tion seem to have been tested before. For an anonymous Dictator Game, where allocators had to decide whether to divide $20 with $18 for themselves and $2 for the recipient, or $10 for each, 76 per cent of the allocators chose to split the cake evenly (Kahneman, Knetsch and Thaler, 1986). A concentration of offers of equal division could also be observed in other anonymous Dicta-tor Games, even though an equal split is not always the model result. In the experiments presented here, non-verbal communication is able to increase 'other-regarding' behaviour, though not quite to the same extent as when the participants do not only identify each other, but are also able to communicate verbally.

RELEVANCE OF DISCUSSION AND IDENTIFICATION FOR DEMOCRACY

The experimental results reveal a strong positive effect of face-to-face discussion on cooperative behaviour. Such verbal interaction is restricted to small groups. In representative democracies, this condition only exists in particular aspects of the political process. In government, it mainly takes place in the inner cabinet, as many of today's governments have grown so large in size that face-to-face discussions are rare. Discussion is also important in parliamentary commissions which, depending on the constitutional rules and traditional procedures, may play an important decision-making role. There are institutions specially designed to establish intensive discussion among ordinary citizens. There are also mediation processes, or 'discourse groups', which have been created to transfer the concept of discursive rationality into reality.

The notion that discussion induces more 'other-regarding' behaviour and therewith 'better' political decisions does not, however, necessarily hold. Two propositions may be advanced regarding the possibility of discussion having destructive effects.

- *Proposition 1: Democratic decisions become more difficult.*
  An open discussion broadens the range of issues considered to such an extent that the complexity becomes unmanageable and confusion arises. It also allows the participants to insist more on their own personal preferences and desires, so that a convergence on mutually shared values (moral standards) is less likely.
- *Proposition 2: Exclusion produces more inequality.*
  Discussion among a selected group of citizens (or politicians) results in an implicit or explicit coalition against those excluded from the discussion, and worsens the relative position of the persons excluded.

These two propositions will be discussed in the following section, concentrating on the Dictator Game, as possible effects on 'other-regarding' behaviour may best be shown when we use the pure form of altruism.

Democratic Decisions become More Difficult

Our experimental results lend support to proposition 1. In the Dictator Game, discussion leads to a larger variability (standard deviation) of outcomes compared with the identification situation, as shown in Table 8.3.

As may be seen from Table 8.3, the standard deviation of the outcomes is raised from 2.43 when the allocator and the recipient may identify with one

*Table 8.3   Effects of identification and discussion on the variability of
outcomes (Experiments at the University of Zurich, November
1993)*

	Identification	Discussion
Dictator Game: Standard Deviation	2.43 (*N*=56)	3.71 (*N*=34)

another, to 3.71 when they may talk to each other. While, in the identification setting, the vast majority of the groups converge to the mutually shared norm of equal division (71 per cent), only 47 per cent of the groups choose a 'half-and-half' split in the discussion framework. Discussion leads to the introduction of a greater number of issues into the decision process, thereby preventing the participants from converging on one particular solution. As social choice theory has shown, increasing the number of issues (alternatives) given the number of participants raises the probability of not reaching a stable equilibrium outcome. Voting cycles become more likely. Thus, whenever a clear focal point like, for example, a sharing norm exists, discussion tends to make it more difficult to find an acceptable solution.

Proposition 1 is in contrast to the economic conception of the effects of discussion. According to the orthodox economic view, the exchange of information is expected to lead to learning. The participants' perception of the world is approximated to reality, consequently it is expected that a discussion meeting reasonable standards of equality and fairness leads to more efficient outcomes. Considering our results, this is not necessarily the case. More information increases the complexity of a decision task and may lead to more undesired and less stable outcomes. This reminds one of the notion that 'optimising with no uncertainty in choosing more preferred alternatives does not tend to produce systematic and stable regularity in behaviour. Rather, it tends to destroy such regularity as successively more information can be reliably interpreted in guiding more complex behavior' (Heiner, 1983, p. 572).

Exclusion Produces More Inequality

The 'destructive' effect of communication by exclusion may be demonstrated by using a slightly different experimental design: individuals do not play a two-person Dictator Game but a three-person game, where identification and communication are only allowed for two of the participants (the allocator and the first 'included' recipient), while the second 'excluded' recipient remains isolated and anonymous. Comparing these treatment conditions with a frame-

Table 8.4   Effects of identification and discussion on 'other-regarding' behaviour in a three-person Dictator Game (Experiments at the University of Zurich, November 1994)

Treatment condition	No identification and no discussion	Identification	Discussion
Share of sum allocated to recipient 1	14%	24%	37%
Share of sum allocated to recipient 2[a]	14%	19%	17%
	(N=21)	(N=36)	(N=66)

Note: [a] Recipient 2 is excluded from discussion in both the identification and the discussion treatment.

work where all subjects are anonymous, reveals the results shown in Table 8.4.

A decision situation where the allocator may only interact with one out of two possible recipients, leads to the recipient with whom the allocator talks receiving significantly more ($p < 0.001$) than in the anonymous situation where nobody talks (37 per cent instead of 14 per cent). The recipient excluded from the discussion receives less: 17 per cent (compared with 37 per cent, $p < 0.001$). This outcome supports the notion that a *partial* introduction of communication creates more inequality than when there is no communication at all. This negative externality on the 'outsider' is less severe in the identification situation: the identified recipient on average receives 24 per cent, while the anonymous one receives 19 per cent. In both cases, the recipient involved in the interaction can increase his or her gain relative to the one excluded, but this unequalizing effect is *smaller* in the case of identification. Nevertheless, it may also be observed that, under both types of direct interaction, there is a positive 'norm activation externality'; that is, compared with a treatment without identification and discussion, the excluded second recipients benefit from the first recipient's interaction with the allocator.

The experiments undertaken highlight the potential of communication to lead to unreliable decisions and more unequal outcomes. The experiments reveal, however, a positive aspect of communication not considered so far. In the experiment just discussed (Table 8.4), the recipient excluded from the discussion receives less than the one included, but receives more than under anonymous conditions. The discourse between the allocator and one of the recipients has a 'spillover' or 'motivational transfer effect' on the excluded recipient. The Schelling norm activated by identification and communication seems to include all recipients, even those not taking part in the interaction, as the allocators share the pie almost equally between themselves and the two other recipients: they keep 57 per cent when they are identified with the recipients, and 46 per cent when they talk to one of the recipients. On the other hand, in an anonymous situation, they keep 72 per cent for themselves.

It must be emphasized that discursive theory stipulates that all parties concerned must be part of the discussion. No indication is given, however, of how this goal can be reached in the democratic setting. In a practical application of discursive theory to a siting or NIMBY (Not-In-My-Backyard) problem (see Chapter 6), this condition is clearly violated, as only a selected number of citizens affected by the location of the refuse disposal plant can participate in the discussion groups. Quite generally, it is impossible to include certain 'interests' in the discussion process because they can, by nature, not be represented at all, or only partially. This applies in particular to consumers and taxpayers, who are difficult to represent by a spokesperson because their interests are so diverse. In any case, there is a fundamental principal–agent problem. The representatives of consumers and taxpayers cannot easily be given an incentive to speak in the interest of their principals, not least because they often do not know what these interests really are. Exclusion from the discussion thus represents a serious limit to discursive democracy.

CONSEQUENCES FOR DEMOCRATIC DESIGN

The results of the experiments suggest the following (tentative) conclusions for the role of communication in democracy:

- Discussion and identification raise cooperation and sharing ('other-regarding' behaviour). Discussion does so more strongly than identification if behaviour needs to be coordinated by a 'psychological contract'. Voluntary public good provision is an important case. For democracy, discussion is important, as it supports civic virtues in the form of cooperation and sharing. Discussion can to some extent be substituted by identification, so that the favourable effects can be transformed to democratic processes beyond face-to-face interactions.
- Discussion makes the convergence on mutually shared values more difficult and may produce inconsistencies of preference aggregation. It favours the consideration of a varied set of individually relevant issues and preferences. On the other hand, identification facilitates the convergence on general norms of cooperation and sharing.

  Personal interaction between citizens, in the form of identification, supports democracy, especially when decisions can only be reached by recourse to mutually shared social norms. Discussions, on the other hand, should in this case be given a restricted role. They tend to increase the diversity of opinions and interests proclaimed and are more strongly geared to particularistic motives, making consistent social choices more difficult.

- The outcome level for persons not included in the communication process is improved by the communication of the other persons engaged via a spillover effect.

    Communication should be supported in a democracy because it tends to improve the lot even of those not taking part in the process. It is thus favourable to groups of persons who cannot be suitably organized by their very nature (above all, consumers and taxpayers), or who participate little or not at all in the political process (especially the lower classes in society).

- Discussion produces more unequal distributions of outcomes to the disadvantage of those excluded from this communication. A disequalizing effect also holds for the case of identification, but it is weaker than for discussion.

Democracies, strongly based on notions of fairness and equality, should make an effort to have all relevant persons participate in the communication process. Those not participating lose relative to the others, which may create social upheaval. Where a general participation in communication is not possible, for whatever reason, it is preferable not to promote discussion by institutionalizing it (for example bargaining between established social groups such as in incomes policy), because partial representation in verbal and nonverbal communication tends to increase inequality.

The design or reform of constitutions should take the relative advantages and disadvantages of the various forms of communication into account. Discussion clearly has its merits and is indispensable for democratic institutions, but it needs to be harnessed by clearly defined rules prescribing where discussion is appropriate. In addition to being time intensive and sometimes exhausting, discussion often cannot be suitably arranged in a large-scale society. We propose that identification may supplement and even be a substitute for discussion.

APPENDIX 8.1

1. Agreement with the Participants in the Experiments

1. You are taking part in an experiment and get SFr 7 (in small coins) as your endowment capital. With that you can cover the expenditures arising during the experiment.
2. You agree to follow the *rules* of the experiment. The main rule is to *remain silent during the experiment*. Talk is allowed only if explicitly introduced by the experimenters.
3. You may earn more money in this experiment: additionally up to SFr 22.
4. The results of the experiments will be used for scientific purposes only.

Signature of the experimenters

I am taking part in the experiment and I confirm having read the agreement.

Signature of the student

2. Explanation of the Prisoner's Dilemma Game with Identification

What it is about
In this experiment, you form a group with three other persons. You may decide between the alternatives X and Y. Your gain or loss depends on how you and the other three members of your group act.

- If you and the other three members of the group choose X, each person gets SFr 2.50.
- If you choose Y, but the other three stay with X, you will get SFr 9, while the others pay SFr 0.50 each.
- If you and another person choose Y and the other two choose X, you (and the other person choosing Y) get SFr 6 each, while the other two choosing X pay SFr 3.50 each.
- If you and two others choose Y and the fourth decides on X, then you (and the two others choosing Y) get SFr 3 each, and the fourth choosing X pays SFr 6.50.
- If all four persons of the group choose Y nobody gets anything.

These results are summed up in the following table:

Persons choosing X	Result for X	Persons choosing Y	Result for Y
4	2.50	0	–
3	–0.50	1	9.00
2	–3.50	2	6.00
1	–6.50	3	3.00
0	–	4	0.00

Before you make the decision, you will get to know who the other members of your group are.

The procedure
- Stage 1: You and all other members of your group get up in order to identify each other. You may look at the other persons, but you cannot talk to the members of your group.
- Stage 2: Next, you have to decide between the alternatives X and Y. Please indicate your choice on the blue sheet enclosed. You make the choice on your own; nobody else knows what you choose (not even after the experiment).
  That marks the <u>end</u> of the experiment.
- Stage 3: Put all the documents into the white envelope and hand it in.

3. Explanation of the Anonymous Dictator Game: Allocator Instruction

What it is about
In this experiment, the team consists of you and one other person. You get the amount of SFr 13, which you may allocate between yourself and the other person <u>as you like</u>.

- You may keep the whole sum of SFr 13 for yourself.
- You may also give the whole sum of SFr 13 to the other person.
- Finally, you may also divide the sum of money exactly as you wish between yourself and the other person; for example SFr 2 for yourself and SFr 11 for the other one.

During the experiment, you remain completely anonymous. The other person does not know who allocated the sum determined by you (possibly zero) to him/her. The other person remains anonymous as well.

The procedure

- Stage 1: You run the experiment without knowing the other member of the group (you are not known by him or her either). The other person is not necessarily in the same room.
- Stage 2: Now you have to decide how much of the SFr 13 you want to forward to the other person. Please put the corresponding amount of money into the coloured envelope and hand it in (it will be given to your designated recipient).

  That marks the <u>end</u> of the experiment.
- Stage 3: Put all the documents into the white envelope and hand it in.

4. Explanation of the Anonymous Dictator Game: Recipient Instruction

What it is about

In this experiment, the team consists of you and another person. The other person gets a sum of SFr 13. He or she may give part of it, or the whole amount to you.

During the experiment, you remain completely anonymous. The other person does not know to whom he/she allocates the sum determined by him/her (possibly zero). The allocator remains anonymous as well (even after the experiment).

The procedure

- Stage 1: You run the experiment without knowing the other member of the group (you are not known by him or her either). The other person is not necessarily in the same room.
- Stage 2: You get an envelope from the experimenters with the sum of money that has been allocated to you by the other member of your group. Please note on the green sheet enclosed how much money you got.

  That marks the <u>end</u> of the experiment.
- Stage 3: Put all the documents into the white envelope and hand it in.

SUGGESTIONS ON THE LITERATURE AND SOURCES

For the philosophical foundations of discourse theory, see
Habermas, Jürgen (1987), *Die Theorie des kommunikativen Handelns*, Frankfurt a. M: Suhrkamp.
Habermas, Jürgen (1992), *Faktizität und Geltung: Beiträge zur Diskurstheorie des Rechts und des demokratischen Rechtsstaates*, Frankfurt: Suhrkamp.

The importance of discourse in the political setting has been treated, for example, by
Dryzek, John S. (1990), *Discursive Democracy: Politics, Policy and Political Science*, Cambridge: Cambridge University Press.

The effect of pre-play communication on other-regardedness in Prisoner's Dilemma games has been analysed using laboratory experiments by
Ostrom, Elinor, Roy Gardner and James Walker (1994), *Rules, Games, and Common-pool Resources*, Ann Arbor: University of Michigan Press.

See also the survey of results in
Ledyard, John O. (1995), 'Public Goods: A Survey of Experimental Research', in John Kagel and Alvin E. Roth (eds), *Handbook of Experimental Economics*. Princeton, NJ: Princeton University Press, pp. 111–94.

For the effect of group identity, see
Dawes, Robyn M., Alphons J.C. van de Kragt and John M. Orbell (1988). 'Not Me or Thee but We: The Importance of Group Identity in Eliciting Cooperation in Dilemma Situations – Experimental Manipulations', *Acta Psychologica*, **68**, 83–97.

A useful meta-analysis on the increased cooperation effect of communication is due to
Sally, David (1995), 'Conversation and Cooperation in Social Dilemmas. A Meta-analysis of Experiments from 1958 to 1992', *Rationality and Society*, **7** (1), 58–92.

The Zurich experiments reported are more fully presented in
Bohnet, Iris (1997), *Kooperation und Kommunikation. Eine ökonomische Analyse individueller Entscheidungen*, Tübingen: Mohr (Siebeck).
Frey, Bruno S. and Iris Bohnet (1995), 'Institutions Affect Fairness: Experimental Investigations', *Journal of Institutional and Theoretical Economics*, **151** (June), 286–303.

The concept of equity or fairness is developed in
Homans, George C. (1961), *Social Behavior. Its Elementary Forms*, New York: Harcourt Brace Jovanovich,

and has been experimentally tested in

Fehr, Ernst and Georg Kirchsteiger (1994), 'Insider Power, Wage Discrimination, and Fairness', *Economic Journal*, **104**, 571–83.

A practical application of 'discourse groups' to a Not-In-My-Backyard, or NIMBY problem, has been undertaken by
Renn, Ortwin (1993), 'Public Participation in Decision Making: A Three-step Procedure', *Policy Sciences*, **26**, 189–214.

9. Popular referenda and institutional reform

On 6 December 1992, the Swiss citizens voted in a referendum on whether their country should join the European Economic Area (EEA). This date was preceded by a heated discussion in the public media (radio, television and newspapers), in the political parties and interest groups (who organized a large number of contradictory meetings and who engaged in a lot of propaganda activity), as well as among individuals (the issue was discussed everywhere from restaurants to trains and private homes). The position of the Swiss political, economic and cultural leadership was as unanimous as never before: the national and cantonal governments and parliaments, the political parties, the pressure groups involving both the manufacturers and the trade unions, academics, artists and sports people, and whoever else 'mattered' in society, solidly supported Switzerland's entry into the EEA. The popular referendum witnessed an extraordinarily high participation rate of 78 per cent. This compares with an average voting participation between 1985 and 1992 of only 42 per cent. The result was that 50.3 per cent of the population, and 16 out of the 23 cantons, were against the proposal, so it was rejected by the citizens.

Such a clear-cut difference between what the leaders or the 'classe politique' want and what the population want is no rare event in Switzerland. Thus it was in 1986 that the government decided the country should become a member of the United Nations. Again, the political, economic and social elite solidly supported this move, but the proposal was rejected by no less than 75 per cent of the popular vote. Only one canton mustered a majority for entry. In the history of Swiss voting, many more such clashes between the opinions of the leaders and of the citizens are to be found.

This chapter argues that the observations made for Switzerland are of great importance for all democracies. Four aspects will be the focus of attention.

1. A major deviation between what the 'classe politique' want, and the population want, is no rare event in all-representative democracies, but it is not observable because the issue is not tested by referenda. More generally, the following proposition can be advanced:

Proposition 1. Popular referenda are an effective, and perhaps unique, means of breaking the cartel of the 'classe politique' versus the general population. This proposition will be discussed in the first section that follows.

2. A referendum should not be looked at as simply a decision taken at a given point in time. The discussion taking place before, and the political adjustments undertaken thereafter, form an essential part of it.

    Proposition 2. A referendum is a process composed of three steps, each of which is of great importance:

    (a) an institutionalized discussion before the referendum;
    (b) the referendum vote itself;
    (c) the reactions of the political decision-makers after the referendum.
    This proposition forms the content of the second section.

3. The institution of referenda is closely linked to the institution of federalism. In a unitary national government, referenda tend to degenerate to plebiscites; that is, to a vote of confidence for the politicians in power, who initiate it whenever they expect it to be advantageous to them.

    Proposition 3. Referenda require federalism and must be possible at all levels of government. The population therewith is able to decide on substantive issues wherever they arise. The third section will deal with these issues.

4. Many arguments are popularly raised against referenda, often by intellectuals. But there are valid and convincing counter-arguments.

    Proposition 4. Referenda should be evaluated in a comparative perspective. The most frequently used arguments against popular referenda refer to

    (a) the low rate of participation;
    (b) the missing competence and level of information of voters; and
    (c) the high cost of organization.

    They then appear in a different light and are refutable. These aspects will be the subject of the fourth section.

Before embarking on the discussion of these four propositions, I want to repeat my scientific and moral position. My analysis is based on methodological individualism: persons are actors and individual preferences count exclusively. This position stands in stark contrast to a holistic conception of the state, where 'the state' is an acting entity with values and goals of its own (including the 'raison d'état' or 'Staatsraison' current in large parts of constitutional law). My position corresponds to modern political economy, or (as the Americans call it) Public Choice, but deviates in various respects from an orthodox interpretation. The analysis is strongly influenced by the role of institutions in the political process, that is, by constitutional economics.

REFERENDUM AGAINST POLITICIANS' CARTEL

Politicians Against the Voters

Persons acting within the confines of the political system have incentives to exploit it to their advantage. It need not be assumed at all that politicians are 'bad', or any worse than other persons, but they tend to be – as everyone else – self-regarding. They endeavour to further their own interests, which consist not only of material wealth, but also recognition and prestige.

In a democracy, politicians can use three main ways of gaining benefits at the citizens' expense, or 'exploiting' the general population:

1. Politicians may take decisions which they know to deviate from the voters' preferences. Political actors may do so because they have an ideology of their own, or because they reap material and non-material advantages by so doing. For instance, politicians systematically prefer direct interventions in the economy to employing the price system, because regulations generally allow them to derive larger rents.
2. Politicians secure themselves excessive privileges in the form of direct income for themselves or their parties, pensions, and fringe benefits, such as cars and houses.
3. Citizens' exploitation may take the form of corruption; that is, direct payments for special services provided to payers but not to others.

Politicians have a common interest to protect and, if possible, to extend these rents; that is, they have an incentive to form a cartel against the ordinary citizens. There is, however, a public good problem involved: an individual politician has an incentive to break out if such action is positively sanctioned by the electorate. Such action can regularly be observed in democracies, but it is rarely of much consequence for the cartel. The politicians in many countries form a close-knit group of people clearly differentiated from the rest of the population. They mainly have contact with each other so that the social disapproval of those few who dare to break out of the cartel is strongly felt and carries a high cost. Moreover, the cartel is administered by the leaders of the parties so that, in most countries and periods, only a small number are involved and the break-out of a politician is quickly and effectively sanctioned by the other members of the cartel, for instance by restricting access to parliamentary positions (in particular membership of powerful commissions), or by reducing the monetary support provided by the state to the parties. An individual politician finds it equally hard not to be a part of the cartel, because the leadership of his or her party has many means at their disposal to control him or her, including enforced resignation.

Constitutional Provisions Against the Politicians' Cartel

All the actors involved, in particular the voters, are well aware that there are strong and ubiquitous incentives for the politicians to form a cartel and to exploit the voters. In response, one finds three quite different forms of institutions in democratic constitutions designed to check such action:

1. *Rules* prohibiting the (excessive) appropriation of rents by the politicians, the most stringent ones being against corruption. Obviously, such rules are only effective if they cannot easily be circumvented and if they are well enforced. Such provisions are completely useless against the first type of exploitation mentioned, namely the systematic deviation from citizens' preferences. As the privileges accorded by the politicians to themselves are of an extremely varied kind and are made difficult to detect (especially with respect to pensions), experience shows that politicians' rent-seeking can thereby scarcely be prevented. With respect to corruption, only the most blatant cases are found out. It must be concluded that, while such rules are of some use, they certainly are not able to prevent the exploitation of citizens to any significant degree.
2. The establishment of special *courts*, with the task of preventing citizens' exploitation. All democratic countries know some institution of courts of accounts, but it may well be shown that they fulfil their role only to a limited extent. They are obviously the less effective, the more directly they depend on the politicians they are supposed to control. In this respect, it does not help much if the members of the court of accounts are elected by, and must answer to, the parliament (instead of to the government), because the cartel includes politicians inside and outside the government. Even courts of accounts formally independent of government and parliament have little incentive and possibility of checking the

exploitation of the citizens by the politicians. This applies particularly to
the deviation from citizens' preferences; it may indeed be shown that
courts of accounts, which necessarily have to focus on the formal cor-
rectness of politicians' and administrators' behaviour, in some respects
tend to widen the gap between what politicians provide and what the
population wishes.

3. The *competition between parties* is the classical institution in representa-
    tive democracies to prevent politicians from pursuing their own goals at
    the population's expense. Constitutions know various devices to further
    competition and to make a coalition between the politicians more difficult
    – one is the division of power between the executive, legislative and
    jurisdictional branches; another is the establishment of two houses of
    parliament. Because of the many types of interactions existing, and the
    well-defined gains to be expected, these devices are rather ineffective in
    checking the interests of the 'classe politique'.

An important constitutional device for stimulating the competition between parties is to guarantee, and to facilitate, the entry of new politicians
and parties into the political system. While this certainly forces the established parties in a democracy to take better care of the population's wishes
and to be more careful with regard to privileges and corruption, the effect
tends to be short lived. The previous outsiders quickly realize that many
advantages are to be gained by tolerating the politicians' cartel, and even
more by participating in it. The experience of many countries supports this
theoretical proposition. An example are the 'Green' parties, who at first
fought against the political establishment, but within surprisingly little time
have learned to take advantage of the taxpayers' money for their own purposes.

On the basis of these arguments, it must be concluded that neither constitutional rules, nor courts, nor party competition are particularly successful in
reducing the possible exploitation of the general population by the politicians. It is not argued, of course, that the constitutional features elaborated
are useless, but that they do not provide a sufficient safeguard against politicians' rent-seeking. It is therefore desirable to search for, and to seriously
consider, other constitutional means of fighting the politicians' cartel.

Referenda as a Constitutional Provision Against the Politicians' Cartel

A referendum, in which all the citizens have the possibility of participating,
meets the crucial requirement that it gives decision-making power to people
outside the politicians' cartel. The individuals making the decision are not
integrated into the 'classe politique' and they avoid the control of politicians.

In an *initiative*, the demands are explicitly directed against the political establishment represented in parliament and government. *Optional* and *obligatory* referenda serve more of a controlling function as, if successful, they overrule the decisions taken by the executive and the legislative bodies.

A popular referendum (in the widest sense of the word) can only serve its purpose if the 'classe politique' cannot block it. In many countries, the Supreme Court or, even worse, the parliament, has the power to decide whether a referendum is admissible. The criteria appear to be purely formal, but in fact the members of the 'classe politique' have considerable possibilities and incentives to forbid referenda threatening the position of the politicians' cartel. Often vague concepts, based on what *they* consider to be the 'raison d'état', are employed. In other countries, such as Switzerland, almost no such possibility exists, and therefore issues may be brought to the vote which are not desired, and are sometimes even strongly disliked, by the politicians.

Empirical evidence shows that referenda are indeed able to break the cartel among the politicians by getting through constitutional provisions and laws totally against the interests of the 'classe politique'. The following cases refer to Switzerland, the referenda nation par excellence. The first two cases concern important historical episodes.

1. During the 19th century, the house of representatives (Nationalrat) was elected according to the majority rule. The largest party greatly benefited therefrom; throughout seven decades the Radical-Democratic Party secured a majority of the seats. When the idea was raised that the elections should follow proportional representation in order to allow small parties to enter parliament, the then 'classe politique' in the executive and jurisdiction strongly rejected this proposal for obvious reasons of self-interest. Nevertheless, in 1918, the corresponding referendum was accepted by the majority of the population and by the cantons. In the subsequent elections, the Radical-Democratic Party lost no less than 40 per cent of their seats.

2. Up until World War II, Urgent Federal Laws (Dringliche Bundesbeschlüsse) were not subject to the (optional) referendum. In order not to have to seek the population's approval and in order to pursue policies in their own interest, the 'classe politique' in the government and parliament often declared federal laws to be 'urgent', even if that was not in fact the case. In 1946, an initiative was started with the objective of preventing this disregard for the interests of the population. Again, the executive and legislative bodies urged the voters to reject the initiative, which was clearly one of self-interest. However, the initiative was accepted by the voters, and the politicians are now forced to take the citizens' interests into account when they decide on federal laws.

Referenda were not only able to break the politicians' cartel in the past, but continue to do so regularly, as the two more recent cases mentioned at the beginning show: both the referendum on Switzerland joining the United Nations (1986), and on joining the European Economic Area (1992) were strongly supported by the 'classe politique', but were nevertheless rejected by the voters. On the other hand, the class politique, after responding to this situation, found substantial support (67 per cent 'yes' votes) when bilateral contracts between the European Union and Switzerland were brought before the voters in May 2000.

In that sense, the politicians are well aware that the institution of popular referendum severely restricts their possibility of exploiting the citizens/tax-payers. It may be argued that this is one of the reasons why a large number of Swiss politicians quite like membership of the European Union (where the institution of referendum has no place whatsoever). They also make great efforts to endorse as quickly as possible any movements originating from outside the cartel. Sometimes it is established parties (but usually at the fringes of the cartel) or associated interest groups which initiate referenda. If this strategy is to be successful, the politicians have to at least partly take into account the population's preferences, and have to reduce the extent of their rent-seeking. The institution of the referendum in this case leads indirectly to the desired outcome that the politicians' cartel has less leeway.

THE REFERENDUM AS A PROCESS

The Traditional Public Choice View

The Economic Theory of Politics looks at direct democracy in terms of preference aggregation and the choice of voting rules, but does not consider referenda in this context. In the few places where referenda are considered in the Public Choice literature, the emphasis lies on the resulting decision. The pre-referenda and post-referenda processes are totally neglected. It is argued here that important insights can be gained by interpreting referenda to be more than just a decision outcome.

The Pre-referendum Process

The constitutional setting determines to a large extent which issues are placed on the political agenda, and which are prevented from appearing. In representative democracies, politicians are often very skilled at not letting problems be discussed in the democratically legitimized institutions that would be to their disadvantage. For example, they usually succeed in not having their privileges (such as their income and pensions) discussed in an open parliamentary session. If they cannot prevent it, they then restrict the discussion to scandals already known to the public, and the same applies to outright corruption. In direct democracies, however, in which the citizens may put any issue to the ballot, the agenda is much less under the control of the 'classe politique'. As has been shown both theoretically and empirically, agenda setting power has a significant effect on voting outcomes.

An important feature of referenda is the discussion process stimulated among the population, and between politicians and voters. Pre-referendum discussion may be interpreted as an exchange of arguments among equal citizens, taking place under well-defined rules. This institutionalized discussion meets various conditions of the discourse process, as discussed in the previous chapter. Compared with a philosophical discourse, the pre-referendum discussion has a crucial advantage. The exchange of arguments does not take the form of an academic seminar without any consequences, because at the end of the process the voters have the final decision. The relevance of the discussion for politics induces citizens to participate, depending on how important the issue in question is considered to be. The experience of Switzerland shows that some referenda indeed motivate intensive and far-reaching discussions. An example is the above mentioned referendum on whether to join the European Economic Area, which resulted in a participation rate of almost 80 per cent, compared with an average of roughly 40 per cent. On the other hand, referenda which are considered of little importance by the voters engender little discussion and low participation rates (as low as 25 per cent). This variability in the intensity of discussion and participation overrides the much studied 'paradox of voting'.

The main function of the pre-referendum process is certainly to raise the level of information of the participants. It may, moreover, be hypothesized that the exchange of arguments also shapes the participants' preferences. What matters is that such preference formation – provided it happens at all – can be influenced, but not be controlled, by the 'classe politique' in a constitutional state which advocates freedom of the media and communication.

Post-referendum Adjustments

In a referendum, a political decision is formally made, but this does not necessarily mean that the politicians and the public administration take the appropriate action to implement it. The more legitimate the constitution is taken to be in a political system, the higher are the costs of not following it. The politicians may also be induced to act by the threat of not being reelected by the voters, but ultimately the extent of implementation depends on the extent to which the constitutional rules are voluntarily obeyed by the persons in power.

The question of which side gets a majority in a referendum is not the only thing that matters. A referendum also clearly reveals how the population feels, and where and how large the minorities are. Groups dissenting from the majority are identified; their preferences become visible and become part of the political process. This makes it more likely that particular parties start to champion their cause in order to win additional support, and for referenda in particular regions to take place.

Switzerland again provides a suitable example. In 1989, a popular initiative demanded that the Swiss Army be completely dismantled. This was considered by many Swiss as an attack against one of the most essential, almost sacred, institutions of the country. The 'classe politique' was again solidly against the initiative, and the generals threatened that they would retire if the initiative was not overwhelmingly rejected (they spoke of between 80 and 90 per cent 'no' votes). The referendum outcome was a surprise to all because one-third of the voters, and a majority of the young voters eligible for service, voted for the dissolution of the army. After a brief period of shock, several parties suggested changes in the army, which were implemented within a short period of time – changes which, before the referendum, were considered by everyone to be impossible to achieve.

REFERENDUM AND FEDERALISM

The institution of citizens directly deciding on an issue and the decentralization of decision-making are closely connected. On the one hand, federalism is an alternative means for better fulfilment of the voters' preferences: individuals tend to leave dissatisfying jurisdictions, while they are attracted to those caring for the population's preferences at low cost. The possibility of voting with one's feet tends to undermine regional cartels by politicians, provided, of course, the persons concerned have political rights.

In more important respects, on the other hand, federalism is a *prerequisite*, rather than a substitute, for effective referenda. In small communities, much knowledge needed for informed political decision-making is impacted in everyday life: as consumers, producers and persons doing the housework, the people are well aware of the benefits and costs of particular public programmes and, as taxpayers, they immediately have to carry the burden, provided a sufficient amount of fiscal equivalence exists (see Chapter 11). Referenda undertaken on communal and regional issues help the citizens to evaluate political questions to be decided at a higher federal level, and make referenda a more effective institution for undermining the politicians' cartel against the voters.

ARGUMENTS AGAINST AND COUNTER-ARGUMENTS FOR REFERENDA

Referenda can hardly be considered a popular institution in democracies, not to speak of authoritarian systems. Not surprisingly, the members of the 'classe politique' are quick to raise many objections because they realize that referenda constitute a threat to their position, by limiting their rent-seeking potential. Many intellectuals – even those who do not share in the spoils of the politicians' cartel, and even those opposing the political establishment – also reject referenda, with a variety of arguments. The basic reason is that they consider themselves to be better judges of what is good for the people than the citizens themselves. They tend to see themselves in the role of 'philosopher-king', determining what 'social welfare' is. Consequently, they prefer decision-making systems where they have a larger say. Thus they oppose referenda for the same reasons as they oppose the market. It has often been claimed that referendum democracy lowers governmental efficiency of performance and reduces the capacity for innovation. This is, however, a technocratic view of efficiency, completely disregarding the tendency among politicians to deviate from citizens' preferences, as well as to grant themselves undue privileges and to engage in corruption. The following five arguments are often raised against the institution of the referendum.

'Voters Do Not Understand the Complex Issues'

The average voter, so it is argued, is not well informed and educated, so that he or she cannot reasonably be allowed to determine political issues; this is the task of a specialized group, the politicians who represent the voters. This view can be refuted in various respects.

First of all, it is not clear why the citizens are trusted to be able to choose between parties and politicians in elections but not between issues in referenda. If anything, the former choice is the more difficult one, because one must form expectations about politicians' choices on future issues.

Second, the voters need not have detailed knowledge about all the issues at stake, but just on the main questions involved. These main questions are not of a technical nature, but involve decisions of principle, which voters are just as qualified to make as politicians. It may even be argued that the politicians are a group of people particularly ill equipped to take such decisions. As professionals, they know much less than ordinary people what reality is about. After all, they have passed their whole lives in sessions and commissions, meetings and other social gatherings, mostly among their peers.

Third, the general intelligence and qualification of politicians should not be overrated. Most members of the 'classe politique' have not exactly excelled in any particular job. Moreover, the average cabinet minister and member of parliament has little choice; he or she is normally forced to go along with what their party superiors and a few specialists have decided before.

Finally, the voters are helped in reaching a reasoned decision by a number of institutions that emerge in a direct democracy: to a certain extent, citizens take into account the suggestions made by the parties and interest groups. Even more importantly, the discourse in the pre-referendum stage brings forth the main aspects and puts them in perspective. The intensity of the discussion should not be compared with the one taking place in representative democracies, because the citizens there have less incentive to get informed and to take a decision, as their position on a particular issue is anyway of little or no consequence to the outcome.

'Voters Are Manipulated'

Financially potent parties and pressure groups are better able to start initiatives and to engage in referendum propaganda than are the poor and badly organized interest groups. This cannot be denied. However, the perspective is mistaken because it takes an absolute stance: it is always true that the rich and well-organized wield more power. The crucial question is whether they have more or less power in a direct democracy than in a representative democracy. If one looks from this perspective, it is no longer evident that this argument speaks against referenda. It is well known that skilfully organized and financed pressure groups exert a lot of power over the politicians sitting in parliament and in government. Most parties and politicians are amenable to the influence exerted, particularly because the 'classe politique' is of long standing and often has close personal contacts with the lobbyists. As the experience of Switzerland shows, even when pressure groups and the political class are united, they do not always get it their own way, particularly where important issues are concerned.

'Referenda Are Inadequate for Major Issues'

As the voters are taken to be badly educated, ill informed and subject to manipulation, it is often maintained that referenda are admissible for small and unimportant issues, but that issues of great consequence – such as changes in the constitution, or the membership of an international body – should be left to the professional politicians. However, the opposite makes more sense. Major issues are reducible to relatively simple questions, where evaluation does not depend on details but rather on fundamental value judgements. Following methodological individualism, only the citizens may be the final judges when it comes to preferences, and a substitution by representatives is, at best, a second best solution. As the politicians have a systematic incentive to deviate from the voters' preferences, a substitution leads to biased outcomes.

There has been a recent trend in Europe to refer the really important political issues to the population, as is borne out by the popular referenda on entry into the European Community undertaken in Scandinavian countries, Ireland and Austria, on remaining in the EC in the United Kingdom, on enlarging the EC in France, and on specific aspects of the constitution of the EC and the EU, such as on the single European Act, Treaties of Maastricht and Amsterdam in Denmark, Italy, France and Ireland. Popular referenda have also gained in importance in other continents, as well as within particular countries, such as, for instance, in Germany (see Appendix 9.1).

'Referenda Hinder Progress'

Asking the population to make a decision is often rejected because it is argued that the 'ordinary citizens' do not like changes and that they prevent the adoption of 'bold, new ideas'. It may well be true that many new propositions are rejected in referenda, but this does not mean that it constitutes a disadvantage. That proposals contain new ideas is no proof of their quality. Indeed, the citizens are right in rejecting them when they are in favour of the 'classe politique'. The concept of 'bold, new' solutions is often the natural outcome of technocratic thinking and of a planning mentality which strengthens the politicians' and bureaucrats' position, but is not necessarily in the voters' best interests.

Referenda are a well-proven procedure to break deadlocks in societal decision-making and, in this sense, are progressive. There are cases in which an issue is difficult to resolve in parliament and by the government, and where a referendum helps to clear the issue. In many countries, the demands of some regions to become more independent are accompanied by much violence and bloodshed. In a referendum democracy, such heated issues may be brought more easily to a solution acceptable to a large majority of the parties involved. In Switzerland, for instance, the secession of the Jura from canton Bern was achieved by undertaking a number of referenda. While some minor violence was involved, the issue was settled with less strife and bloodshed than normally occurs in democracies in which referenda are uncommon, or used only in the form of a plebiscite.

'Referenda Are Costly'

The last argument against referenda is the alleged high administrative cost of undertaking them. It is argued that parliamentary decisions are much less expensive, and should therefore be favoured. There are two reasons why this reasoning is fallacious:

1. From the empirical point of view, referenda are not so expensive compared with the immense cost of entertaining a professional parliament with its accompanying party system. As in a direct democracy the final say is with the citizens, less money needs to be spent on parliament and the parties. Moreover, the administrative costs of referenda are not all that high because several propositions can be bundled together in one weekend, and citizens can be asked to actively participate in organizing the vote and counting the distribution of votes. While the citizens drafted suffer some opportunity cost, such a participation has the advantage of getting them more directly involved in governing their state, which tends to raise their sense of a citizen's duty.
2. The administrative costs of running referenda are immaterial compared with their major advantage, namely to significantly reduce the deviation of political decisions from individual preferences.

A comparison of Swiss communes and cantons with different degrees of institutionalized forms of citizen participation in political decisions reveals (ceteris paribus) that:

●   The outcomes correspond more closely to the voters' preferences, the more directly democratic they are;
●   The growth of public expenditure is more strongly determined by the citizens' willingness to pay than by the politicians' and bureaucrats' own interests;
●   Public supply is less costly, the more direct the democratic institutions are;
●   Tax morale is better, and therefore tax evasion lower;
●   Per capita public debt is lower;
●   Per capita income is higher;
●   Citizens reveal a higher level of subjectively perceived well-being or happiness (for a more extensive description, see Chapter 10).

These results provide strong evidence that the deviations from the citizens' preferences are indeed significantly lower in a referendum compared with a representative democracy, which constitutes a major advantage of direct democracy that most likely overrides the alleged (but unproven) higher administrative costs of referenda.

CONCLUSION

The theoretical implications, as well as the empirical results reported, are clear: referenda are a crucial constitutional means of restricting the cartel of politicians against ordinary citizens. Direct democracy therefore constitutes an essential element in a constitutional reform designed to improve democracy.

APPENDIX 9.1

Facts on the use of direct democracy all over the world are available at http://c2d.unige.ch, prepared by the 'Centre d'études et de documentation sur la démocratie directe' located at the University of Geneva.

The leading role of Switzerland among all nations with respect to referenda is shown in Table A9.1. As can be seen, even confined to the national level only, more than half of all referenda were undertaken in Switzerland. If the very large number of referenda at the cantonal and communal level were considered, the predominance of Switzerland with respect to direct democracy would be even stronger.

Table A9.1   Referenda around the world, pre-1900 to 1993

	Switzerland	Rest of Europe	Australia and New Zealand	Rest of the world	Total
Up to 1900	57	11	–	3	71
1901–50	99	48	32	18	197
1951–93	258	90	32	151	531
Per cent of total	51.81	18.65	8.01	21.53	100
Total	414	149	64	172	799

Source: Butler and Ranney (1994; p. 5).

For Switzerland between 1848 (when direct democracy was introduced) and 2000, Table A9.2 shows the popular referenda (in the broad sense) that were undertaken.

Table A9.2   Popular referenda in Switzerland, 1848–2000

	Number	Accepted	Rejected
Obligatory referenda	207	152	55
Facultative referenda	132	65	67
Popular referenda	127	12	115
Total	466	229	237

Source: http://c2d.unige.ch

SUGGESTIONS ON THE LITERATURE AND SOURCES

Authoritative surveys of Political Economy or Public Choice are provided in
Mueller, Dennis C. (1989), *Public Choice II*, 2nd edn, Cambridge: Cambridge University Press.
Mueller, Dennis C. (ed.) (1997), *Perspectives on Public Choice*, Cambridge: Cambridge University Press.

Constitutional political economy is treated in
Buchanan, James M. and Gordon Tullock (1962), *The Calculus of Consent. Logical Foundations of Constitutional Democracy*, Ann Arbor: University of Michigan Press.
Buchanan, James M. (1991), *Constitutional Economics*, Oxford: Basil Blackwell.
Brennan, Geoffrey and James M. Buchanan (1985), *The Reason of Rules. Constitutional Political Economy*, Cambridge: Cambridge University Press.

The theory of rent-seeking is due to
Tullock, Gordon (1967), 'The Welfare Costs of Tariff, Monopolies and Theft', *Western European Journal*, **5** (June), 224–32,.

and is surveyed in
Tollison, Robert D. (1982), 'Rent Seeking: A Survey', *Kyklos*, **35** (4), 575–602.

The extent of rent appropriation for instance in the German Federal Republic is documented in
Von Armin, Hans Herbert (1997), *Fetter Bauch regiert nicht gern: Die politische Klasse – selbstbezogen und abgehoben*, München: Kindler.

The behaviour of the Courts of Account is analysed in
Forte, Francesco and Giuseppe Eusepi (1990), 'La corte dei conti: Un "agente" alla ricerca del vero "principale"', *Giornale degli Economisti e Annali di Economia*, **49** (7–8), 315–29.
Frey, Bruno S. (1994), 'Supreme Auditing Institutions: A Politico Economic Analysis', *European Journal of Law and Economics*, **1**, 169–76.

Opening political markets has been proposed by
Eichenberger, Reiner (1999), 'Dereguliert, liberalisiert und globalisiert die Politik. Ein politisch-ökonomischer Reformvorschlag', *Studia Philosophica*, **58**, 99–121.

The political system of Switzerland is described in
Klöti, Ulrich et al. (1999), *Handbuch der Schweizer Politik*, Zürich: Verlag Neue Zürcher Zeitung.
Linder, Wolf (1999), *Schweizerische Demokratie: Institution, Prozesse, Perspektiven*, Bern/Stuttgart/Wien: Paul Haupt.

Popular referenda are discussed in

Cronin, Thomas E. (1989), *Direct Democracy. The Politics of Initiative, Referendum and Recall*, Cambridge, MA: Harvard University Press.
Budge, Ian (1996), *New Challenge of Direct Democracy*, Cambridge: Polity Press.

Empirical facts on referenda the world over are collected in

Butler, David and Austin Ranney (eds) (1994), *Referendums Around the World. The Growing Use of Direct Democracy*, Washington, DC: AEI Press.

The historical episodes of breaking the politicians' cartel by referenda are treated in

Blankart, Charles B. (1992), 'Bewirken Referenden und Volksinitiativen einen Unterschied in der Politik?', *Staatswissenschaften und Staatspraxis*, **3**, 509–24.

The role of agenda setting power has been discussed in the American context by

Romer, Thomas and Howard Rosenthal (1978), 'Political Resource Allocation, Controlled Agendas, and the Status Quo', *Public Choice*, **33** (4), 27–43.
Weingast, Barry R. and Mark J. Moran (1983), 'Bureaucratic Discretion or Congressional Control? Regulatory Policymaking by the Federal Trade Commission', *Journal of Political Economy*, **91** (5), 765–800.

The paradox of voting is treated in

Tullock, Gordon (1967), *Towards a Mathematics of Politics*, Ann Arbor: University of Michigan Press.

An empirical analysis of pressure group activity in the referendum democracy of Switzerland has been undertaken by

Schneider, Friedrich (1985), *Der Einfluss der Interessengruppen auf die Wirtschaftspolitik: Eine empirische Untersuchung für die Schweiz*, Bern: Haupt.

Research on the outcome of direct democracy has been collected in

Kirchgässner, Gebhard, Lars Feld and Marcel R. Savioz (1999), *Die direkte Demokratie: Modern, erfolgreich, entwicklungs- und exportfähig*, Basel: Helbing and Lichtenhahn/Vahlen/Beck.

10. What are the sources of happiness?

with Alois Stutzer

HAPPINESS MATTERS

To analyse the sources of people's happiness is an issue of major interest. Accordingly, there has been a constant enquiry into the determinants of individual well-being in the social sciences. One of the crucial questions has been what kind of institutions lead to people being happier. In particular, the role of democratic institutions in people's well-being has been speculated about.

Over the last few years, extensive econometric research has convincingly demonstrated the beneficial effects of democratic institutions on political outcomes (see Chapter 9). The more developed the possibilities for direct political participation via popular initiatives and referenda are, the more strongly government policy reflects the preferences of the voters. These results are based mainly on cross-sectional data for the United States and Switzerland, the two countries with by far the greatest number of referenda.

This chapter goes one step further. It is argued that the more developed direct democracy is, the happier the citizens are. The analysis moreover suggests that the higher level of happiness associated with more extensive democracy is partly due to the utility produced by the political process itself, and is not only due to favourable political outcomes.

In addition to institutional determinants, the influence of economic variables on happiness is shown. Unemployment considerably lowers happiness. Higher income raises subjective well-being, but not by very much. In addition, the effects of demographic variables, such as age, sex and family status on happiness, are demonstrated.

The next section presents a short overview of important determinants of happiness. The following sections discuss the theoretical and empirical basis for the proposed factors. The third section surveys the effects of direct democracy on political outcomes, both theoretically and empirically and the next section emphasizes the utility gained by participation possibilities in the political process. Its effect on happiness is analysed by distinguishing between citizens and foreigners. The latter are excluded from political participation as a source of utility. The fifth section deals with the effects of unemployment and income on well-being and the sixth section presents the data for Switzerland and the empirical results derived by an econometric cross-section analysis among the 26 Swiss cantons. The final section draws conclusions.

DETERMINANTS OF HAPPINESS

Three sets of sources of individual well-being may usefully be distinguished.

1. The first set of influences on happiness relates to the *institutional* (or constitutional) *conditions* in an economy and society, of which democracy is of greatest importance. The impact of the extent and design of democratic institutions on subjective well-being has, at best, been alluded to, but has not been empirically analysed in previous research.
2. *Micro- and macroeconomic factors.* In most nations, individuals belonging to the upper income groups report somewhat higher subjective well-being than persons with low income. The often dramatic increase in per capita incomes in recent decades has not raised happiness in general; the national indices for subjective well-being have remained virtually flat over time. In contrast to these longitudinal findings for single nations, per capita income levels and happiness are more strongly positively related across nations.

     The influence of the other two major economic variables, *unemployment* and *inflation*, is clear cut. Unemployment is correlated with substantial unhappiness. As the income level is kept constant, that influence is not due to lower revenue, but to non-pecuniary stress. In terms of a trade-off, the results suggest that a much higher income would be required to compensate people for being out of work. Individuals also have a strong aversion to inflation, reflected in lower satisfaction in times of high inflation.
3. *Personality and demographic factors.* For many decades, these factors have been extensively studied by psychologists. They comprise such factors as health, age, gender and family circumstances.

   The determinants of happiness are usually investigated under the assumptions that subjective well-being is cardinally measurable and interpersonally comparable; that is, two claims economists are likely to be sceptical about. To avoid problems with regard to a cardinal interpretation of subjective variables, it is often possible to treat the subjective data qualitatively in econometric analyses. In contrast, it is more difficult to assess whether or not people associate the same degree of subjective experience with a certain score on a ladder for life satisfaction. However, there is a lot of indirect evidence that cardinalism and interpersonal comparability are much less of a problem practically than theoretically. The measures of subjective well-being have high consistency, reliability and validity. Happy people are, for example, more often smiling during social interactions, and are rated as happy by friends and family members, as well as by spouses. Furthermore, the measures of subjective well-being have a high degree of stability over time and are not systematically biased with regard to social desirability. Some of the problems connected with the measurement of happiness are of lesser importance, as the main use of happiness measurements here is to identify the determinants of happiness rather than to compare levels of happiness between persons and periods.

EFFECTS OF DIRECT DEMOCRACY

Three revolutionary stages in the development of democracy may be distinguished. The first is Athenian democracy, characterized by the citizens' assembly. The second was brought about by the French revolution. Its principle of representation allowed democracy to extend over a wide area. The third stage is (semi-) direct democracy, in which the citizens may decide on political issues via initiatives and referenda. Parliament and government make most current decisions, but the voters always have the final say and must always support proposed changes in the constitution, as well as major laws. The professional politicians are thus in a more direct way the agents of the voters, who resume the role of the principals.

A large number of empirical studies have convincingly shown that the institutions of direct democracy lead to outcomes that benefit the voters. Thus it has been shown for American states that per capita debt is substantially lower with a referendum requiring a qualified majority. In contrast, educational public expenditures are higher when a referendum is possible. For Switzerland, the econometric evidence is even more compelling, one reason being that the institutions of direct democracy are more developed than in the US. It has been established that public expenditures are lower by 14 per cent, and that public expenditures exhibit significantly lower growth in Swiss cities with well-established direct democracy. Moreover, these cities have a 5 per cent higher share of self-financing and, as a consequence, the per capita debt is no less than 45 per cent lower. Other studies conclude that tax evasion is significantly lower in cantons with a higher degree of direct participation rights for voters. Finally, it has been established that gross domestic product per capita is about 5 per cent higher in cantons with more extended direct democratic institutions. All these results are based on estimates which carefully control for influences unrelated to direct democracy. They establish a causal effect between direct democracy and political outcomes, and their consequences in terms of behaviour (tax evasion) or economic activity (income).

If direct democracy does indeed produce political outcomes, and therewith economic and social conditions more favourable to citizens, it can be expected that they enjoy a higher level of reported subjective well-being or happiness than in political jurisdictions with less extensive participation rights.

PROCEDURAL EFFECTS OF DIRECT DEMOCRACY

Citizens do not only gain utility from the outcome of the political process and its material consequences, but also from the democratic process itself. Citizens value the possibility of engaging themselves directly with politically relevant issues, quite irrespective of the outcome.

The essence of procedural aspects in direct democracy lies in the discussion brought about by initiatives and referenda. A direct democracy produces the conditions for a serious discursive process, which is in principle open to the whole population, and which ends in a well-defined decision. This ongoing political process is able to provide utility not only to the 'winners' but also to the 'losers', because both feel that their preferences have been seriously taken into account in a fair political process. The utility derived from the possibility of participating in the direct democratic process thus supports the subjective well-being of the citizens. The foreigners living in the same canton, who are excluded from this process, experience lower happiness compared with the citizens.

ECONOMIC DETERMINANTS OF WELL-BEING

The evaluation of the state of the economy by the people has been analysed from several different perspectives. Three major approaches – individual welfare functions, reaction functions and election and popularity functions – use econometric methods to empirically capture the influence of unemployment, income and inflation. Citizens' reactions to economic conditions in the voting booth or in regular political surveys are usually attributed to the 'responsibility hypothesis'. Voters are taken to express a general dissatisfaction with the existing state of the economy and to make the government responsible for it. The economic variables, unemployment and inflation, have been shown most strongly to reduce the proportion of votes going to the party in power. A 1 percentage point increase in the rate of unemployment lowers the vote or popularity share of the government by approximately 0.4 to 0.8 percentage points. The same holds for a 1 percentage point increase in the rate of inflation.

In contrast, a change in the growth rate of per capita real income often has no statistically significant effect on voting and popularity shares, even though the relationship is positive. In the studies which have found statistically significant positive effects, the size of the effect varies across a much wider range than the ones for unemployment or inflation.

The economic variables are likely to have an effect on reported subjective well-being similar to the effect they have on government popularity.

EMPIRICAL ANALYSIS

The empirical work presented here is based on the survey results of more than 6000 Swiss inhabitants. The dependent variable called 'happiness' is based on the answers to the following question: 'How satisfied are you with your life as a whole these days?' Simultaneously, the respondents were shown a table with a 10-point scale, where only the two extreme values ('completely dissatisfied' and 'completely satisfied') were verbalized. The survey reveals a high general life satisfaction in Switzerland for the years 1992 to 1994, on average 8.2 out of 10. As many as 29 per cent of the interviewees reported a satisfaction level of 10 ('completely satisfied'), 17 per cent reported 9, and 27 per cent reported 8. At the lower end of the happiness scale, score 1 ('completely dissatisfied'), score 2 and score 3 were indicated only by 0.4 per cent, 0.5 per cent and 0.9 per cent, respectively.

The major explanatory variables focused on here are the institutional possibilities for individual political participation, which vary considerably between the 26 Swiss cantons. Due to the federal structure of Switzerland, major competences remain with the cantons (states). As on the national level, strong direct democratic instruments exist besides representative democratic parliaments and governments. The most important direct democratic instruments in the cantons are the popular initiatives to change a canton's constitution or laws, and compulsory and optional referenda to prevent new laws, or to change existing laws, and to decide on new state expenditure. Citizens' access to these instruments differs from canton to canton. Thus, for example, the number of signatures required to launch an initiative, or an optional referendum, or the time span within which the signatures are to be collected, vary. The referendum on public expenditures may be launched at different levels of additional outlays. An index was constructed to reflect the extent of direct democratic participation possibilities. This index is defined over a six-

Table 10.1   Direct democracy and satisfaction with life in Switzerland

Variable	Coefficient	*t*-value	Marginal effect (score 10)
	Weighted ordered probit Std. error adjusted to clustering in 26 cantons		
Institutional variable			
Direct democratic rights	0.082**	3.054	0.028
Economic variables			
Unemployed	−0.841**	−5.814	−0.211
Equiv. income SFr 2000–3000	0.084*	2.199	0.029
Equiv. income SFr 3000–4000	0.143**	3.169	0.050
Equiv. income SFr 4000–5000	0.258**	5.382	0.092
Equiv. income SFr 5000 and more	0.192**	4.277	0.068
Demographic variables			
Age 30–39	−0.079	−0.865	−0.027
Age 40–49	−0.008	−0.106	−0.003
Age 50–59	−0.081	−1.275	−0.027
Age 60–69	0.206**	2.903	0.073
Age 70–79	0.295**	3.401	0.106
Age 80 and older	0.273**	2.968	0.099
Female	0.043	1.211	0.015
Foreigner	−0.284**	−5.048	−0.091
Average education	0.113**	3.143	0.039
High education	0.119*	2.472	0.042
Single woman	−0.258**	−6.294	−0.083
Single man	−0.174*	−2.589	−0.057
Couple with children	−0.068	−1.777	−0.023
Single parent	−0.372**	−3.602	−0.113
Other private household	−0.128	−1.664	−0.042
Collective household	−0.413**	−3.432	−0.124
Self-employed	0.072	1.413	0.025
Housewife	0.123*	2.463	0.043
Other employment status	−0.129[(*)]	−1.911	−0.044
Observations	6134		
Prob > F	0.001		

Notes:
Dependent variable: level of satisfaction on an eight point scale (scores of 1, 2 and 3 were aggregated). White estimator for variance. Included in the reference group are 'employed people', 'people with a lower equivalence income than SFr 2000', 'people younger than 30', 'men', 'Swiss', 'people with low education', and 'couples'. Additional control variables (not shown) for size of community (5 variables) and type of community (7 variables).
Significance levels: [(*)] 0.05 < p < 0.10, * 0.01 < p < 0.05, ** p < 0.01.

Data source: Leu, Burri and Priester (1997) and Stutzer (1999).

point scale with 1 indicating the lowest, and 6 the highest degree of participation possibilities of the citizens.

The purpose of the econometric estimate is to show that the extent of direct
democratic participation possibilities exerts a statistically significant, robust
and sizeable effect on happiness over and above the demographic and economic determinants so far taken into account in the literature. The estimation
equations regress the scores of individual happiness according to three sets of
determinants:

1. Political institutions in the form of the extent of direct democracy;
2. Economic variables; and
3. Demographic variables.

Table 10.1 presents the results.

The Effects of Direct Democratic Participation Rights on Happiness

The index of the extent of direct democracy has a statistically highly significant positive effect on happiness, keeping all other influences constant. An
increase in the value of the direct democracy index by one unit (on a possible
six-point scale) raises the proportion of persons stating themselves to be
'completely satisfied' (score 10) by 2.8 percentage points. This result clearly
suggests that the institutions of direct democracy do indeed make people
happier. In addition, the effect itself is sizeable.

*   The effect of direct democratic rights on happiness is as large as the
    effect of living in the second lowest income category (SFr 2000–3000)
    instead of the lowest income category (<SFr 2000).
*   The effect is even larger when the full range of the institutional vari-
    able is considered; that is, when individuals in canton Basle-Land
    (with the highest democracy index of 5.69) are compared with citizens
    in canton Geneva (with the lowest direct participation rights of 1.75).
    Citizens living in Basle-Land have an 11 percentage points higher
    probability of stating that they are completely satisfied than citizens
    living in Geneva.
*   Such an institution-based improvement affects everybody, that is, the
    institutional factor is important in an aggregate sense. In comparison,
    getting a job 'only' raises the subjective well-being of the unemployed.

Do happy people choose direct democratic institutions? Or, in other words,
does the causality between direct democracy and subjective well-being work
in reverse? Direct democratic participation possibilities in the form of refer-

enda and initiatives in Switzerland started to develop in the middle of the 19th century. The adoption of some of the instruments of direct popular participation reflects the spread of the spirit and ideas behind the American and the French revolutions. Equally important were political movements among the citizens. Citizens fought for direct democratic instruments to gain political power against arbitrary decisions by parliaments and the influence of industrial pressure groups on these authorities in the cantons. This historic perspective suggests that the democratic institutions are not simply the result of happy, satisfied citizens. Especially during the last decades, institutional conditions in Swiss cantons have been quite stable, which suggests that causality runs unambiguously from direct democratic rights to satisfaction with life.

Two alternative explanations are often put forward against the empirical findings described above. These explanations emphasize the possibility of spurious regression due to missing variables, in our case the income level and the degree of urbanization in a canton.

- *Income level in cantons*: it is hypothesized that in cantons where in-habitants are richer than the Swiss average, the public provision of goods can be quantitatively or qualitatively augmented. Thus if the index of direct democratic rights and the income level in Swiss cantons are highly correlated, the former variable just captures different wealth levels in Swiss cantons. However, the inclusion of national income per capita in the estimation equation does not change the results significantly. The aggregate income variable itself is negatively correlated with subjective well-being, whereby the coefficient is small.
- *Urbanization*: if direct democracy were a phenomenon restricted to rural areas, the index for direct democratic rights might just capture a negative effect of urbanization, rather than the beneficial outcome and process due to political participation rights. To separate these two possible sources of individual utility and disutility, the variable 'urbanization' is included in the microeconometric happiness function. The results show that the positive effect on happiness of direct democracy does not change significantly, and that people living in urban areas are somewhat less happy.

Direct democracy thus has a robust and sizeable effect on satisfaction with life over and above cantonal differences with regard to wealth and urbanization.

Do citizens derive procedural utility from the possibility of participating in the direct democratic process? To investigate this question a control group has to be found. Foreigners are an optimal control group because, on the one hand, they generally have no political participation rights and, on the other

Table 10.2   Outcome and process utility in direct democracy

Variable	Weighted ordered probit Std. error adjusted to clustering in 26 cantons		
	Coefficient	*t*-value	Marginal effect (score 10)
Institutional variable			
Direct democratic rights	0.097**	3.384	0.033
Direct democratic rights x foreigner	−0.067	−1.699	−0.023
Economic variables	Yes		
Demographic variables	Yes		
Foreigner	−0.042	−0.283	−0.014
Observations	6134		
Prob > F	0.001		

Notes and data source: See Table 10.1.

hand, they cannot be excluded from the favourable outcome of direct democracy (outcome utility). Due to the fact that foreigners cannot reap procedural utility from political participation, they are expected to gain less from direct democracy than Swiss citizens do.

The econometric analysis presented in Table 10.2 suggests that foreigners are less happy, relatively speaking, than Swiss citizens in cantons in which the institutions of direct democracy are well developed. However, foreigners are still better off in a more directly democratic canton than in a less directly democratic canton. This result suggests that procedural utility, in addition to outcome utility, is an important source of satisfaction related to direct democracy.

Economic Determinants of Happiness

Unemployment
Unemployed people report a statistically highly significant lower level of subjective well-being than those who are employed. It should be remembered that this result refers to the state of being unemployed, and not the resulting lower income level. Not having a job imposes high non-pecuniary stress and unhappiness.

The size of the drop in happiness due to unemployment is substantial. Comparing the people looking for a job with other respondents, a 10.4 percentage points higher share reports to be unhappy (scoring 1, 2, 3 or 4). Interestingly enough, the effect on the upper range of happiness is huge: a

21.1 percentage points lower share indicates being completely satisfied. In other words, very few people seem to really enjoy the state of being unemployed (independent of the income level effects).

Income
Higher income correlates positively with higher happiness in a statistically significant way. However, the differences in subjective well-being are not very large. Consider, for example, the highest income group, with a monthly equivalence income above SFr 5,000. Compared with persons with low income, only a 6.8 percentage points larger share reports being 'completely satisfied'. Interestingly enough, an even larger additional percentage of persons (namely 9.2 percentage points), belonging to the second highest income group, reports a satisfaction score of 10. However, the marginal effects are much smaller than for being unemployed. This illustrates that employment is far more important than income for perceived satisfaction with life.

   These results are in line with the results of election and popularity functions mentioned above, as well as with happiness functions for other periods and countries.

Demographic Influences on Happiness

Several demographic characteristics are systematically related to reported subjective well-being.

- *Age.* People over 60 are happier than people under 30.
- *Gender.* Women are not happier than men, if the positive effect of their being a housewife is considered separately.
- *Nationality.* Foreigners are subject to a significantly lower probability of reaching high happiness scores compared with the Swiss.
- *Education.* People with higher education report significantly higher subjective well-being.
- *Family.* Couples with and without children are happier than singles, single parents and people living in collective households.

These results are quite similar to those found by other researchers on happiness for other countries and periods.

CONCLUSIONS

Based on data from interviews of more than 6000 Swiss residents, there is strong evidence that institutional (or constitutional) factors exert a systematic and sizeable influence on reported happiness. The existence of extended individual participation possibilities, in the form of initiatives and referenda, raises the subjective well-being of people.

Politicians in a strongly developed direct democracy are forced to follow the preferences of the voters more closely than where direct popular participation rights are less well developed. Citizens gain procedural utility from the fuller possibilities of directly participating in the political process. Foreigners living in Switzerland are more likely to benefit from the outcome than from the process (from which they are excluded). Foreigners therefore tend to reap systematically positive but lower satisfaction from living in a canton with strongly developed direct participation rights than do the Swiss.

In agreement with other happiness studies, unemployment is associated with a considerably lower level of subjective well-being. A higher income has a statistically significant positive but small effect on happiness.

For a sample of 12 European countries, additional interesting results for economic variables have been found (DiTella, MacCulloch and Oswald, 2000). Inflation is an important determinant of subjective well-being in the sense that it lowers subjective well-being. The following subjective trade-offs between unemployment and inflation can be deduced:

- A one percentage point rise in the inflation rate must be compensated by about $150 (in 1985 dollars) in additional per capita income.
- A one percentage point rise in the unemployment rate must be compensated by about $165 (in 1985 dollars) in additional per capita income.

The cost of a one percentage point increase in inflation or unemployment is thus quite similar. This corresponds to the results found for election and voting functions. Political-institutional factors in the form of direct democracy, as well as economic and demographic factors, exert a systematic and sizeable effect on happiness.

SUGGESTIONS ON THE LITERATURE AND SOURCES

A good summary of the present state of research on happiness is provided in
Lane, Robert E. (2000), *The Loss of Happiness in Market Economies*, New Haven and London: Yale University Press.

The psychological point of view is discussed in
Argyle, Michael (1987), *The Psychology of Happiness*, London: Methuen.
Kahneman, Daniel, Ed Diener and Norbert Schwarz (1999), *Well-being: The Foundation of Hedonic Psychology*, New York: Russell Sage Foundation.

A corresponding survey article is
Diener, Ed, Eunkook M. Suh, Richard E. Lucas and Heidi L. Smith (1999), 'Subjective Well-being: Three Decades of Progress', *Psychological Bulletin*, **125** (2),
276–303.

Happiness between nations is discussed in
Veenhoven, Ruut (1993), *Happiness in Nations: Subjective Appreciation of Life in 56
Nations 1946–1992*, Rotterdam: Erasmus University Press.

The effect of income on happiness is the subject of
Diener, Ed and Shigehiro Oishi (2000), 'Money and Happiness: Income and Subjec-
tive Well-being Across Nations', in Ed Diener and Eunkook M. Suh (eds), *Subjective
Well-being Across Cultures,* Cambridge, MA: MIT Press, 185–218.

The first economist to seriously study happiness was
Easterlin, Richard A. (1974), 'Does Economic Growth improve the Human Lot?
Some Empirical Evidence', in Paul A. David and Melvin W. Reder (eds), *Nations
and Households in Economic Growth: Essays in Honour of Moses Abramowitz*,
New York: Academic Press.

See also his more recent contribution
Easterlin, Richard A. (1995), 'Will Raising the Incomes of All Increase the Happiness of All?', *Journal of Economic Behavior and Organization*, **27**, 35–48.

Recent analyses by economists are, for example,
Oswald, Andrew J. (1997), 'Happiness and Economic Performance', *Economic Jour-
nal*, **107** (445), 1815–31.
Di Tella, Rafael, Robert J. MacCulloch and Andrew J. Oswald (2001), 'Preferences
over Inflation and Unemployment: Evidence from Surveys of Happiness', *Ameri-
can Economic Review*, forthcoming.
Frey, Bruno S. and Alois Stutzer (2000), 'Happiness, Economy and Institutions',
Economic Journal, **110**, 918–938.

The relationship between utility and happiness is discussed in
Ng, Yew-Kwang (1997), 'A Case for Happiness, Cardinalism, and Interpersonal
Comparability', *Economic Journal*, **107** (445), 1848–58.
Frank, Robert H. (1997), 'The Frame of Reference as a Public Good', *Economic
Journal*, **107** (445), 1832–47.

Popularity and election functions are surveyed by
Nannestad, Peter and Martin Paldam (1994), 'The VP-function: A Survey of the
Literature on Vote and Popularity Functions after 25 Years', *Public Choice*, **79** (3-
4), 213–45.

11. FOCJ: competitive governments for Europe

with Reiner Eichenberger

LIBERALIZED ECONOMIC AND RESTRICTED POLITICAL MARKETS IN EUROPE

European integration was outstandingly successful at granting the four 'freedoms' related to the movement of goods, services, labour and capital. As a result of establishing a single, competitive European economic market, the citizens of the countries forming the European Union have certainly experienced a significant increase in welfare.

In contrast, no such open and competitive market for *politics* has been established: the competition between governments was successfully restricted by the various European treaties and institutions. While the European Union's power in politics, including economic policy, is still quite limited, no steps have been undertaken to actively institutionalize competition between all levels of governmental units. Such competition has, at best, been considered for national governments, but there are strong efforts to undermine it by 'harmonizing' or 'equalizing' taxes.

Other forms of political competition should be envisaged, too. Welfare can be improved substantially by promoting competition between newly emerging jurisdictions that are organized by functions instead of territories. The fifth freedom suggested here allows for such Functional, Overlapping, Competing Jurisdictions. They will be called by their acronym FOCJ (one such jurisdiction will be called FOCUS). FOCJ form a federal system of governments that is not dictated from above, but emerges from below as a response to citizens' preferences. This fifth freedom requires a constitutional decision, ensuring that the emergence of FOCJ is not blocked by existing jurisdictions. Every citizen and community must have the right to appeal directly to the European Court if barriers to the competition between governments are established. The European Constitution must give the lowest political units a measure of independence so that they can engage in forming FOCJ. The citizens must be given the right to establish FOCJ by popular referenda, and political entrepreneurs must be supported and controlled by the institution of popular initiatives. FOCJ themselves must have the right to levy taxes to finance the public services they provide.

These FOCJ strongly contrast with the concepts of federalism currently existing, or being proposed in the European Union. We intend to show that FOCJ are well grounded in economic theory. Successful precursors of these institutions exist in European history. Indeed, Europe owes its rise as an economic and intellectual centre to the competition among governmental units. Moreover, such functional competing units already partially exist in present-day Europe, and elsewhere, where they perform well within the room accorded to them. The idea of completing the European integration at different speeds, and thus having various subgroups of countries within the European Union, is also related, though it is far more restrictive than our concept of FOCJ.

The next section specifies the concept of FOCJ, and puts it into theoretical perspective; our concept of competitive federalism is contrasted with all-purpose jurisdictions confined to one particular geographical area. The third section shows that FOCJ partially exist, both in European history and today. The relationship to US special districts, and in particular to functional communities in Switzerland, is emphasized. The next section compares FOCJ to existing federal institutions in the European Union. The fifth section analyses the working of FOCJ and discusses how the problems associated with this type of jurisdiction may be overcome. Concluding remarks are offered in the last section.

CONSTITUTING ELEMENTS

The Four Characteristics

The federal units proposed here have four essential features: they are

- *Functional (F)*: that is, the new political units extend over areas defined by the tasks to be fulfilled;
- *Overlapping (O)*: that is, in line with the many different tasks (functions), there are corresponding governmental units extending over different geographical areas;
- *Competing (C)*: that is, individuals and/or communities may choose to what governmental unit they want to belong, and they have political rights to express their preferences directly via initiatives and referenda;
- *Jurisdictions (J)*: that is, the units established are governmental, they have enforcement power and can, in particular, levy taxes.

FOCJ are based on theoretical propositions advanced in the economic theory of federalism. They nevertheless form a governmental system completely different to the one suggested in that literature. While the economic theory of federalism analyses the behaviour of given political units at the different levels of government, FOCJ emerge in response to the 'geography of problems'. As always, there are precursors to FOCJ. The general idea has already been advanced by Montesquieu. In the economics literature, a related concept has been pioneered by Tullock, who somewhat misleadingly speaks of 'sociological federalism'. A recent Centre for Economic Policy Research publication (CEPR, 1993) briefly mentions the possibility of establishing overlapping jurisdictions in Europe (pp. 54–5) but does not work out the concept, nor does it refer to previous research.

The four elements of FOCJ are now related to economic theory, as well as to existing federal institutions, pointing out both similarities and differences to existing concepts.

Functions

A particular public service, which only benefits a certain geographical area, should be financed by the people living in this area, that is there should be no spillovers. Under this rule, the different political units can cater for differences in the populations' preferences or, more precisely, to its demands. To minimize cost, these units have to exploit economies of scale in production. As these may strongly differ in function (for example between schools, police, hospitals, power plants and defence) there is an additional reason for unifunctional (or few-functional) governmental units of different sizes. While this idea is central to 'fiscal equivalence', the adjustment of the size of governmental units to varying conditions constitutes an essential part of FOCJ.

However, fiscal equivalence theory has been little concerned with decision-making within functional units. The supply process is either left unspecified, or it is assumed that the mobility of persons (and of firms, a fact rarely mentioned) automatically induces these units to cater for individual preferences. This criticism also applies to a closely related concept of fiscal federalism, namely 'voting by foot'. This preference revealing mechanism makes comparatively efficient suppliers grow in size, and the others shrink. According to this model of federalism, the political jurisdictions are exogenously given, are multi-purpose, and do not overlap, while the political supply process is left unspecified. In contrast, we emphasize the need to explicitly study the political supply process. Exit and entry is considered insufficient to eliminate rent extraction by governments. Individuals must have the possibility of raising their voices in the form of voting. Clubs are similar to FOCJ, because their size is determined endogenously by the benefits and costs of the club members.

Overlaps

FOCJ may overlap in two respects:

- Two or more FOCJ catering for the same function may geographically intersect (for example a multitude of school FOCJ may exist in the same geographical area);
- FOCJ catering to different functions may overlap.

The two types of overlap may coexist; however, a constitutional decision can be taken to restrict FOCJ of specific functions to the second type because this alleviates free riding problems (see below). An individual, or a political community, normally belongs to various FOCJ at the same time. FOCJ need not be physically contiguous, and they do not have a monopoly over a certain area of land. Thus this concept completely differs from archaic nationalism with its fighting over pieces of land. It also breaks with the notion of federalist theory that units at the same level may not overlap. In this respect, FOCJ are similar to clubs, which may intersect.

Competition

The heads of FOCJ are induced by two mechanisms to conform closely to their members' preferences: while the possibility of individuals and communities to exit mimics market competition, their right to vote establishes political competition. It should be noted that migration is only one means of exit; often, membership in a particular FOCUS can be discontinued without changing one's location. Exit is not restricted to individuals or firms; as indicated before, political communities as a whole, or parts of them, may also exercise this option. Moreover, exit may be total or only partial. In the latter case, an individual or community only participates in a restricted set of FOCUS activities. This enlarged set of exit options makes 'voting by foot' function properly.

  Secession, that is the exit of jurisdictions or individuals from a jurisdiction, has been recognized as an effective means for restricting the power of central states. The right to secede stands in stark contrast to the prevailing concepts of nation states and federations, where this is strictly forbidden and often prevented by force, as is illustrated, for example by the American Civil War (1861–65), by the Swiss 'Sonderbundskrieg' (1847), or more recently by the wars in Katanga (1960–63), Biafra (1967–70), Bangladesh (1970–71), and recently in ex-Yugoslavia and Chechnya. Current European treaties do not provide for the secession of a nation from the European Union, and a fortiori for regions within a nation. The possibility of lower-level jurisdictions to exit at low cost from the European Union as a whole, as well as from particular subunits (nations, states, Länder, autonomous regions and so on), thus depends strongly on the future European constitution.

For FOCJ to establish competition between governments, exit should be as unrestrained as possible. In contrast, entry need not necessarily be free. As for individuals in clubs, jurisdictions may impose a price if they want to join a particular FOCUS and benefit from its public goods. The existing members of the particular FOCUS have to decide democratically whether a new member pays an adequate entry price, and is thus welcome. 'Free' mobility, in the sense of a disregard for the cost imposed on others, is overcome by internalizing the external cost of movement. In addition, FOCJ do not have to restrict entry by administrative and legal means such as zoning laws. Explicit, openly declared entrance fees substitute implicit restrictions, resulting in high land prices and housing rents. The commonly raised concern that pricing could be exploitative and mobility strongly curtailed, is unwarranted as FOCJ are subject to competitive pressure. Moreover, the possibility of imposing an explicit entrance fee gives incentives to FOCJ governments to care not only for the preferences of actual members, but also of prospective members.

Competition needs to be furthered by political institutions, as the exit option does not suffice to induce governments to act efficiently. The citizens should be able to elect directly the persons managing the FOCJ, and should be given the right to initiate popular referenda on specific issues. These democratic institutions are known to raise efficiency, in the sense of taking care of individual preferences (see Chapter 9).

Jurisdictions
A FOCUS is a democratic governmental unit with authority over its citizens, including the power to impose taxes. According to the two types of overlap, two forms of membership can be distinguished:

1. The lowest political unit (normally the community) is a member, and all corresponding citizens automatically become citizens of the FOCJ to which their community belongs. In that case, an individual can only exit via mobility.
2. Individuals may freely choose whether they want to belong to a particular FOCUS but, while they are its citizens, they are subject to its authority. Such FOCJ may be non-voluntary in the sense that one must belong to a FOCUS providing for a certain function, for example a school FOCUS, and must pay the corresponding taxes (an analogy here is health insurance, which in many countries is obligatory, but where individuals are free to choose an insurance company). The citizens of such a school FOCUS may then decide that everyone must pay taxes in order to finance a particular school, irrespective of whether one has children or not. With respect to FOCJ providing functions with significant redistributive effects, a minimal regulation by the central government may be in order

so that, for example, citizens without children do not join so-called 'school FOCJ', which in effect do not offer any schooling, but have correspondingly low (or zero) taxes. In this respect, Buchanan-type clubs differ from FOCJ, because they are always voluntary, while membership in a FOCUS can be compulsory.

FOCJ, as jurisdictions, provide particular services, but do not necessarily produce them themselves if contracting out to a public or private enterprise is advantageous. It is noteworthy that present-day outsourcing by communities does not automatically lead to FOCJ. The former is restricted to production, while FOCJ care for provision and are directly democratically controlled. FOCJ also differ from existing functional and overlapping institutions, such as the various kinds of specific administration unions (or Zweckverbände as they are aptly called in German speaking countries). These institutions normally do not have the legal status of governments, but are purely administrative units. The same applies to the many types of corporations, which usually have no power to impose taxes, but have to rely on charges.

Beneficial Effects

Due to their four essential characteristics, FOCJ compare favourably to traditional forms of federalism. One aspect concerns the governments' incentives and possibilities to satisfy the heterogeneous preferences of individuals. As a consequence of the concentration on one functional area, the citizens of a particular FOCUS have better information on its activity, and are in a better position to compare its performance with other governments. As many benefits and costs extend over a quite limited geographical area, we often envisage FOCJ to be small, which is also helpful for voters' evaluations. The exit option opened by the existence of overlapping jurisdictions is not only an important means to make one's preferences known to governmental suppliers, but it also strengthens the citizens' incentive to be informed about politics.

On the other hand, FOCJ are able to provide public services at low cost, because they are formed in order to minimize interjurisdictional spillovers and to exploit economies of scale. When the benefits of a specific activity indivisibly extend over large areas, and there is decreasing cost, the corresponding optimal FOCUS may cover many communities, several nations, or even Europe as a whole. An example may be defence against outward aggression, where the appropriate FOCUS may most likely extend over the whole of Europe (even beyond the European Union). That such adjustment to efficient size is indeed undertaken in reality is shown by the Swiss experience. Communities decided by referendum whether they wanted to join the new canton, Jura, established in 1978, and in 1993 communities in the Laufental opted to belong to the canton Basle-Land instead of Bern. Communities also frequently change districts (the federal level below cantons) by referendum vote, which suggests that voters perceive the new size of jurisdictions and the new bundle of services to be more efficient. The same holds for American special districts.

The specialization in one or more functions further contributes to cost efficiency, due to the advantages of specialization. As FOCJ levy their own taxes to finance their activity, it pays to be economical. In contrast, in all-purpose jurisdictions financed from outside, which lack such fiscal equivalence, politicians have an incentive to lobby for ever increasing funds, thereby pushing up government expenditure. The incentive to economize in a FOCUS induces its managers to contract out whenever production cost can thereby be reduced.

While FOCJ are more market oriented than all-purpose jurisdictions, they reduce the size of the public sector. However, they differ from today's one-shot privatization, which usually does not impact on the government's basic incentives, and thus is often reversed by reregulation and deprivatization. In contrast, in a system of FOCJ, privatization emerges endogenously and is sustainable, as the politicians' incentives are changed dramatically.

The threat of dissatisfied citizens or communities exiting the FOCUS, and the benefit of new citizens and communities joining, gives an incentive to take individual preferences into account and to provide efficient public services. Quite another advantage of FOCJ is that they open up the politicians' cartel ('classe politique') to functionally competent outsiders. While all-purpose jurisdictions attract persons with broad and non-specialized knowledge to become politicians, in FOCJ it tends to be persons with a well-grounded knowledge in a particular functional area (say education or refuse collection) who are successful.

The possibility of forming FOCJ also helps to deal with issues raised by fundamentalist sentiments. Political movements focused on a single issue (for example, ethnicity, religion, environment and so on) are not forced to take over governments in toto, but can concentrate on those functions they are really interested in. An ethnic group need not disassociate itself from the state they live in as a whole, but may found FOCJ which care for their particular preferences. South Tyroleans, for example, unhappy with the language domination imposed by the Italian state, need not leave Italy in order to have their demands for cultural autonomy fulfilled, but may establish corresponding FOCJ. Such partial exit (for example only with respect to ethnic issues) does not lead to the trade barriers often going with the establishment of newly-formed all purpose political jurisdictions. FOCJ thus meet the criterion of market preserving federalism.

A REALISTIC CONCEPT

It could be argued that FOCJ and the fifth freedom break away too radically from present realities to have much chance of being implemented, thus being too utopian a concept. However, from a more historical and international point of view, things look different.

European History

Decentralized, overlapping political units have been an important feature of European history. The competition between governments in the Holy Roman Empire of German Nations, especially in today's Italy and Germany, has been intensive. Many of these governments were small. Quite a number of scholars attribute the rise of Europe to this diversity and competition of governmental units, which fostered technical, economic and artistic innovation. While the Chinese were more advanced in very many respects, their superiority ended with the establishment of a centralized Chinese Empire. The unification of Italy and Germany in the 19th century, which has often been praised as a major advance, partially ended this stimulating competition between governments and led to deadly struggles between nation states. Some smaller states escaped unification; Andorra, Liechtenstein, Luxembourg, Monaco, San Marino and Switzerland stayed politically independent, and at the same time grew rich.

The governmental units just mentioned are not FOCJ in the sense outlined in this contribution, but they shared the characteristic of competing for labour and capital (including artistic capital) among each other. However, history also reveals examples of jurisdictions close to FOCJ. The problems connected with Poland's strong ethnic and religious diversity (Catholics, Protestants and Jews) were at least partly overcome by jurisdictions organized according to these features, and not according to geography. The highly successful Hanse prospered from the 12th to the 16th century, and comprised inter alia Lübeck, Bremen, Köln (today German), Stettin and Danzig (today Polish), Kaliningrad (today Russian), Riga, Reval and Dorpat (today parts of the Baltic republics) and Groningen and Deventer (today Dutch); furthermore, London (England), Bruges and Antwerp (today Belgian) and Novgorod (today Russian) were 'Handelskontore' or associated members. It was clearly a functional governmental unit, providing for trade rules and facilities, and was not geographically contiguous.

Contemporary Examples

The European Community started out as a FOCUS designed to establish free trade in Europe, and was from the very beginning in competition with other trade areas, in particular North America, Japan, and EFTA. Due to its economic success, it has attracted almost all European countries. Entry has not been free. The nations determined to enter had to pay a price. They have (with few exceptions) to accept the 'acquis communautaire', as well as to pay their share of the Community's outlays, which to a large extent serve redistributive purposes. In several respects, FOCJ-like units exist within Europe, such as with the police force, education, environment, transport, culture or sports, though they have been prevented from becoming autonomous jurisdictions with taxing power.

There are two major examples of functional, overlapping and competing jurisdictions (though they do not in all cases meet the full requirements of FOCJ specified above). One relates to the US special districts, with which American readers are familiar. The other relates to Switzerland. Many Swiss cantons have a structure of overlapping and competing functional jurisdictions, which share many features of FOCJ. In canton Zurich (with a population of 1.2 million), for example, there are 171 geographical communities, which in themselves are composed of three to six independently managed, directly democratically organized jurisdictions, devoted to specific functions and levying their own taxes on personal income: besides general purpose communities, there are communities that exclusively provide for elementary schools and other ones that specialize in junior high schools, and there are the communities of three different churches. All these governmental units have widely differing rates of income tax. Moreover, there are a vast number of 'civil communities' (Zivilgemeinden) providing water, electricity, TV antennas and so on, which are directly democratic but finance themselves by user charges. These communities often overlap with neighbouring political communities. In addition, there are 174 functional units ('Zweckverbände'), whose members are not individual citizens but communities. These Zweckverbände take care, for example, of waste water and purification plants, cemeteries, hospitals and regional planning. Canton Zurich is no exception in Switzerland, where the multitude of types of functional communities are concerned. A similar structure exists, for example, in canton Glarus or Thurgau. Various efforts have been made to suppress this diversity of functional communities, usually initiated by the cantonal bureaucracy and politicians. However, most of these attempts have been thwarted because the population is to a large extent satisfied with the public supply provided. The example of Switzerland – which is generally considered to be a well-organized and administered country – shows that a multiplicity of functional jurisdictions under democratic control is not a theorist's wishful thinking, but has worked well in reality.

COMPARISON WITH FEDERALISM IN EUROPE

While institutions similar to FOCJ play an important role in European history and in today's USA and Switzerland, they are largely absent from the EU's political landscape and the intellectual debate. Most notably, FOCJ differ in many crucial respects from scholarly proposals for a future European constitution. One of the most prominent is Buchanan, who stresses an individual nation's right to secede but, somewhat surprisingly, does not build on Buchanan-type clubs. The European Constitutional Group focuses on the example of the American constitution, and presents detailed proposals with respect to the houses of parliament and the respective voting weights of the various countries. Overlapping jurisdictions and referenda are not allowed for, and the exit option is strongly restricted. Other economics scholars suggest a strengthening of federalism in the traditional sense (that is with multi-purpose federal units), but do not envisage overlapping jurisdictions. The report by the Centre for Economic Policy Research (1993) criticizes 'subsidiarity' (as used in the Maastricht Treaty) as an empty concept, arguing that good theoretical reasons must be provided for central government intervention. But the report does not deal with the institutions necessary to guarantee that policy follows such theoretical advice. The idea of overlapping, not geographically based, jurisdictions is briefly raised but is not institutionally or practically worked out, nor is the need for a democratic organization and the power to impose taxes acknowledged.

Recent proposals from political bodies mainly deal with the organization of the parliamentary system (the houses of parliament and the national voting weights) and to a substantial extent accept the existing treatises as the founding stones of the European constitution. The idea of competition between governments (which is basic for FOCJ) is neglected, or even rejected, in favour of 'cooperation' between governments.

FOCJ are also quite different from the regions envisaged in existing European treaties and institutions. A major difference is that FOCJ emerge from below, while the 'European regions' tend to be established from above. Moreover, their existence strongly depends on subsidies flowing from the European Union and the nation states. In contrast, the concept of FOCJ corresponds to a non-constructivist process view. It cannot a priori be determined from outside and from above, which FOCJ will be efficient for dealing with in the future. This must be left entirely to the competitive democratic process taking place at the level of individuals and communities. The central European constitution must only make sure that no other government units, in particular nations, may obstruct the emergence of FOCJ. Our scheme allows for a (closely restricted) set of central regulations, as mentioned above. Efficiency should not only be judged by its capacity for survival in the evolutionary process; efficiency is therefore more directly defined in terms of the fulfilment of citizens' demands.

'Subsidiarity', as proclaimed in the Maastricht Treaty, is generally recognized to be more of a vague goal than a concept with content. Even if subsidiarity were taken seriously, it would not lead to a real federal structure, because many (actual or prospective) members of the European Union are essentially unitary states without federal subunits of significant competence. Examples are the Netherlands, France or Sweden. 'Regions' existing in the European Union (examples are Galicia and Cataluña in Spain, or South Tyrol and Sicily in Italy) are far from being units with significant autonomous functional competencies.

The idea of FOCJ also contrasts with the EU's reluctance to grant exceptions to specific aspects of agreements reached (as in the Maastricht Treaty concerning the European Monetary Union and the Protocol on Social Policy, or in the Schengen Treaty concerning the free movement of persons). Indeed, they are seen as damaging the 'spirit of Europe'. Whether differential degrees of European integration are framed as models of variable geometry, multi-track, multi-speed, two-tier, hard core, concentric circles, or as Europe à la carte, the subject regularly evokes fierce opposition from European politicians. In a system of FOCJ, in contrast, functional units not covering everyone are taken as a welcome expression of heterogeneous demands among Europeans.

FOCJ are relevant for all levels of government and major issues. An example would be Corsica, which could form an independent region of Europe because of its dissatisfaction with France. However, the Corsicans are most likely only partially dissatisfied with France. This suggests that one, or several, FOCJ provide a better solution in this case; they may, for example, especially focus on ethnic or language boundaries, or on Corsica's economic problems as an island. This allows the Corsicans to exit France only partially instead of totally. Generally speaking, tourism and transport issues, in particular railways, are important areas for FOCJ. It should be noted that, despite the membership of various countries in the (then) European Community, railway policy was not coordinated to exploit possible economies of scale; a FOCUS may constitute a well-suited organization to overcome such shortcomings.

OVERCOMING PROBLEMS

Up to this point, the beneficial effects of FOCJ have been emphasized. However, there are also some alleged problems with our concept, which will now be discussed.

Overburdened Citizens

In a federal system of FOCJ, each individual is a citizen of various jurisdictions. As a consequence, individuals may be overburdened by voting in elections and referenda taking place in each FOCUS. However, citizens in a directly democratic FOCUS find it much easier to participate politically, as they have only to assess one or two concrete issues at a time. In contrast, in representative, democratic, all-purpose jurisdictions, citizens have to evaluate all political aspects simultaneously, and they have to speculate what position a political candidate will take in his or her next term of election. If the citizens do find it burdensome to vote on each governmental function separately, they can rely on emerging institutions to deal with the problem. For instance, in referenda they may simply follow parties' recommendations.

An individual is confronted with a multitude of suppliers of public services, which is argued to make life difficult. This is the logical consequence of having more options to choose from, and is similar to supply in the private sector. If citizens find it nevertheless to be a problem, a governmental or a private advisory service can be established, to offer information and support for the consumers' decisions. It should, moreover, be observed that in all-purpose jurisdictions the same problem exists. There is no all-enhancing administration managing all public services. Rather, the responsibility is divided up among specialized government departments, so that the citizens/consumers are also effectively confronted with many different agencies supplying public services.

'Need' to Coordinate the Activities of FOCJ

While coordination is obviously often needed, coordination between governments is not a good as such. It sometimes serves to build cartels among the members of the 'classe politique', who then evade or even exploit the population's wishes. As far as welfare increasing coordination is concerned, its need is reduced compared to all-purpose jurisdictions, because the FOCJ emerge in order to minimize externalities. If major spillovers between FOCJ exist, new FOCJ will be founded, taking care of these externalities. As the number of FOCJ is restricted due to the transaction costs involved, less important externalities between FOCJ will remain. However, spillovers also exist in a system of all-purpose jurisdictions between administrative units, for example between the department for environment and the department of transport. The crucial question, therefore, is in what system interfunctional bargaining is more likely to arise. The respective civil servants in all-purpose jurisdictions have a muted incentive to take these spillovers into account by bargaining. On the one hand, their sphere of influence may be curtailed if they coordinate decisions among various departments effectively. On the other hand, their income and other benefits are essentially unconnected to the possible benefits to the citizens. In contrast, the political managers of a FOCUS have a self-interest to seriously engage in bargaining, as the support received from the members of their FOCUS depends on how much they raise their members' utility. This responsiveness is achieved by the institutions of re-election, and by popular initiatives and referenda on specific issues. To the extent that the citizens of a FOCUS value coordination, it behoves FOCJ governments to provide it. Thus, coordination among FOCJ is not inherently different from coordination in economic markets, where similar problems occur all the time and are analysed in depth by much recent research in industrial organization.

Redistribution

It is claimed that all forms of federalism – including FOCJ – undermine redistribution. Moreover, FOCJ are said to emerge on the basis of income. As far as redistribution is based on the citizens' solidarity, or on insurance principles, this fear is unwarranted. Only as far as redistribution is a pure public good, and must thus be enforced to prevent free riding, may a problem arise. However, empirical research suggests that substantial redistribution is feasible in federal systems. In the USA, and especially in Switzerland, lower level and even local governments strongly engage in redistribution activities and are responsible for a substantive share of redistribution. In these countries, mobility is obviously not high enough to render redistribution impossible. Where Europe is concerned, mobility is also quite low. Fewer than 5 per cent of EU citizens live outside their country of citizenship. This low level of mobility can be interpreted in two ways.

1. In decentralized systems, mobility by persons (and to a lesser extent also firms) is countervailed by strong local attachment.
2. Redistribution does not constitute a pure public good, but provides localized benefits. However, if decentralized redistribution is considered insufficient, a FOCUS specialized on interregional redistribution may emerge, but this presupposes barriers to entry (in analogy to insurance systems with cross-subsidization). Moreover, centralization of redistribution is still possible, of course. The European constitution may give central government the power to impose a limited amount of income redistribution.

CONCLUSIONS

Europe owes its position as an economically rich and intellectually and artistically powerful continent in large measure to the great variety of governmental jurisdictions in competition with each other. This basic insight was overshadowed by the unification movements, especially in Italy and Germany. The European movement follows the historic lesson by opening up trade barriers and supporting economic competition, with great success. However, the historic lesson has not been followed with respect to establishing competition between existing and new governments.

This chapter proposes that the future European constitution should allow, and actively promote, the evolution of functional, overlapping and competing governmental jurisdictions (FOCJ). They fulfil many of the welfare-enhancing qualities of theoretical concepts, such as voting by foot, fiscal equivalence, or clubs. It is shown that FOCJ are feasible, that there are successful historical examples, and that they partially exist in the form of US special districts and Swiss functional, democratic and overlapping communities. In particular, FOCJ represent a new way of planning a future, more citizen-oriented Europe.

SUGGESTIONS ON THE LITERATURE AND SOURCES

The idea of competition between governments has been championed and analysed by
Hayek, Friedrich A. von (1960), *The Constitution of Liberty*, London: Routledge.
Jones, Eric L. (1981), *The European Miracle*, Cambridge, UK: Cambridge University Press.

Recent contributions are contained in
Bernholz, Peter, Manfred E. Streit and Roland Vaubel (1998), *Political Competition, Innovation and Growth. A Historical Analysis*, New York: Springer.

Precursors to FOCJ are
Burnheim, John (1985), *Is Democracy Possible?: The Alternative to Electoral Politics*, Cambridge: Polity Press.
Casella, Alessandra and Bruno S. Frey (1992), 'Federalism and Clubs: Towards an Economic Theory of Overlapping Political Jurisdictions', *European Economic Review*, **36**, 639–46.
Drèze, Jacques (1993), 'Regions of Europe: A Feasible Status, to be Discussed', *Economic Policy*, **17**, 266–307.
Tullock, Gordon (1994), *The New Federalist*, Vancouver: Fraser Institute.

A more complete discussion with many further references is offered in

Frey, Bruno S. and Reiner Eichenberger (1999), *The New Democratic Federalism for Europe: Functional Overlapping and Competing Jurisdictions*, Cheltenham, UK and Northampton, US: Edward Elgar.

Surveys on the economic theory of federalism are

Breton, Albert (1996), *Competitive Governments. An Economic Theory of Politics and Public Choice Finance*, New York: Cambridge University Press.
Oates, Wallace E. (1999), 'An Essay on Fiscal Federalism', *Journal of Economic Literature*, **37** (3), 1120–49.

The concept of fiscal equivalence is due to

Olson, Mancur (1969), 'The Principle of "Fiscal Equivalence": The Division of Responsibilities among Different Levels of Government', *American Economic Review*, **59** (2), 479–87.

Voting by foot and clubs have been studied by

Tiebout, Charles M. (1956), 'A Pure Theory of Local Expenditure', *Journal of Political Economy*, **64** (October), 416–24.
Buchanan, James M. (1965), 'An Economic Theory of Clubs', *Economica*, **32** (February), 1–14.

Exit and voice have been analysed by

Hirschman, Albert O. (1970), *Exit, Voice and Loyalty*, Cambridge, MA: Harvard University Press.

For the concept of market preserving federalism, see

Weingast, Barry R. (1993), 'Constitutions as Governance Structures: The Political Foundations of Secure Markets', *Journal of Institutional and Theoretical Economics (JITE)*, **149** (1), 286–311.

For the beneficial effects of competition between government jurisdictions, see for the Holy Roman Empire of German Nations

Baumol, William J. and Hilda Baumol (1994), 'On the Economics of Musical Composition in Mozart's Vienna', *Journal of Cultural Economics*, **18**, 171–98.

The bad effects of destroying such competition by centralization is shown for China by

Pak, Hung Mo (1995), 'Effective Competition, Institutional Choice and Economic Development of Imperial China', *Kyklos*, **48**, 87–103.

There are many proposals for a European Constitution. See, for example,

Buchanan, James M. (1991), 'An American Perspective on Europe's Constitutional Opportunity', *Cato Journal*, **10** (3), 619–29.
Vibert, Frank (1995), *Europe: A Constitution for the Millennium*, Aldershot: Dartmouth.
Schneider, Friedrich (1996), 'The Design of a Minimal European Federal Union: Some Ideas Using the Public Choice Approach', in José Casas Pardo and Friedrich

Schneider (eds), *Current Issue in Public Choice,* Cheltenham, UK and Brookfield, US: Edward Elgar, pp. 203–22.

European Constitutional Group (1993), *A Proposal for a European Constitution,* London: Policy Forum.

A proposal by the European Parliament is

Herman, Fernand (Reporter) (1994), 'Zweiter Bericht des Institutionellen Ausschusses über die Verfassung der Europäischen Union', Sitzungsdokumente A3-0064/94, Europäisches Parlament.

European regions are discussed in

Adonis, Andrew and Stuart Jones (1991), 'Subsidiarity and the European Community's Constitutional Future', *Staatswissenschaft und Staatspraxis,* **2** (2), 179–96.

The dangers of harmonization and coordination, from the point of view of European citizens, are pointed out in

Vaubel, Roland (1995), *The Centralisation of Western Europe: The Common Market, Political Integration, and Democracy,* London: Institute of Economic Affairs.

That income redistribution is possible in a federal structure is empirically shown by

Kirchgässner, Gebhard and Werner W. Pommerehne (1996), 'Tax Harmonization and Tax Competition in the European Community: Lessons from Switzerland', *Journal of Public Economics,* **60**, 351–71.

12. The political economy of stabilization programmes in developing countries

with Reiner Eichenberger

PROBLEMS AND ISSUES

Developing countries are faced with severe economic problems: high, galloping rates of inflation, large shares of the population without adequate employment, and low real growth or even declining standards of living. The balance of payments and budget are regularly in deficit. The developing countries' governments may turn to various sources of outside help. Some countries were fortunate enough to receive substantial help from industrial countries for strategic political reasons (Israel and Cuba are, or were, good examples of this). Most countries' governments have to resort to the international credit market. However, due to the high country risk typically attributed to nations in trouble, either the interest rates demanded are very high, or credits are not available at all. Governments must then turn to international financial institutions, most importantly the International Monetary Fund and the International Bank for Reconstruction and Development (World Bank). The cost of the credit to the government of the recipient developing country is then not so much (or not at all) reflected in the interest rate, but rather in the conditionalities attached, that is in the adjustment programme the country is contractually obliged to undertake. In such programmes, three kinds of action are normally required of the developing country's government: the currency must be devalued in order to balance external accounts, the budget must be balanced, and the distorted price structure must be reformed, involving, in particular, a heavy reduction or discontinuation in subsidies to specific households and firms.

Experience shows convincingly that such adjustment programmes meet with limited or no success.

- Economic conditions in the countries receiving the credits improve only slightly, or not at all;
- The suppression of the population by the recipient countries' rulers often increases, and human and democratic rights are increasingly violated; and

- The conditionalities to which the recipient countries' governments formally agree are met to a small degree only, and many, if not most, programmes are abandoned after a relatively short period of time.

The unsatisfactory results achieved by credits and adjustment programmes in developing countries are likely to have a politico-economic explanation; all the same, Public Choice theorists have been rather mute on the issue, even though the crucial influence of governments on economic development has long been recognized. However, political economy as it presently exists may not be directly applied to the analysis of developing countries since, unlike most industrialized countries, they are usually *non-democratic*. Recently, some Public Choice literature explicitly modelling the behaviour of authoritarian governments, has been published. But there are only a handful of studies analysing the attempts at reforming and stabilizing the economy of developing countries within a politico-economic framework, drawing explicitly on the peculiarities of the developing countries' institutions and policies. This chapter endeavours to diminish this gap in the literature.

In the next section, a general framework is established for the analysis of the basic interaction between the economy, the polity and the main actors. The third section develops a simple interactive model in terms of the demand for and the supply of government support. The following section focuses on two fundamental features; *attributability* and *appropriability*, which can be looked at as essential filters through which the politico-economic interaction passes. The fifth section analyses attributability and appropriability in the case of stabilization programmes. The last section draws conclusions.

GENERAL FRAMEWORK

The Basic Relationships

The state of the economy, and the resources flowing from the economy to interest groups, influence the polity through their impact on the utility and survival probability of the government. The reverse causation originates from the government which seeks to influence the economy in order to improve its own welfare and, above all, in order to remain in power.

Figure 12.1 represents the circular flow between the economy and the polity. The government is seen as an endogenous part of the politico-economic relationship. Its survival depends on the support (or opposition) provided by the various groups. The government therefore influences its own utility and survival by using the classical economic policy instruments. This affects the state of the economy and the utility of the different groups. Governments

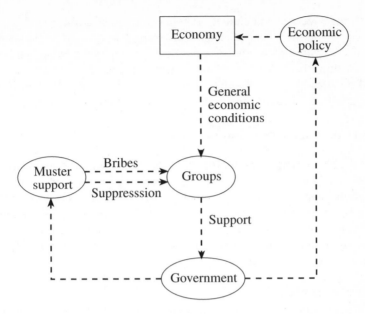

Figure 12.1   Politico-economic interdependence in an authoritarian developing country

also sanction groups by means of suppression and/or bribes in order to muster support. The possibility of imposing direct negative sanctions on opposing groups distinguishes this politico-economic model from more traditional ones better suited to democratic countries.

This outline of the basic features of the politico-economic model of developing authoritarian countries illuminates that the working of the system depends crucially on the institutional conditions. In authoritarian political systems typical in developing countries, elections play a lesser role than in democracies, or are even non-existent. They do not necessarily determine who is in power; that is, a government can be disposed of without election defeat, can come to power without having been (freely) elected, or can stay in power despite an election defeat. An example is the military regime in Burma after the election victory by the opposition in 1990. Accordingly, group influence goes much further than in a democracy. In the extreme, a group such as the military, or part of it, may take over the government by force. Authoritarian systems are thus characterized by the dominant position of the government and the limited constitutional role of the citizens, who therefore must put more emphasis on expressing their wishes via demonstrations, strikes or revolts, rather than by participating in free elections. The government, in turn, resorts to all kinds of force to suppress the population in general, but also specific opposition groups.

While democratic and authoritarian political systems differ fundamentally with respect to the extent of actual and potential force used, in both systems the government seeks to influence political outcomes by handing out benefits to, or calling back benefits from, specific groups. Such transfers are not usually called 'bribes', but the term is nevertheless used here in order to highlight their function, namely that of supporting the government's survival.

Government and Other Institutions

Figure 12.1 demonstrates the central role of government in the political economy of developing countries: government is influenced by economic conditions, and in turn affects economic conditions via its economic policy. The politicians in power are taken to maximize their own utility subject to constraints. The government politicians enjoy pursuing a certain ideology, but also consuming and maintaining power. The government is faced with three main types of constraint.

Political constraints

While politicians are subject to re-election constraints in liberal democracies, politicians in power in developing countries are aware that they can be over-thrown by a 'coup d'état', an uprising or a revolution. They therefore provide against this threat by transferring (often large) sums of money to foreign countries. A government's survival depends on a sufficiently high level of support, or on a sufficiently low level of opposition, from the various groups of society. Obviously, the groups are not equally capable of threatening the government's survival; the support by some groups – in many developing countries in particular by the military – is essential, while other groups can be suppressed more easily. The support or opposition of groups depends not only on the absolute level of the net benefits they receive from the government, but also on the relative level. The benefits received by the groups are compared with those they could obtain from an alternative government. These alternatives therefore shape the constraints of the government. Interestingly, most modelling attempts do not explicitly endogenize these alternatives.

Technical constraints

The government is also limited by the instruments available for pursuing its goals. Its possibility set may be further limited by an inadequate bureaucratic structure. These restrictions are summarized under the term 'technical constraints', but it should be borne in mind that these constraints are only partly given exogenously. They are also influenced by the interaction of the actors involved. Thus, the government's goals can be aided, or hindered, by the bureaucracy, depending on the latter's benefit–cost calculus.

Resource constraints

The government has limited means at its disposal for pursuing its goals. The extent to which a government can appropriate resources for its own purpose is of crucial importance in understanding the politico-economic interactions. Suffice it here to remark that the possibilities of taxation are often severely limited, and the government must resort to other modes of financing its expenditure.

The general framework in which government behaviour is analysed applies equally to the various groups distinguished. Their members are also taken to pursue their own interests, in particular to raise their income and wealth, and are subject to similar constraints which, in turn, are shaped by the behaviour of the government and the other groups.

Contrast to Existing Approaches

The discussion of the perspective employed here makes it clear that it differs markedly from those traditionally used for analysing developing countries and, in particular, from the analysis of stabilization programmes.

- Our approach stands in stark contrast to 'traditional' economic models of developing countries, where the focus is on purely economic aspects. In these models, the interaction between the economy and the polity are disregarded, and government – in so far as it is considered at all – is explicitly or implicitly assumed to pursue the general welfare of the population. It is taken not to react in any systematic way to changes in its survival probability or possibilities to raise its members' income and wealth. The traditional economic theory of developing countries, while certainly noting the importance of groups for economic events, does not consider them to be independent actors in the sense of pursuing their own interests. In particular, the economics literature does not take into account the behaviour of those groups which critically determine a government's possibility set, the military being a case in point.
- Our approach also differs significantly from the 'politico-economic' models in Public Choice, which have almost without exception been designed for either representative or direct democracies of western, market-oriented countries. While these models (rightly) disregard the suppression of certain groups by force, this plays a major role in our analysis. Accordingly, the traditional politico-economic models have assumed that governments are able to raise revenue by taxation or minting money. This chapter focuses instead on the various possibilities with which the government tries to get hold of a share of the resource flows (the question of appropriability). Moreover, in politico-economic models, cognitive aspects have been restricted to voters'

myopia and to the perceived difference between general and particular economic conditions. In contrast, here the question of attributability forms a central part of the analysis.

A SIMPLE MODEL OF AN AUTHORITARIAN GOVERNMENT

Authoritarian governments depend on the support that the population and the various groups are willing to provide. The interaction between the government on the one hand, and the population and groups on the other hand, can therefore conveniently be looked at in a demand and supply framework.

The Demand for and Supply of Support by the Government

In a politico-economic framework, the two main arguments in the government's utility function are its own consumption and the likelihood of its survival. The demand for support curve (Figure 12.2) identifies the government's optimal demand for support in terms of the amount of its own consumption the government must forgo.

Both the population and the various groups benefit from the government's policy. They compare the utility they get from a government with the alternatives that they would get were the opposition in power, and then act accordingly. In authoritarian systems, individuals can rarely vote, or the voting outcome is of little consequence. But they can provide support, and thereby increase the probability that the preferred government stays in, or comes to, power. Normally, individuals and groups face higher costs by supporting the government or some opposition group than in a democracy.

To increase its support, the government has to increase the net benefits to the population. For this purpose, the government has three instruments at its disposal: *economic policy* to improve general economic conditions; *bribery* as positive sanction; and *suppression* as negative sanction. The government is faced with a classical problem: it has to muster a sufficient amount of support from the population and the various groups in society in order to stay in power, but its possibilities, or the resources at its disposal, are limited. No government is certain to remain in power because either an organized, or a non-organized, opposition always exists which can topple it. The politicians, or the dictator in power, are therefore forced to use the resources available as efficiently as possible.

Groups respond positively to an improvement in the general economic conditions, as well as to suppression and/or bribes, but the marginal benefit of each decreases. Therefore, the supply function of support for the govern-

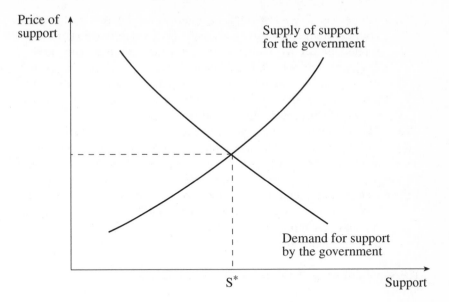

Figure 12.2   Equilibrium support S for the government by the population
and groups*

ment curves upward; that is, the marginal cost to the politicians in power of
mustering higher levels of support increases. The equilibrium level of support
for the government is shown in Figure 12.2.

Institutional Conditions Determining the Demand for and the Supply of Support

The government's demand for support function depends on two main factors.

1. The extent to which the government can appropriate the resources with
    which it musters the groups' support. This possibility depends on, among
    others things, the efficiency of taxation, the extent of public ownership of
    resources, and also the conditions imposed by creditors. An increase in
    appropriability will shift (ceteris paribus) the demand curve outwards. In
    the new equilibrium, the government enjoys a higher level of support,
    and its chances of survival are larger. The concept of appropriability will
    be discussed extensively below.
2. The political institutions determining the conditions under which a change
    of government takes place. Two characteristics of the political system are
    especially important.

(a) The stronger developed the institutional safeguards are to secure political competition between government and opposition, the more support is (ceteris paribus) needed for the government to survive. The government therefore demands a higher level of support; that is, the demand curve shifts to the right. At the other extreme, a government which has strong institutions to safeguard its power is more independent of support and seeks it less.

(b) The higher the cost for government politicians is in losing power (for example being killed, exiled, and/or deprived of their property), the more support will be demanded; that is, the demand function shifts to the right. This also means that government politicians who are able to move their money abroad will demand less support. This may be called the Duvalier–Marcos effect: neither fought to the bitter end, that is neither mustered all the support they could, because they had the means to live well in another country.

The supply of support for the government function depends on four factors.

1. The economic possibilities, in particular the natural and human resources in a country. When the resources available to the population increase, a given amount of support can be provided at lower cost. The supply of support function shifts to the right.

2. The politico-economic institutions; that is, the relationship of market vs. planning, the extent of federalism, as well as a multitude of microeconomic conditions such as the existence of well-defined, tradable and enforceable property rights. Examples are:

   (a) The better the population's private sector alternatives to pursue its utility are (for example, the better-defined private property rights in private markets are), the higher the opportunity cost of supporting the government is; the supply of support function shifts to the left.

   (b) The more decentralized a state is, the more difficult it is for the government to use negative sanctions against the population – the supply of support function shifts to the left.

   (c) When the population's trust that support provided today will be honoured by the government in the future increases, the supply of support curve shifts to the right.

3. The effectiveness with which the government influences the state of the economy by its economic policy measures. This determines the extent to which interference in the economy is productive or stifling, which in turn

depends on the quality of public administration. When the government's efficiency at influencing general economic conditions rises, it can produce more benefits to the population for a given amount of input, shifting the supply function to the right. The same mechanism holds for positive and negative sanctions.

4. The extent to which an improvement, or a deterioration, of the general economic conditions affects the government. The crucial question is: to what extent can such changes in general economic conditions be attributed to the government? There may be cases in which the state of the economy improves, but the groups judge this improvement to be due to external forces, for instance to an improvement in the world economy or an increase in natural resource prices. In this case, the government is likely not to be rewarded, because the groups feel that the opposition would have done equally well. The opposite case may be even more important: the state of the economy worsens, but the groups judge this to be the effect of external forces which neither the government in power, nor the opposition, is able to control. Examples are natural disasters, recessions in the world economy, or intervention by potent foreign countries (for example the imposition of trade barriers or boycotts). In this case, the government loses little or no support from the groups. Therefore, an increase in the extent to which an improvement of the economic conditions is attributed to the government strengthens its position. The supply of support curve shifts outside.

The choice made by the government – whose members are assumed to act rationally – is determined systematically by relative prices. These in turn depend on the factors determining the supply of support curve just listed. Any government, even a dictatorial one, is subject to the generalized law of demand: an activity which becomes more expensive is undertaken less in comparison with other activities. If, for instance, an improvement in economic conditions is attributed less to the government than before, the productivity of investing resources into general economic conditions falls. The politicians in power will then resort more to directly seeking group support by either bribing or suppressing certain groups. The government may substitute the support of one group for the support of another. This decision is also influenced by the expected return in the form of the additional support forthcoming relative to the cost of suppressing or bribing one particular group.

The government makes another choice of great importance for the effect of stabilization programmes on developing countries. Given general economic conditions, the politicians in power may attain a certain level of support from groups, either by suppressing or bribing them. Both sanctioning activities

consume resources, and the government is again faced with a trade-off. As
the resources available to the government are not completely fungible between suppression and bribes, there are diminishing marginal returns. It is
therefore not generally optimal for the government to rely solely, or even
mainly, on suppressing the population or certain groups.

ATTRIBUTABILITY AND APPROPRIABILITY

The population and the various groups do not invariably hold the government
fully responsible for the general economic conditions. Rather, the perception
of the respective benefits and costs is determined by a filter: *attributability*
influences the extent to which the groups feel that the existing state of the
economy is due to the workings of the government, and therefore influences
the amount of support given to the government.

The groups are not only rewarded by changes in general economic conditions, but also by the income flows specifically directed to them through
government intervention. *Appropriability* decides the extent to which the
government can raise and distribute income flows in its favour. What matters,
however, is not what the government does for a particular group, but rather
how such a group accounts for these flows. Thus the filter of attributability is
relevant. A group might take an income flow from the government for granted
or, conversely, might perceive it as a reward or 'price' for 'services' rendered,
namely for political support for the government.

The revenue appropriated by the government may be used (1) to sanction
groups by rewarding or suppressing them or (2) to pursue ideologically
oriented policies and/or to enrich the members of the government. The government must decide what share of revenues appropriated should be allocated
to increase the support by groups and thus the likelihood of its survival, and
what share can be used for the politicians' individual current consumption.
Expenditures for raising the support by groups enable the government to
increase its members' wealth in the future. Moreover, the government is able
to affect attributability to some extent, thereby influencing the political effectiveness of the income flows directed at particular groups. The two crucial
aspects, attributability and appropriability, will now be discussed in turn.

Attributability

Governments which obtain credits from international monetary institutions,
usually have to face a short-term deterioration in general economic conditions caused by the conditionalities they have to meet. In particular, the need
to balance the budget results in a recession hitting the various groups in the

population. The standard of living falls, support for the government declines and opposition rises. Reduced support often manifests itself in the form of demonstrations, strikes and uprisings. The extent to which the government is held accountable for the deterioration of economic conditions depends on four institutional conditions.

1. The government in power is made less responsible for the economic crisis if it is able to convince the groups that this has been caused by the former government. This is all the easier, the more visible the distinction is between the present and the former government. Even if the present government is forced to undertake a stabilization programme, it can, at least to a certain extent, attribute the negative consequences to its predecessor, provided it disassociates itself clearly from the previous government. The same holds for the cost of paying back and servicing debt, which can partly be attributed to the former government.

2. The present government can attribute the cost of undertaking the stabilization programme to foreign forces. The better the foreign events claimed to be responsible are identifiable, the easier it is to reduce attributability. Among suitable foreign events are oil price increases, wars and boycotts, the international economic situation, or the terms of trade. The government faces a trade-off: if it claims to be in control of everything, it is correspondingly less able to attribute the cost of stabilization programmes to foreign sources. In contrast, it can attribute the cost of stabilization programmes to foreign sources only if it admits that there are forces beyond its control.

3. The lower the expectations are, the less the government undertaking the restrictive measures is politically burdened. This effect has been empirically shown to hold for industrial democracies, but is sure to hold for developing countries as well. A government's popularity with the voters depends on deviations from the longer-term economic trend which shapes expectations. There is also evidence of asymmetric reactions to economic fluctuations due to a different adjustment of expectations; the government is made more responsible for a deterioration rather than for an improvement in economic conditions.

4. The population and groups may distinguish between general economic conditions, which they attribute more strongly to the government and their own economic conditions, for which they make the government less accountable. It is therefore especially troubling for a government when losses due to economic policy hit the members of a group, or even diverse groups simultaneously. In that case, people could realize that the losses are not due to their own behaviour or to bad luck. The more diverse the effects of a stabilization programme are, and the less concen-

trated the losing groups are, the less relevant is the concept of 'general' economic conditions, and the better are the government's chances of not having to deal with the negative consequences of conditionalities.

The attributability filter is also relevant for the income flows appropriated by the government and directed to specific groups. In its efforts to survive, every government wants to make it clear to the recipients that they owe this income to the government, and that they risk losing it if they reduce the political support provided to the government.

Appropriability

The ability of a government to raise resources and use them for its own purpose – to raise its consumption and/or to improve the chances of staying in power – depends on the conditions described below.

The developing country's economic structure

It can be hypothesized that it will be easier for the government to appropriate such resources,

- the more closed an economy is, because firms and individuals then find it more difficult to get the resources under their control beyond the reach of their government;
- the more immovable the natural resources (such as oil) located within the country are;
- the fewer possibilities there are to switch economic activities into the shadow economy where the resources are, by definition, beyond the reach of government;
- the larger the share of the economy that is controlled by the state; that is, not left to the price system. This enables the government to appropriate resources via allocating jobs, creating contracts favourable to specific groups, granting licences or foreign exchange dealings, and implicitly subsidizing goods and services by selling them below cost. More generally, the larger the directly controlled sector of the economy is, the more easily the government can raise revenue and allocate rents to supporting groups;
- the better developed the system of taxation is, and the more efficient the tax bureaucracy is. In many developing countries, such conditions exist only to a limited extent, so that the government is forced to resort to means of raising revenue which have high transaction costs and particularly strong negative side effects for the economy, such as the taxation of goods for export.

The developing country's political and legal structure
A government finds it easier to appropriate resources for its own use,

- the less powerful the groups are from which the resources are taken. A group wields less influence, the less concentrated its members' interests are, and the less cohesion there is due to bounds of ethnicity and tradition;
- the less political competition there is. The fewer institutional possibilities there are for an opposition to form and to act in a politically effective way, the more easily the government is able to appropriate resources. The government can do so more easily in a strong dictatorship, for example, where no opposing views are allowed to be voiced or organized, rather than in a politically more open system with regular elections;
- the more flexible jobs in the governmental bureaucracy are, that is the less life tenure that exists;
- the more developed organizations able to exploit the difference between artificially lowered prices for domestic goods and higher world market prices are. In many African countries, government appropriation of revenue is facilitated by the existence of marketing boards which pay low prices for domestic agricultural products and export them at considerable profit.

Attributability and appropriability form essential elements in the politico-economic interdependence of developing countries. Both concepts are, in principle, amenable to quantitative testing. Cases have been adduced demonstrating the empirical relevance of the two concepts. Moreover, it has been suggested that the extent of attributability, as well as of appropriability, depends on empirically observable institutional conditions. The next section applies the concepts of attributability and appropriability to the case of stabilization programmes.

STABILIZATION PROGRAMMES

Attributability of Recession

Recession induced by conditionalities
The politicians in power do not in every case lose the support of the different groups in society when a stabilization programme leads to recession. Whether opposition arises depends on the extent to which the government is made responsible for the short-term deterioration of the state of the economy due to

the conditionalities imposed by the other political actors. The question, more precisely, is what conditions tend to exonerate the government in power for the cost involved? The following hypotheses may be advanced.

1. The government is perceived to be less responsible for the recession when more possibilities exist to shift the blame to the international financial institutions setting the conditionalities. Such a shift will be the more probable, the less likely the government is to need another credit in the near future. In this case, the expected cost of making it more difficult to receive credits, and defending the decision to take a further credit is smaller. It is easier for non-market-oriented governments to blame the international financial institutions; a pro-market government could be charged with being inconsistent if it were to put the blame on these institutions.

2. The government may be lucky enough to profit from beneficial economic effects from abroad, for instance from a boom in the world economy. This mitigates the domestic recession induced by the conditionalities. The government can then claim that the costs of raising the credit and enacting the conditionalities have been low. This hypothesis depends on the notion that it is difficult, or impossible, to establish how economic conditions would have been in the absence of the conditionalities imposed. Rather, the groups on whose support the government depends, evaluate the state of the economy according to whether it is better or worse than before, and to what extent. While such a before/after comparison is scientifically unsound, and a careful analysis would be based on a comparison between being with and without a stabilization programme, even professional economists are often not able to undertake the latter due to theoretical and empirical limitations. Rather, they tend to rely on the much simpler before/after comparison. Obviously, such behaviour is even more likely for non-economists.

    Econometric evidence for popularity and election functions supports this hypothesis. It is also consistent with the observation made in psychoeconomic experiments, where it has been found that people do not generally take missed opportunities into account. For example, opportunity cost is of smaller relevance than more direct, especially monetary, cost, and people evaluate the behaviour of others by putting too much emphasis on the outcomes of their actions. The first two hypotheses imply an asymmetry in attributability between harmful and beneficial external effects: an authoritarian government in control of the mass media may, to a certain extent, manipulate the relevant information.

3. There are other conditions under which the government is less likely to be burdened by the recession:

(a) The weaker the political opposition, the more the government is able to frame the credit decision in an advantageous way. A well-organized, vocal opposition makes it difficult for the government to attribute the cost of the recession to other actors;

(b) The more unusual events that happen, such as wars, natural catastrophes or failed harvests, the easier the government can argue that such exogenous shocks are the origins of the economic hardships;

(c) If it is abundantly clear to all relevant groups that it is absolutely necessary to raise credit from an international financial institution. The government is then held less responsible for the bad short-term economic effects than if there had been other courses of action available.

Price reforms

Conditionalities regularly require that the distorted price structures existing in some (or many) sectors of the economy be corrected. The question is to what extent the resulting benefits and costs are attributed to the government. The following hypotheses can be advanced.

1. When the price system is used for the allocation of resources, the *benefits* of the market tend to be attributed to impersonal forces, and the government is given little credit for these benefits. Only if the opposition champions a planned economy are the benefits of the market attributed to the government that introduced it.

2. The *cost* of changing the price structure, and the move towards a competitive market are the more strongly attributed to the government, the more counter-intuitive the mechanism of the changes is. If the groups find it very difficult to understand why the prices of until now much subsidized goods are being raised, they will perceive the cost all the more and be even more likely to blame the government. Attributability (to the government) is thus the larger,

(a) the less educated in economics the population is;

(b) the less favourable past experiences with moving to a market economy have been (for example if the supply response to the higher prices has been slow and/or negligible);

(c) the stronger the 'socialist' ideology and, therewith, a statist, antimarket view is in the population;

(d) the stronger a technocratic illusion of control is among the elite.

3. The cost of introducing the price system is attributed the more to the government, the larger and politically more influential are the groups

who in their consumption depend essentially on the goods whose prices have risen as a consequence of the reforms. The most important goods of that kind are the staples, which make up around 70 per cent of total consumption expenditures of the urban dwellers in developing countries.

4. Undesirable consequences of price reforms are attributed the more to the government, the greater losses are weighted relative to gains by the population. There is extensive literature in cognitive psychology based on experimental results, suggesting that individuals evaluate losses as larger changes in welfare than equal-size gains. This effect is the stronger:

    (a) The more rapidly expectations adjust to gains rather than losses. With the reference point shifting in this way, more changes in the economic situation are accounted for as losses, and fewer as gains. In particular, expectations are raised more quickly, the more promises the government makes concerning future improvements in economic conditions. The government is the more tempted to make such promises, the lower its expectations of staying in power are. A government seriously doubting its survival tends to undertake the risky strategy of making high promises. It calculates that if the promises are not kept, another government must deal with the dissatisfied population.

    (b) The losses will be felt more strongly than equivalent gains if the groups burdened are easily able to compare their situation with those favoured. This is the case if the urban working population is strongly hit by the price rises, while the rich profit visibly.

    (c) The perception of losses is also increased relative to the gains, the more apparent the additional cost going with the price rises is, such as crime and begging. These consequences lower the information cost.

5. Another perception problem is also likely to raise the cost of the price reforms attributed to the government; people resent the price rises induced because many of them are unable to buy the goods now visibly displayed in the stores, and weigh less heavily the fact that, at the previous low prices, many of the goods were not available or were rationed by waiting in queues.

6. The extent of the shadow economy existing before the price reform – when prices were controlled – may also influence the extent to which the government is made responsible for the cost of the price reform. 'Reality' may be revealed to the consumers in the shadow economy, where prices are much higher but goods are available. A price increase in the

direction of black-market prices is then likely to be less resented. An example is the normally strongly overvalued exchange rate, a fact which is well understood by most people because the much lower value of the domestic currency on the black market is clearly visible. In these circumstances, the cost attributed to the government of adjusting from the official to the free-market rate may be relatively small.

Appropriability of Credits

The extent to which the government can use the given credits depends on three main factors.

Differences between lenders

By attaching conditionalities to the credits, the International Monetary Fund (IMF) places restrictions on the 'political' use to which loans can be put. An effort is made to commit the funds as much as possible to productive economic purposes, so that the existing government cannot easily use the credit to enhance its own chances of survival or for consumption by reigning politicians (nor for ideologically motivated prestige projects). The question is, of course, to what extent the IMF is able, and willing, to enforce these restrictions. The behaviour of the lending institutions is assumed to be exogenous. The authors are well aware that the political views of the IMF directorate enter into the picture here, but the analyses of them are beyond the scope of this chapter. It may be hypothesized that the conditionalities are the better observed by the recipient government,

- the more monopolistic the IMF's position is; that is, the more it can force the developing country's government to accept restrictions;
- the less the IMF is interested in the survival of the politicians in power, compared with a government made up of other politicians;
- the more the credits can be divided into tranches – the idea being that future tranches are only paid out if the recipient government has complied with the IMF's stipulations.

The credits given by the World Bank (IBRD) are mostly project-related, which restricts the amount the recipient government can appropriate for its own purposes. However, evidence (see for example Neue Zürcher Zeitung, 100, 1988, p. 7 on Brazil) suggests that only 25–50 per cent of the funds actually reach the project level; that is, the government, as well as other groups (to whom partly the government, in its own interest, grants this possibility), are able to appropriate a significant portion of the World Bank credits. Moreover, the government can indirectly appropriate part of the funds by selecting contractors whom it wants to benefit from the projects, and by allowing them to overcharge for their services.

The extent to which project funds can be appropriated is the larger,

- the higher the domestic rate of inflation and therewith the interest rate. Funds can be appropriated by simply holding back the credit for a period and appropriating the interest payments;
- the larger the share of nationalized firms, or private domestic firms that are taxable, among the contractors. It seems to be more difficult to appropriate funds from foreign contractors;
- the larger the share of domestic inputs whose price the government can raise; and
- the less a project can be split up into tranches, thus confronting the World Bank with an all-or-nothing proposition.

Private lenders (for example banks) find it even more difficult than the international financial institutions to restrict the appropriation of the credits by the recipient government. While one specific creditor has no incentive to monitor the government, private creditors as a group are interested in an efficient use of the resources because the repayment of the loan then becomes more probable. But because the restriction of appropriation is a public good, private creditors have difficulty organizing themselves. Moreover, the recipient government may be able to exploit the competition among lenders, which induces the lenders to alleviate the conditions under which the loans are granted.

Differences between recipients
A credit from the International Monetary Fund nominally goes to the central bank of the recipient country. If the central bank were independent, the government would find it difficult to appropriate the funds. However, in virtually all developing countries, the central bank strongly depends on the government, and can often simply be regarded as a branch of public bureaucracy.

In the case of World Bank credits, the credits nominally go to the ministries in charge of the projects. The head of a ministry can, in general, easily be forced by the government to give it part, or all, of the funds. Heads of ministries have little interest in resisting such appropriation if their political survival is linked with the government; they may only make an effort to resist if they can keep their position, whatever group of politicians may be in power, which is rarely the case.

When a credit goes to a business actor, the government is more easily able to appropriate the funds if the firm in question is wholly or partially nationalized. This has often been the case in developing countries such as Brazil. Appropriation is also made easier when the government is able to tax the recipient private firm (which includes bribes to the government).

Differences in forms of credit
Credits given solely to service overdue foreign debt (interest and capital repayments) are difficult, or impossible, for the government to appropriate because such credits do not enter the country but are used directly as settlements among the creditors.

CONCLUDING REMARKS

Developing countries are looked at from the rational choice perspective. Positive incentives in the form of bribes are distinguished from negative incentives in the form of suppression. Both affect an authoritarian government's survival. A crucial aspect is identifying the conditions which determine the extent to which the government can appropriate resources, in particular from foreign sources, in the form of development credits.

In addition to the rational choice considerations used in orthodox economic theory, but rarely applied to developing authoritarian countries, much emphasis has been put on cognitive or psychological aspects in decision-making. Attributability plays a central role in the model: the extent to which the government is held accountable for positive and negative events depends on a number of identifiable factors which the government can at least partially influence. Such events are, in particular, the positive impacts of the credits received, and the short-term negative impacts. Change in economic conditions may thus have a quite different impact on the government's chances of survival, and therewith on its behaviour. It is crucially dependent on how far the government is able to appropriate resources, and how far good and bad economic conditions are attributed to the government.

SUGGESTIONS ON THE LITERATURE AND SOURCES

The nature and results of conditionalities and adjustment programmes are, for example, discussed in
Edwards, Sebastian (1989), *The IMF and the Developing Countries: A Critical Evaluation*, Carnegie-Rochester Conference Series on Public Policy.
Nelson, Joan M. (ed.) (1989), *Fragile Coalitions: The Politics of Economic Adjustment*, New Brunswick: Transaction.

The role of government in developing countries has been taken into account in the survey by

Stern, Nicholas (1989), 'The Economics of Development: A Survey', *Economic Journal*, **99** (Sept.), 597–685,

as well as in

Krueger, Anne O. (1992), *Economic Policy Reform in Developing Countries*, Oxford: Blackwell.
Nelson, Joan M. (1990), *Economic Crisis and Policy Choice*, Princeton: Princeton University Press.

The role of international financial agencies is analysed in

Dreyer, Jacob S. and Andrew Schotter (1980), 'Power Relationships in the International Monetary Fund. The Consequences of Quota Changes', *Review of Economics and Statistics*, **62** (February), 97–106.
Schneider, Friedrich and Bruno S. Frey (1985), 'Economic and Political Determinants of Foreign Direct Investment', *World Politics*, **13**, 161–75.
Frey, Bruno S. and Friedrich Schneider (1986), 'Competing Models of International Lending Activity', *Journal of Development Economics*, **20**, 225–45.
Palda, Filip (1993), 'Can Repressive Regimes be Moderated through Foreign Aid?', *Public Choice*, **77** (3), 535–50,

and more generally in

Frey, Bruno S. (1994), *International Political Economics*, Oxford: Blackwell.

For models of government behaviour using concepts of political economy, see

Paldam, Martin (1994), 'Political Business Cycles', in Dennis C. Mueller (ed.), *Handbook of Public Choice*, Oxford: Blackwell.
Schneider, Friedrich and Bruno S. Frey (1988), 'Politico-economic Models of Macroeconomic Policy: A Review of the Empirical Evidence', in Thomas D. Willett (ed.), *The Political Economy of Money, Inflation and Unemployment*, Durham and London: Duke University Press, pp. 240–75.
Hibbs, Douglas A. (1987), *The Political Economy of Industrial Democracies*, Cambridge, MA: Harvard University Press.
Frey, Bruno S. (1983), *Democratic Economic Policy*, Oxford: Blackwell.

Public Choice models of authoritarian and dictatorial governments are due to

Tullock, Gordon (1987), *Autocracy*, Dordrecht: Kluwer.
Wintrobe, Ronald (1998), *The Political Economy of Dictatorship*, Cambridge: Cambridge University Press.

Applications of such models to developing countries have been undertaken by

Paldam, Martin (1987), 'Inflation and Political Instability in Eight Latin American Countries 1964-83', *Public Choice*, **52**, 143–68.

Bernholz, Peter (1988), 'Hyperinflation and Currency Reform in Bolivia: Studied from a General Perspective', *Journal of Theoretical and Institutional Economics*, **144** (5), 747–71.
Bates, Robert H. (ed.) (1988a), *Toward a Political Economy of Development. A Rational Choice Perspective*, Berkeley: University of California Press.

The effects of general and of personal economic conditions on the government's popularity and voting are discussed in
Kinder, Donald R. and D. Roderick Kiewit (1979), 'Economic Discontent and Political Behavior: The Role of Personal Grievances and Collective Judgements in Congressional Voting', *American Journal of Political Science*, **23** (3), 495–527.
Nannestad, Paul and Martin Paldam (1997), 'The Grievance Asymmetry Revisited: A Micro Study of Economic Voting in Denmark, 1986–92', *European Journal of Political Economy*, **13** (1), 81–99.

For the policy of marketing boards to lower the prices for domestic agricultural products, see
Bates, Robert H. (1988b), 'Governments and Agricultural Markets in Africa', in Robert H. Bates (ed.), *Toward a Political Economy of Development. A Rational Choice Perspective*, Berkeley: University of California Press.
Nelson, Joan M. (1988), 'The Political Economy of Stabilization: Commitment, Capacity and Public Response', in Robert H. Bates (ed.), *Toward a Political Economy of Development. A Rational Choice Perspective*, Berkeley: University of California Press.

The concept of 'framing' is due to
Kahneman, Daniel and Amos Tversky (1984), 'Choices, Values, and Frames', *American Psychologist*, **39** (April), 341–50.

For the observation that losses loom larger than gains, see also
Harless, David W. (1989), 'More Laboratory Evidence on the Disparity between Willingness to Pay and Compensation Demanded', *Journal of Economic Behavior and Organization*, **11** (3), 359–79.

Behavioural anomalies are more generally discussed in Chapter 3 of this book.

Theoretical and empirical aspects of the underground economy are treated in
Schneider, Friedrich and Dominik Enste (2000), 'Increasing Shadow Economy All Over the World – Fiction or Reality?', *Journal of Economic Literature*, **38** (1), 77–114.
Frey, Bruno S. and Friedrich Schneider (2001), 'Informal and Underground Economy', *International Encyclopedia of the Social and Behavioral Sciences*, forthcoming.

13. Bond values and World War II events

with Marcel Kucher

THE BASIC APPROACH

Economists assume that price movements on financial markets and, in particular, the value of stocks and bonds, reflect economic and political events. They affect current returns (and interest payments) as well as the probability that the capital sum is paid back by the due date. Looking at government bond prices of European countries traded on the Swiss stock exchange during World War II (WWII) therefore provides a useful way of interpreting the importance attributed to various events during the war.

The link between financial markets and historical events has been observed for a long time. The story of Baron Rothschild making huge gains by speculating on the change in bond prices induced by the outcome of one of Napoleon's decisive battles, is famous. Recently, this relationship has been systematically exploited by applying advanced econometric techniques to identify break points in financial values. A good example would be the impact of the United Nations' peacekeeping policy on exchange rates: while the missions in Lebanon resulted in a long-lasting positive effect on the exchange rate, no systematic changes induced by the UN sanctions could be identified in the South African exchange rates (Sobel, 1998). Willard, Guinnane and Rosen (1996) demonstrate that events occurring during the US Civil War (1862–6) systematically affected the rate of exchange of greenbacks relative to the gold dollar. In some instances, the events identified by break points in the exchange rate have not been found noticeable by traditional historians and, conversely, with hindsight they have taken different events during the war as crucial.

This chapter empirically analyses the relationship between financial markets and history for a particular asset and a particular period. We are especially interested in how far major events of World War II are reflected on capital markets, and to what extent fluctuations of capital market values can be related to major events in that war. During World War II (as well as in other wars), capital markets were either heavily controlled, or altogether suppressed, by the governments involved. An exception was the bourse in

Switzerland (Zurich), which remained in operation during the whole war (with the exception of two months in 1940), and where the government, for reasons of neutrality, did not interfere in its operation. To our knowledge, this is the only major financial exchange where a primary market for assets involving several nations operated during that period.

As we are interested in the relationship between historical events occurring among the nations directly involved in the war, and fluctuations in capital markets, we direct our attention to value changes in the government bonds of five different nations. On the side of the Axis, there are Germany and Austria which, after March 1938, formed 'Grossdeutschland'; on the side of the Allies is France, the major opponent on the western continental front; and then there are the two neutral countries, Belgium and Switzerland, of which the former was occupied by Germany in 1940, while the latter was spared direct involvement. Too few government bonds for other important nations involved in the war, in particular Great Britain and the United States, but also The Netherlands and Italy, were traded on the Swiss stock exchange to allow a statistical analysis.

We chose to look at government bond prices rather than at shares, since prices of the latter might be influenced by firm specific factors which we do not know about, but which most likely have nothing to do with historical events. On the other hand, prices of government bonds reflect to a great extent the risk that traders attach to them; since our primary interest lies in the historical determinants of the perceived risk, it therefore seems natural to look at government bonds.

Our results lead us to the conclusion that major political events related to WWII are clearly reflected in the values for government bonds. A particularly strong effect on the bond market was exerted by the official outbreak of war in September 1939 (causing the government bond values to drop by between 46 per cent and 25 per cent) in *all* the countries at war (that is Germany, Austria, Belgium and France). Investors thus took war to be an unwelcome event, threatening the servicing of government bonds. This result suggests that historians' dating of the beginning of the war with hindsight corresponds well to the gloomy evaluation of the persons acting without knowledge of the future.

A second strong change in the value of government bonds is associated with losses and gains of national sovereignty. When Austria lost its independence and became part of 'Grossdeutschland' (March 1938), the value of its government bonds fell by 46 per cent (though the German government guaranteed the servicing of the Austrian debt). When it regained its nationhood in the Potsdam Conference (August 1945), the value of Austrian government bonds rose by 12 per cent. Similarly, when Belgium and France were beaten and occupied by the German forces in the 'Blitzkrieg' of May 1940, their government bond values fell by no less than 35 per cent and 31 per cent, respectively.

Conversely, we have found only two statistically significant breaks in government bond values, according to our econometric procedures, which could not be related to any significant historical event. These results suggest that the type of capital market studies undertaken here can serve a useful complementary role in historical research. At the same time, it helps to bridge the gap currently existing between economic and historical analysis.

The next section of this chapter investigates the relationship between financial markets and historical events. A short description and overview of the data is given in the following section and the fourth section presents the econometric methods used. The fifth section discusses the break points identified, as well as the corresponding changes in government bond values, for each of the four nations included in our study. The next section analyses how far major pre-war, war, and post-war events are reflected in statistically significant break points. A short summary of what happened to the government bonds after the war is given in the seventh section, while the final section draws conclusions.

FINANCIAL MARKETS AND HISTORY

Financial markets reflect historical events in a special way. It is useful to differentiate two aspects.

1.   A chosen group of persons, the traders, act on financial markets. They are far from representative of the population, but they have a strong monetary interest to take into account the evaluations of other traders in the market. A wrong forecast, for example, directly affects their own income and wealth. This strong incentive constitutes a major difference to surveys.
2.   The traders deal partly for themselves, but mostly for investors, that is a much wider group of persons. They comprise not only private capital owners, but also persons acting for institutional investors, such as firms and pension funds. In most cases, it is not known who the investors are; in principle, the final actors may be situated anywhere in the world. Movements on financial markets are therefore driven not only by expectations of the people directly engaged in trading, but also actors less directly affected. This is another major difference to most surveys, where the set of respondents is well determined and where usually only people from the region or country affected by a particular event are questioned.

Financial markets reflect the actual and expected future development of the assets in question, in particular the probability that they are serviced, paid back (in the case of bonds), and remain tradable (for instance that no currency restrictions prohibit the repatriation of the funds invested).

Financial markets are thus not per se related to the nation and population. A nation may disappear, but the respective financial assets may survive. Normally, however, there is a strong correlation between the fate of a population and/or nation and the values of traded assets. In most cases, when a nation is destroyed, its public debt is neither serviced any longer nor paid back at maturity, a fact which the financial markets reflect by a drop in value to zero (if there is no hope that the debt will ever be honoured). Similarly, if the population of a country is negatively affected (say by natural catastrophes or a war), the respective government may be unable to service its public debt, so that the population's fate is again reflected in the financial market.

Historians deal with past economic and political events in quite a different way. They carefully collect and select facts and interpret them in the light of their general knowledge of the field and the particular circumstances prevalent. Such interpretation is necessarily ex post facto, that is after the consequent development is known. This knowledge may bias the evaluation of the events, and may lead to 'facts' being overlooked or over-emphasized, as the case may be. This problem is most obvious in the case of wars. Once the outcome is known, say a crushing defeat of the country under consideration, it is difficult to analyse objectively why the decision-makers of the country engaged in the war in the first place. To simply refer to a misjudgement is unsatisfactory because it would have to be explained why such an error could possibly happen. In order to evaluate the historical situation existing at a given moment in time, historians have to take care not to impute information to the then decision-makers which was only revealed by subsequent developments.

Historians are, of course, well aware of this problem. Marwick (1970, p. 146), for example, states: 'Essential to historical thinking, and therefore to historical writing, is the avoidance of anachronism, that is the imputing into the past of concepts which only have reality in the present'. Historians therefore make a great effort to capture the information, views, sentiments and feelings existing at the respective time. The major avenue is to turn to written documents, but sometimes surveys are used (oral history). Both approaches may be biased by strategic considerations of the writers and speakers. Thus, as Carr (1961, p. 8) put it, 'Our picture has always been pre-selected and predetermined for us, not so much by accident as by people who were consciously or unconsciously imbued with a particular view and thought the facts which supported that view worth preserving'.

Some of the problems mentioned can be overcome by analysing data from financial markets. As a complementary method of evaluating particular sentiments existing at a given moment of time, this has at least three advantages.

1. By analysing financial markets, we direct our attention towards the actual behaviour of thousands of people directly and indirectly engaged in stock markets (compared with only intentions, ideas or comments of the writers of historical documents). This, of course, greatly reduces the incentives to behave strategically.
2. People who are active on financial markets bear a high monetary risk. As already pointed out above, this gives them a strong incentive to gather all the relevant information.
3. Financial markets usually exhibit a high predictive power, resulting from the existence of so-called marginal traders. This type of trader decides on a relatively unbiased basis and collects the important information carefully. In the extreme case, only one such trader could drive the market price to the underlying equilibrium price.

The analysis of financial markets is certainly no substitute for the traditional enquiries undertaken by historians. But as a complementary method it has the advantage of being quantitative; that is, it is in the tradition of the new economic history or cliometrics.

Two kinds of questions may be posed when using financial market data:

1. Can breaks in financial markets be related to historical 'facts'? And if so, are the changes in financial values consistent with historians' interpretations of the 'facts'?
2. Are the historically established 'facts' reflected by financial markets? And if so, did a specific event raise or lower asset values?

For both types of questions, care must be taken to allow for time delays. Thus, a historical fact may have been predicted in advance by the people active on the financial markets, in which case the break should be visible *before* the event, or be completely absent, depending on the speed of adjustment. Either way, no break will be visible at the date of the event itself. An example is the end of a war which, in many cases, is foreseen far in advance. Evidence suggests, however, that financial markets tend to overreact to the arrival of news. The overreaction hypothesis implies that, even though many investors have predicted an event way in advance and financial markets have adjusted accordingly, a break in the price series can still be identified.

Our approach is based on the general premise that 'facts' considered important by historians are reflected in changing bond prices (provided the

respective historical occurrence has not been predicted by the market participants, and therewith has already been integrated in the data). However, for a
number of reasons, historical 'facts' may not show up as break points.

1. The quality of the bond market data is lacking, for example because
    there are too few transactions.
2. Governments have intervened in the bond market either as buyers or
    sellers, or by imposing controls of one sort or another. An important case
    occurs when governments want to prevent the reflection of a political (or
    economic) event on the financial market. What might particularly affect
    our analysis is changes in capital market restrictions imposed by govern-
    ments.
3. The particular econometric method applied is unable to identify break
    points relating to historical events, even though they are in the data.
4. A 'fact' may be important from the historians' point of view (it relates to
    the fate of a nation, country or population), but does not affect the
    servicing and payback of the government bonds.
5. The 'fact' does not exist, nor is it as important as the historians believe.
    Here the quality of historical research is in question. However, it would
    be misleading to assume that all historians identify the same 'facts' as
    being important. So the issue is what historical school or which indi-
    vidual historian has identified what historical 'fact', as well as the
    importance attributed to it.

Obviously, the reverse question: 'What breaks in government bond
values cannot be related to historical facts?' is easy to answer. It is always
possible to find some historical 'fact' that can be related to the break points
identified. This holds, in particular, if time lags in the reactions of capital
market participants, as well as their expectations, are taken into account. It
is nevertheless instructive to search for temporally related events taken to
be important by historical research. The sixth section of this chapter, on
historical facts and bond values, proceeds along this line, but we are well
aware of the ensuing problems. It is again interesting to pose the question:
'What break points are difficult (if not practically impossible) to relate to a
historically significant event?' As before, there are several reasons why this
may be the case.

1. Economists, in this case ourselves, have insufficient historical knowl-
    edge to find the associated 'fact'.
2. While a significant break point exists from the point of view of the
    financial market (relating to servicing and payback), there is no occur-
    rence of special interest from the historians' point of view.

3.   An important historical fact exists, but historical research has not identi-
     fied it or, more likely, 'accepted' historical writing has not paid sufficient
     attention to it (but there will always be some historians, possibly out-
     siders, who have observed the fact).

THE GOVERNMENT BOND MARKET, 1933–48

During World War II, as well as before the war, all governments directly or
indirectly intervened in economic markets, including stock markets. In Germany, in particular, many foreign currency restrictions that had a strong
influence on capital markets were introduced or tightened up soon after the
Nazi take-over, that is in 1933. Many capital restrictions in Germany had
already been introduced during the banking crises in September 1931, and
were only tightened up by the Nazis. There were, however, some additional
regulations, such as restrictions concerning the transfers of interest payments,
that were introduced by the Nazis. The only relevant market on which government bonds of the countries under consideration were freely traded was
the Swiss stock exchange. For reasons of neutrality, the Swiss government
neither controlled price movements nor the extent of trading, and there were
no restrictions for foreign investors. Trading was stopped only during May
and June 1940, when it was unclear whether the German forces would outflank the Maginot line in the South (that is march through Switzerland), or in
the North (which they did by invading Belgium and the Netherlands).

Many countries issued government bonds in Switzerland during the time-
span between the two world wars. The countries that borrowed most from the
Swiss capital market were France and Germany, followed by Belgium and
Austria. The value at time of issue of the 31 German government bonds was
roughly 460 million Swiss Francs in 1934 (which equals about 3 billion of
today's Swiss Francs). The French government debt in Switzerland equalled
approximately 550 million Swiss Francs in 1934 (about 3.6 billion of today's
Swiss Francs) and Belgium and Austria borrowed one billion and 590 million
of today's Swiss Francs, respectively. It is important to note that all of these
bonds were both issued and traded in Swiss Francs, so fluctuating exchange
rates should not have any influence on the bond prices. Our analysis considers a weighted index of the value of all foreign government bonds of these
four countries issued in Switzerland since 1922.

Due to the large number of government bonds issued by Switzerland, we
restrict ourselves to the 12 largest Swiss government bonds. A value index is
constructed by comparing the average rate of return of the 12 government
bonds in each month to the average rate of return of the 12 largest Swiss
government bonds in the period 1906–25 (which was 4.4 per cent). For

December 1939, for example, the average return of the 12 bonds was 4.25 per cent. Comparing this with the 4.42 per cent average return yields an index of 104.00 ((4.42/4.25)*100).

All of the indices are based on end-of-the-month bond prices (usually the 25th of each month). Since the time series are not, as is often the case for historical statistics, based on averages throughout the month, we can assume the series to follow a random walk (for details on the econometric procedure, see the next section).

No information is available on who traded at the Swiss stock exchange during WWII. But, as mentioned before, even if we knew who the actual traders were, it would remain unclear whose money they invested and therewith who their clients were. Given the high degree of openness of the Swiss financial market, it seems likely that investors from all over Europe used this 'safe haven'.

There is, however, limited information available concerning the extent of trading in government bonds on the Swiss stock exchange. Unfortunately, the Swiss National Bank did not keep any records regarding the turnover in stocks or bonds. Turnover was, however, taxed by the Swiss government and the tax information can be used to estimate the extent of trading. According to Schwab's (1948) estimate, the extent of trading in foreign government bonds fell from about 2.8 billion Swiss Francs in 1937 to about 0.5 billion in 1943 and rose back up again to about 1.1 billion in 1946. Adjusting for inflation, these figures correspond to approximately 18 billion, 3.5 billion and 7 billion, respectively, of today's Swiss currency. German and French government bonds each accounted for roughly 30 per cent of the annual turnover, whereas the respective shares of Belgium and Austria stood at 7 and 6 per cent. Trading in Swiss government bonds reached about half the level of all foreign bonds together in 1937. During the war, investing in government bonds of the countries at war became more and more risky, so investors put the money they withdrew from these countries into Swiss government bonds, and hence the extent of trading in Swiss government bonds rose relative to foreign government bonds. The best estimates available indicate an annual turnover of approximately 9 billion of today's Swiss Francs in 1937, 4.5 billion in 1940 and 13 billion in 1946, respectively.

World War II 'officially' started with the German invasion of Poland on 1 September 1939, and ended in the West with the unconditional and complete capitulation of the German forces in Rheims on 7 May and in Berlin on 9 May 1945. In many respects, however, the war started earlier, for example with the occupation of the Rheinland by Germany in March 1936, or the invasion of the Sudetenland and thereafter of the remainder of the Czech Republic in March 1939. It could even be argued that World War II was a direct consequence of the Nazi take-over in January 1933. In order to be able to analyse whether it makes sense to look at this period as a form of war preceding the official war dates, we include monthly data for the Swiss bond index, extending from December 1928 to December 1948. Unfortunately, more frequent data (like weekly or even daily data) are not available. While more frequent data are econometrically not necessary, monthly data might raise two problems: (1) event A in November might raise bond prices and event B lower them. The data will not register this and one might miss two potentially important events; (2) the data might say that something happened in November, but if several things happened in that month, then one might find oneself at a loss (relying on the data only) to say which particular event it was that shifted the prices. However, while we cannot exclude the possibility that we missed some dates in our study due to the usage of monthly data, we never found that two important events happened in the month before a break point. So while daily data might enable us to identify events with greater precision, we do not think that they would lead us to new insights. Due to lack of data, we consider only December 1933 to December 1948 for the foreign government bond indices. The data were collected from the *Monatsberichte der Schweizerischen Nationalbank* (monthly publication of the Swiss National Bank) for January 1929 to January 1949. (Note: Dates shown on the graphs in Figures 13.1 to 13.10 are in the format MM/DD/YYYY throughout.)

Germany

Figure 13.1 shows the monthly index of the 31 German government bonds traded at the Swiss stock exchange. Over the entire period, the bond values take a strong downturn. This also holds for the period 1933–6; that is, for the first years of the Third Reich. The drop in bond values may be considered surprising as the rise of Hitler to power has often been attributed to the 'capitalists', who considered him to be a stronghold against communism. On the other hand, the heavy intervention in, and the strong regulations imposed on, the capital markets by Hitler's government – with Hjalmar Schacht, the president of the Reichsbank, being the leading exponent – may well have depressed the expectations of the bond holders, who suffered a decline in their returns.

The bond values made a marked recovery in 1937/38, but fell drastically from the middle of 1938 to the end of 1939, when WWII broke out. There was again a rise in the value of German government bonds after the successful *Blitzkrieg* at the beginning of 1940. But it did not last long: from the second half of 1941 onwards, there is a permanent fall in German bond values, suggesting that the bond market soon predicted that the Nazis would lose the war, the debt would no longer be serviced and the capital would be lost.

Source: *Monthly publication of the Swiss National Bank (SNB) 1933–48.*

Figure 13.1   Index of the 31 German government bonds traded in Switzerland

Austria

Figure 13.2 shows the corresponding monthly index of the 9 Austrian government bonds traded in Switzerland during WWII. In contrast to Germany, it shows a marked increase in value between 1933 and 1937. There was a huge drop with the *Anschluss* (annexation) by Germany in 1938, and the index remained much depressed thereafter. This drastic fall in the value of Austrian government bonds may not only be attributed to political factors, but may also be due to the fact that, with the annexation, Austrian bonds were subjected to the severe German capital market and foreign currency regulations. It is, however, worth noting that the Austrian index remained much below the respective German index until mid-1944, which suggests that at least part of the 1938 drop was due to political factors.

The evaluation of German and Austrian bond values thus differed significantly, which is an interesting fact in itself because, after 1938, the two countries formally merged into one, *Grossdeutschland*. But the actors in the two bond markets nevertheless maintained the difference.

Source: *Monthly publication of the Swiss National Bank (SNB) 1933–48.*

Figure 13.2   Index of the 9 Austrian government bonds traded in Switzerland

France

As shown in Figure 13.3, the raw data for the French government bonds exhibit a constant value until the middle of 1938, followed by a huge drop with the 'official' outbreak of the war, the invasion by German forces, and the capitulation (22 June 1940). After trading was resumed at the Swiss bourse, the French bonds experienced a continuous increase in value until the end of 1945.

It is interesting to note that the value of the French government bonds remained above 20 per cent of the value at the time of issue, even though France suspended interest payments in November 1942, and did not resume servicing its debts until the end of the period considered. The fact that the price of the French government bonds fell to 20 cents on the dollar indicates an extreme lack of confidence on the part of the traders that France would pay back their debts by the due date and resume paying interest. However, the price did not drop to zero, which shows that investors saw at least some possibility of further debt servicing.

Source: *Monthly publication of the Swiss National Bank (SNB) 1933–48.*

Figure 13.3 Index of the 12 French government bonds traded in Switzerland

Belgium

The values of Belgian government bonds traded in Switzerland exhibit clearly noticeable variations (see Figure 13.4). A marked increase from 1934 to 1937 is followed by an even stronger fall; culminating in a value of about 30 per cent in 1940. Over the course of World War II, the bond values show a continuous recovery, ending in 1947.

Switzerland

The value of Swiss government bonds shows an overall long-term rise of about 30 per cent over the 20-year period from 1928 to 1948 (Figure 13.5). Values tended to fall in the 1930s. The strong increase in value in 1936 can be attributed to a devaluation of the Swiss currency by approximately 30 per cent (27 September 1936). However, this economic event does not show up as a statistically significant break in the data, most probably because it also affected the values of all the other (government) bonds traded in Switzerland. The Swiss government bonds experienced a marked drop in the three years

Source: *Monthly publication of the Swiss National Bank (SNB) 1933–48.*

*Figure 13.4   Index of the 11 Belgian government bonds traded in
             Switzerland*

before the 'official' outbreak of the war, until the invasion of the Benelux
countries and France in May 1940. After trading was resumed later that year,
Swiss government bonds increased in value until they regained the pre-war
level of 1936/37.

ECONOMETRIC TECHNIQUES OF ANALYSIS

The econometric method used is aimed at searching the series of government
bond prices discussed above for structural breaks. In contrast to an event
study, the starting point is not a list of dates, with the data then telling which
ones matter. Rather, the method used here allows the data to speak for
themselves, without *a priori* specification of the dates.

   The sequential test procedure we follow is based on Banerjee, Lumsdaine
and Stock (1992). A similar procedure is also applied by Sobel (1998) or
Willard, Guinnane and Rosen (1996) in their analyses of the US greenback
market. The basic idea behind the procedure used is to estimate conditional
random walks within small time windows, and then test for differences in the

Source: *Monthly publication of the Swiss National Bank (SNB) 1933–48.*

Figure 13.5   Index of 12 major Swiss government bonds, 1928–48

means of the bond prices between these time windows. In order to find all possible turning points, a four-step procedure is applied. Steps one to three are used to isolate 36-month windows within which structural breaks are most likely. The last step then tests for structural breaks within these windows. Applying only the last step of the procedure to the data would yield inappropriate results, since the last step was developed under the assumption that there is only one break point in the series. If there were a second shift, which reversed the first, a 'normal' regression with dummies for possible breaks might very well miss both shifts. To address the problem, we only need look for mean shifts in rather short 'time windows'. Hence we need steps one to three to determine which periods we should look at.

Using data from a 36-month window, and starting with December 1933, we first estimate the regression

$$\ln p_t = \beta_0 + \beta_1 \ln p_{t-1} + \beta_2 \ln \bar{p}_{t-1} + \varepsilon_t \tag{1}$$

for each of the five countries, where p_t stands for the index value of all government bonds of the country considered on date t, $\bar{p}_t$ is the index of all government bonds traded in Zurich (which we use as a measure of the market performance as a whole), the βs are the parameters to be estimated and ε_t is a white noise error term. A Wald test associated with the hypothesis that there was a shift in the mean at the midpoint of the window is then calculated. The idea behind step one is to estimate a random walk and then check for changes in the constant, which is the procedure followed in recent stock market studies. It implies that bond prices follow an exponential Brownian motion. In fact, we also ran regression with auto-regressive processes of up to the sixth order, but did not find different results. The inclusion of a measure of market performance as a right-hand variable allows us to estimate the random walk ceteris paribus, for example we correct for factors that might influence the value of all bonds traded (like changing real interest rates, inflation and so on).

The regression is estimated again in a second step, this time using a 36-month window that begins one month later; that is, in January 1934. Step two is then repeated over and over again, each time moving the window by one month, until the entire period has been covered. The *F*-statistics from all the Wald tests can be seen in the following section. By searching for peaks in the series of *F*-statistics, the first two steps identify the dates where the null hypothesis of no structural breaks is most strongly questioned.

The third stage of the econometric procedure consists of selecting particular 36-month windows on the basis of the *F*-statistics computed in steps one and two. Windows associated with an *F*-statistic exceeding five are considered as dates where structural breaks are most likely.

In the last stage, we test for statistically significant structural breaks within each of the windows isolated in step three. We do this by estimating a series of the following equations which, in comparison with equation (1), have been extended by a dummy variable, as suggested by Perron (1989).

$$\ln p_t = \beta_0 + \beta_1 \ln p_{t-1} + \beta_2 \ln \bar{p}_{t-1} + \gamma_s D_{st} + \varepsilon_t \quad \text{with } s = 6, \dots, 42 \quad (2)$$

where $D_{st} = 1$ if date t is on or after date s, and zero otherwise. The parameter γ_s measures a change in the conditional mean (that is a shift in the mean price index ceteris paribus) that occurs at date s. Since all the prices are in logs, γ_s can be interpreted as the percentage change in the conditional mean. We estimate equation (2) repeatedly, each time moving s by one month. For each resulting equation, it is tested whether γ_s is different from zero using a conventional F test. The date associated with the highest F-statistic is then designated as the date where the most important mean shift took place within each window. Since sequential break tests cannot identify breaks around the beginning or end of a sample, we add six observations at the beginning and at the end of the windows examined in this last step. So, for the first equation estimated in step four, s is set at date six of the new window (which equalled date one in the original window).

Two further points warrant comment: first, since the bond price series contains a unit root, test statistics based on regression residuals will have a non-standard distribution. For step four, we therefore generated Monte Carlo critical values for the Wald test under the null hypothesis of no structural breaks. Critical values for the F-tests of no breaks were approximated with 5000 Monte Carlo simulations of the equation $\ln p_t = c + \ln p_{t-1} + \varepsilon_t$, with $c = 0.1$ and $se(\varepsilon_t) = 0.1$ (the rationale behind the parametric choices being that these are the average parameters resulting from equation (1)). Note that Banerjee et al. (1992) applied a similar test procedure. However, while their test statistic is $\tilde{F}_T^{\max} \equiv \max_k \tilde{F}_T(k)$, we fixed k in the middle of the windows and used $\tilde{F}_T(k)$ instead. The resulting 90, 95 and 99 per cent critical values are 3.14, 4.32 and 8.00 respectively.

Second, we also tried to test for variations of the bond index of a specific country relative to the index of all government bonds traded in Zurich. That is, we rewrote equation (1) as $\ln p_t = \ln \bar{p}_t = \beta_0 + \beta_1 \ln p_{t-1} + \beta_2 \ln \bar{p}_{t-1} + \varepsilon_t$. Such a specification would seem to be more in line with the excess return literature frequently used in finance. We did, however, find the same breakpoints as we did with the procedure first suggested, and the size of the effects did not change dramatically (none was reversed). Since we believe that the coefficients of the specification presented in equation (1) are more easily accessible, we will proceed to present results only from this first specification.

We, of course, fully appreciate that the capital market is simultaneously influenced by a great many factors. The econometric method suggested here allows us to control only for some of them. Nevertheless, the results of our analysis are encouraging.

IDENTIFICATION OF BREAK POINTS

Germany

Steps one to three of our econometric analysis identified seven possible break points for Germany (as exhibited in Figure 13.6 showing the F-statistics), one of which did not prove to be statistically significant in the fourth stage of the estimation procedure. Table 13.1 gives a survey of resulting break points and the corresponding percentage changes in the conditional mean price index.

German government bonds experienced a strong upward surge, beginning in the summer and autumn of 1936. In July/August of that year, the conditional average index rose by more than 7 per cent. This might be attributed to the Olympic Games in Berlin, which took place in August 1936, and which made the Nazi regime look peaceful to many. Thus, for example, the French delegation used the fascist salute upon entering the stadium at the opening

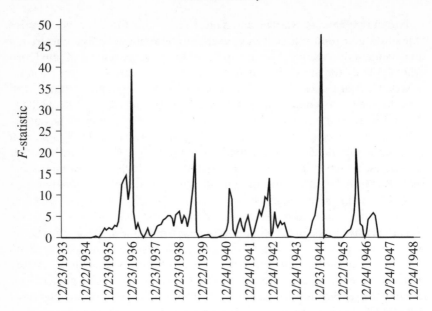

Figure 13.6   F-Tests for structural breaks in the index of government bond prices, Germany 1933–48

Table 13.1   Structural break points and corresponding events for Germany

Date	Percentage change in German bond index	Major events
July 1936	+8**	Olympic Games in Berlin
March 1939	−17**	Invasion of the Czech Republic
September 1939	−39***	Outbreak of WWII
December 1941	−5**	Pearl Harbor, entry into the war of the USA
November 1942	−7***	Russian offensive at Stalingrad
February 1945	−34***	Yalta Conference

Notes:
Column (2) is the percentage change in the conditional mean (i.e. the parameter γ_s from equation (2)).
*, ** and *** indicate statistical significance on the 90, 95 and 99 per cent confidence level, respectively.

ceremony. The market was bullish until January 1937, when it was particularly marked. This latter peak can most likely be attributed to a marked devaluation of the Swiss currency in October 1936. Since this break is not related to any event during the war, we do not consider it further (although it is statistically significant).

In mid-March 1938, the Nazis invaded the remaining parts of the Czechoslovak Republic (after the Sudetenland was handed over to them at the Munich Conference on 29 September 1938). According to many historians, it heralded the beginning of World War II. The government bond markets support this interpretation of history. The value of German government bonds fell by no less than 17 per cent. The actors in these markets thus lost even more of their confidence in the German government's capacity to service and pay back its bonds (which had already been seriously hampered before). The invasion of the Czechoslovak Republic was the first time Hitler annexed territory beyond 'German' lands, which was taken as an indication that he would not stop there and that it was likely that a great war would be initiated. However, some amount of uncertainty remained; some actors on capital markets obviously thought that the annexation of the Czech Republic satisfied Hitler's demands. Accordingly, the value of German government bonds dropped only half as much compared with when World War II 'officially' broke out in September 1939.

The formal outbreak of the war was on 1 September 1939, when German troops invaded Poland, but the stock market had been interpreting the previous actions by the Nazi government in a strongly negative way since the end of 1938. The actual start of the war saw it drop by 39 per cent. Obviously, the capital market was extremely pessimistic about the prospects of a German victory.

As already noted, the Swiss stock exchange was closed in May/June 1940 so the effects of the German *Blitzkrieg* victories are not reflected in our data, but Figure 13.1 shows clearly that the average German government bond values rose back to a level similar to that seen before the war. It is, however, worth noting that it did not rise above that level. This may be interpreted to indicate that, after the *Blitzkrieg*, peace was considered a likely prospect, with 'normal' pre-war conditions expected to resume.

The fourth structural break is identified in November/December 1941, but the decline of average bond prices is rather small (around 5 per cent). It reflects a major event during the war, namely the Japanese attack on Pearl Harbor (7 December) and the consequent declarations of war of the United States (and the United Kingdom) on Japan, and of Germany (and Italy) on the United States (8 and 11 December respectively).

Yet another significant drop in German bond values (about 7 per cent) occurred in November 1942. In that month, the Soviet army started a large counter-offensive against the German 6th army and parts of the 4th panzer army. More than 300 000 German troops were encircled at Stalingrad. The capital market considered the launching of the offensive to be more significant than the capitulation by Field Marshal Friedrich Paulus three months later (2 February 1943). The traders thus predicted the actual defeat when its first signs were visible, and not when it was consummated. There is actually a significant positive break in the index in February 1943 of about 7 per cent, which is rather sensitive to small movements of the estimation window. It may indicate that, while the German defeat was clearly discounted in the German bond values, the unexpectedly large scale capitulation of the German troops engaged was seen as improving the chances of shortening the war.

The last break point indicated by the data took place towards the end of the war, in February 1945. At the Yalta Conference, the Allied powers decided that only a complete capitulation of all German forces on all fronts would be accepted, and that Germany would be divided into three military occupation zones (at that time, France was not yet recognized as one of the world war victors). This was interpreted to be a final blow for the Nazis (more so than the formal capitulation of the German military in May 1945) and resulted in a fall of German bond prices by 34 per cent.

Austria

The econometric analysis of the Austrian government bonds identifies five dates for possible structural breaks, of which three proved to be statistically significant in the fourth step of the econometric procedure – see Figure 13.7 for the F-tests and Table 13.2 for a survey of the results.

On 13 March 1938, Hitler declared the Anschluss of Austria to Germany, now forming Grossdeutschland. The prices for Austrian government bonds fell by no less than 46 per cent in that month. A significant drop is visible from the beginning of the year, when the Nazi government prepared that event. It is worth noting that the traders on the Swiss stock exchange were not fooled by the seemingly enthusiastic support of the Anschluss in Austria at the time. Nor were they fooled by the unanimous support (more than 99 per cent of the votes) for the Anschluss in a plebiscite undertaken on 10 April of the same year. Approximately 4 453 000 of the 4 484 000 electorate voted 'yes', only 11 924 voted 'no' and 5776 spoilt their papers (Henschy, 1989).

Similar to Germany, the outbreak of the war strongly depressed the average Austrian government bond values (again minus 46 per cent in September 1939).

The capitulation of the German forces (May 1945) does not show up in the data for Austria. One reason for this might be that the future of Austria was taken to be uncertain, and traders could not clearly predict how it affected

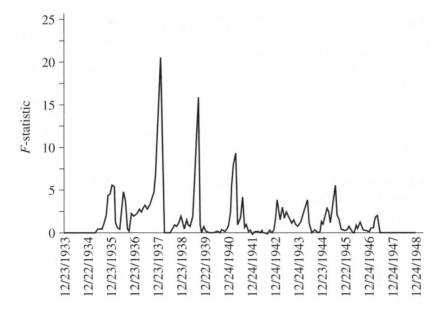

Figure 13.7   F-tests for structural breaks in the index of government bond prices, Austria 1933–48

Table 13.2   Structural break points and corresponding events for Austria

Date	Percentage change in Austrian bond index	Major events
March 1938	–46***	Annexation of Austria
September 1939	–46***	Outbreak of WWII
August 1945	+12**	Potsdam Conference

Notes: See Table 13.1.

that part of the Reich which, after all, was annexed by the Germans. This uncertainty was mitigated in August of the same year when the Potsdam Conference (15 July–2 August) settled crucial issues relevant for Austria. It was decided that Austria would re-emerge as a country of its own, which is reflected in an increase in average bond prices of 12 per cent.

France

Our procedure identifies five statistically significant break points for France, shown in Figure 13.8 and Table 13.3. The French government bond values suffered a blow when the Germans occupied the demilitarized Rheinland. The financial investors may to some extent have lost confidence in the French to successfully oppose the Nazi government's aggressive policy. The 'official' outbreak of World War II reduced its bond values further. An even stronger fall in French government bonds occurred when that country was defeated and occupied by the Germans. The invasion of the Allied troops in Normandy was greeted as a decisive sign of military and political recovery, and raised French bond values.

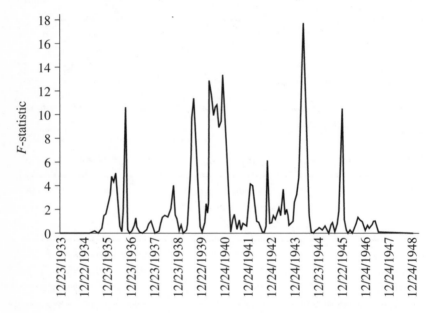

Figure 13.8   F-tests for structural breaks in the index of government bond prices, France 1933–48

The final break is most likely related to the resignation of General De Gaulle who governed France since the liberation as a quasi-dictator. With his resignation, he left France in total chaos since there was no valid constitution at that time. It seems that investors regarded his step (which is nowadays widely seen as a strategic move to put pressure on the constitutional assembly to adopt the presidential system he preferred) as further destabilizing France and therewith lowering the probability of being repaid soon.

Table 13.3   *Structural break points and corresponding events for France*

Date	Percentage change in French bond index	Major events
May 1936	–4**	German occupation of Rheinland
September 1939	–25***	Outbreak of WWII
May 1940	[–31]	German invasion of Belgium, France, Holland
June 1944	+16***	Allied invasion of Normandy
January 1946	–14***	Resignation of General De Gaulle

Notes:
See Table 13.1.
[ ] means the difference in the bond values between the day when trading was stopped and when it was resumed. For methodological reasons, it is not possible to identify such 'breaks' with the econometric techniques used.

Belgium

Our analysis identifies six break points of Belgian government bonds traded in Switzerland – these are shown in Figure 13.9 and Table 13.4. The 'official' start of the war and, to a much greater extent, its invasion by the Germans in May 1940 sent its values plummeting. The victories of the Allies at Stalingrad, on the beaches of Normandy, and the very end of the war predictably pushed up the values of the Belgian government bonds.

Switzerland

The econometric analysis reveals six dates for statistically significant break points, as summarized in Figure 13.10 and Table 13.5. The rise of Hitler to dictatorial power in spring 1933, as well as the reintroduction of the general draft in March 1935, were considered to be negative events from the point of view of investors in Swiss government bonds. The Olympic Games in August 1936 gave the Nazi government a convenient forum for making propaganda. It raised Swiss bond values in September 1936, which perhaps may be interpreted as a sign that Hitler's government was able to gain some goodwill with financial investors (as well as with many British, French and Italian politicians). In view of Switzerland's neutrality, the 'official' outbreak of the war in September 1939 increased Swiss government bond values in October 1939. It is most likely that investments were shifted into Swiss government

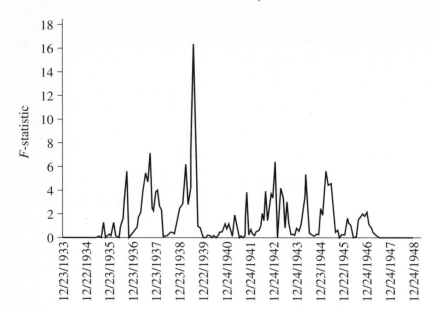

*Figure 13.9   F-tests for structural breaks in the index of government bond
prices, Belgium 1933–48*

Table 13.4   Structural break points and corresponding events for Belgium

Date	Percentage change in Belgian bond index	Major events
September 1937	−3**	Unknown
August 1939	−10***	Outbreak of WWII
May 1940	[−35]	German invasion of Belgium, France, Holland
February 1943	+10**	German capitulation in Stalingrad
June 1944	+6**	Allied invasion of Normandy
April 1945	+7**	German capitulation

Notes: See Tables 13.1 and 13.3.

bonds, which seemed to be safer than those of the four other countries
considered here (all of whose government bond values fell).

A similar reaction on the part of financial investors occurred in June 1940
when first the Benelux countries and France were invaded by German forces

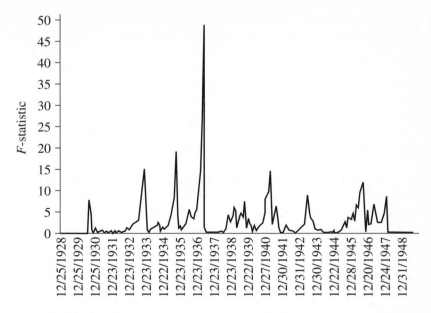

Figure 13.10   F-tests for structural breaks in the index of government bond prices, Switzerland 1928–48

Table 13.5   Structural break points and corresponding events for Switzerland

Date	Percentage change in Swiss bond index	Major events
April 1933	–4**	Nazi take-over and 'Ermächtigungsgesetz'
March 1935	–6**	Allgemeine 'Wehrpflicht' (general draft) in Germany
September 1936	+7**	Olympic Games in Berlin
October 1939	+3*	Outbreak of WWII
June 1940	+4**	German invasion of Belgium, Holland and France
June 1941	+4**	German invasion of the Soviet Union

Notes: See Table 13.1.

and then, in June 1941, the Soviet Union. In both cases, the attacks were directed at countries other than Switzerland, so that this country's position as a safe haven improved. In particular, the decision by Hitler to outflank the Maginot line in the north by moving through Belgium and the Netherlands, instead of in the south by moving through Switzerland, was a lucky event for Switzerland.

HISTORICAL FACTS AND GOVERNMENT BOND VALUES

This section analyses (1) whether and when historical 'facts' related to World War II, and generally considered to be important by historians, show up as statistically significant break points in the government bonds of the four countries under consideration; (2) the direction taken by the bond values, and how much they changed; (3) as pointed out in the introduction, it is also important to consider what historical 'facts' are not reflected as break points in government bond values.

After consulting the literature on World War II (a comprehensive overview can be found in Weinberg, 1994), we take seven 'facts' during the war to be crucial (in view of the capital market data available, we restrict our attention to the western theatre of World War II) (see Table 13.6). One of the interesting features of an analysis based on capital markets is whether the 'official' dates for the beginning (1 September 1939) and the end (7 or 9 May 1945) correspond to the evaluations of capital market participants. As World War II was, according to the opinion of virtually all historians, initiated by the Nazis, we also include seven important historical events occurring in Germany in the period before the war 'officially' broke out. In the same vein, three historical events referring to facts after the official end of WWII are included in order to test whether the 'official' end of the war on 7/9 May 1945 also marks the end, according to capital market data.

So far, we have tested for country specific threats by estimating conditional random walks and then testing for differences in the means of the bond prices for each country. The term 'conditional' must be stressed, since the procedure applied corrects for effects that influence all government bonds traded in a similar way. While this method might be useful in answering a variety of questions regarding events that affected only one country, it also means that nothing can be said about common threats. Events having the same effect on the bond prices of all countries would not be recognized by the econometric method used so far. In order to generate information on common threats for all countries considered, we applied an adapted version of the econometric procedure to the index of all government bonds traded on the Swiss exchange. The only difference between the original and the adapted version lies

Table 13.6 Important historical dates before, during and after WWII

Date	Historical 'facts'
Pre-war	
(1) January/March 1933	Nazi take-over of power in January 1933, and the 'Ermächtigungsgesetz' of March 1933, giving Hitler essentially unlimited power
(2) June/July 1934	'Röhm Putsch' whereby Hitler removed the SA as a relevant military force and re-established the Wehrmacht as the only military force
(3) March 1935	Introduction of the general draft for military service
(4) March 1936	Invasion of the Germans into the demilitarized Rheinland
(5) July/August 1936	Olympic Games in Berlin
(6) March 1938	Annexation ('Anschluss') by Germany of Austria, now forming 'Grossdeutschland'
(7) March 1939	Invasion of the remaining parts of the Czech Republic, whereby Hitler broke his formal promise given at the Munich conference that the Sudentenland was the last territorial demand of Germany
War	
(1) September 1939	'Official' outbreak of the war on 1 September, when the German forces attacked Poland
(2) May 1940	Invasion of Belgium, the Netherlands, Luxembourg and France by Germany
(3) June 1941	Invasion of the Soviet Union by the Germans
(4) December 1941	The United States joined the war following the attack of Japan on Pearl Harbor
(5) February 1943	Defeat of the German Army at Stalingrad
(6) June 1944	Invasion of the Allied forces in Normandy
(7) May 1945	Capitulation of Germany, marking the 'official' end of the war
Post-war arrangements	
(1) February 1945	Yalta Conference, where the principle of the total capitulation of Germany and its division into four occupied sectors was decided upon. This Conference took place before the capitulation, but it referred to post-war arrangements.
(2) August 1945	Potsdam Conference, where (among other issues) the rebirth of Austria as a nation was decided upon.
(3) July 1947	Marshall Plan Conferences in Paris, which were boycotted by the Soviet Union and therewith mark the 'official' beginning of the Cold War in the eyes of most historians

in the fact that we estimate pure random walks. As we do not (and cannot) correct the movements of the index of all government bonds, equation 1 now reads

$$\ln \bar{p}_t = \beta_0 + \beta_1 \ln \bar{p}_{t-1} + \varepsilon_t \tag{1'}$$

where $\bar{p}_t$ stands for the index of all government bonds traded in Zurich on date t, the βs are the parameters to be estimated and ε_t is a white noise error term. All the following steps of the procedure are adapted accordingly.

Table 13.7 takes up the 17 historical events just mentioned and indicates the statistically significant changes in the overall government bond index, as well as in the indices of two of the Axes powers (Germany, Austria), one Allied nation (France) and the one neutral country (Belgium). The table speaks for itself and it therefore suffices to concentrate on the most important aspects.

With respect to common threats (an exception is the Marshall Plan Conferences in Paris), all of the breaks are related to either prolonging or shortening the war. Events that indicate an earlier end to the war, like the Allied invasion in Normandy or, of course, the German capitulation itself, have a positive impact on bond prices. On the other hand, all events that indicated that there would be war, that the war would last longer, or that it would involve more countries than previously thought, had a negative effect on the overall bond index. Most prominently, the actual outbreak of WWII reduced bond values by more than a quarter.

Surprisingly enough, the Marshall Plan Conference in Paris, the major conference deciding on the programme to rebuild Europe, reduced the value of government bonds by more than 5 per cent. However, the conference also marks the beginning of the Cold War. The first conference of the Three Powers, taking place in Paris from 27 June to 2 July, was planned to conceptualize the proposals made by US Secretary of State Marshall in June 1947. It soon turned out that the differences between the United States and England on the one side, and the Soviet Union on the other side, could not be resolved, and the conference ended without the intended results. This failure had important consequences: the common European programme, which Marshall had in mind when making his proposals, had turned into a Western European programme with several anti-Soviet elements. The confrontation culminated as first Poland, and later on all countries under the influence of the Soviet Union, withdrew their promise to participate in the follow-up conference. The negative break in the index of all government bond prices suggests that even in 1947 the negative impact of this withdrawal, which nowadays is widely regarded as the beginning of the Cold War, was understood by the capital markets.

Table 13.7   From events during the war to break points in government bond series

	Overall %	Germany %	Austria %	Belgium %	France %	Switzerland %
Pre-war						
1. Nazi take-over, January 1933 and 'Ermächtigungsgesetz', March 1933	n.d.	n.d.	n.d.	n.d.	n.d.	-4
2. Röhm Putsch, June/July 1934						-6
3. Wehrpflicht, March 1935	-6					
4. Rheinland, March 1936					-4	
5. Olympic Games in Berlin, July/August 1936		+8				+7
6. Anschluss of Austria, March 1938			-46			
7. Invasion Czech Republic, March 1939	-8	-17				
War						
1. Outbreak of WWII, September 1939	-26	-39	-46	-10	-25	+3
2. Invasion Belgium, France, etc. May 1940*		+8		[-35]	[-31]	+4
3. Invasion Soviet Union, June 1941						+4
4. US entry into the war, December 1941	-2	-5				
5. Stalingrad, February 1943 (November 1942) (February 43)	-2	-7		+10		
6. Invasion Normandy, June 1944	+6			+6	+16	
7. Capitulation of Germany, May 1945	+4			+7		
Post-war arrangements						
1. Yalta Conference, February 1945		-37				
2. Potsdam Conference, August 1945			+12			
3. Marshall Plan Conferences July 1947	-5					

Notes:

n.d. = no data available.

* The Swiss Stock Exchange was closed 10 May through 8 July 1940 and there was no trade with French or Belgian Bonds between May 1940 and February 1941.

[ ] means the difference in the bond values between the day when trading was stopped and when it was resumed again. For methodological reasons, it is not possible to identify such 'breaks' with the econometric techniques used.

211

With respect to country specific threats, the pattern evolving from Table 13.7 resembles the one for common threats: events that are related to either prolonging or shortening the war have a significant impact on government bonds. It therefore comes as no surprise that the 'official' outbreak of World War II produced a statistically significant break point in the indices of all four countries at war. It strongly reduced the value of the government bonds on both sides of the conflict; that is, of 'Grossdeutschland' (Germany and Austria), but also of France. The bond investors thus did not 'pick a winner', but considered the war to be a threat to their assets. Neutral Belgium was also negatively affected, probably because investors thought it likely that it would be drawn into a military conflict between Germany and France, a prediction which turned out to be correct. The significant break point in bond values going with the 'official' outbreak of the war (1 September, 1939) speaks for the choice of that date as the beginning of WWII. The analysis of the capital market thus leads to the same evaluation as historical research. It is worth noting, however, that major events before that date are clearly reflected on the bond market, most importantly the German invasions of the Rheinland and of the remainder of the Czech Republic.

Several other events during the war, considered important by historians, had an important influence on the length of the war. In addition to German invasions (Rheinland, Austria, Czech Republic, Benelux, France and the Soviet Union), this also holds for two military battles generally considered decisive: Stalingrad, which marked the turning point of the war in Russia, and the invasion of Normandy, which marked the defeat of the Germans on the western front.

The end of WWII seems to be less defined by the capitulation of the military forces (it only affects Belgian bond values), but by the conferences where the fate of the defeated countries was decided (the Yalta and Potsdam Conferences).

Other historical 'facts' which are well reflected in the capital market are major changes in national sovereignty. When a nation disappears (Austria in 1938, the Czech Republic in 1939, Germany in 1945) or is occupied (Belgium and France in 1940) the respective government bond values experience a very marked drop. When a nation re-emerges (Austria in 1945), its bond values rise sharply.

POST-WAR FATE OF BOND PRICES

What happened to the bond prices after the war? Was the markets' pessimistic assessment correct that most European countries would not service their debt

Table 13.8   *Values of government bonds of four European countries traded in Switzerland after WWII*

Date	Germany	Austria	France	Belgium
December 1945	21.18	39.99	59.67	90.45
December 1947	16.72	30.40	40.41	97.97
December 1949	39.50	49.03	44.65	101.52
December 1951	48.15	64.09	73.72	99.37
December 1953	89.89	102.95	78.70	104.77
December 1955	99.84	108.54	83.89	103.85

Source: 'Monatsberichte' of the Swiss National Bank (SNB), 1948–56.

for a considerable time span, as is suggested by the very low value of the bond prices at the end of the war?

Table 13.8 depicts the value of the government bonds for the four European countries under consideration. Switzerland is not being considered because the Swiss government never stopped interest payments, and values for the Swiss government bonds remained above par almost throughout the war. The most striking feature of the post-war fate of the bond prices is that they developed very differently in the four countries. While Belgium resumed interest payments almost immediately after the war (with the effect that the Belgian bonds had already reached par by 1946), Germany, for example, ceased servicing most of its foreign debt until 1954.

Common to all countries under consideration is the fact that their post-war governments acknowledged all of the foreign debt and did eventually resume servicing it. However, none of the countries offered investors compensation for the forgone interest payments during the war.

There is a large amount of literature on when and why governments repudiate debts (for a good survey on how debts were repudiated in the 1930s, see Eichengreen and Portes, 1986). There are several models asking under what conditions regimes decide to repudiate debt run up either by earlier regimes, or in the service of aims for which they do not think their people should pay (like fighting back the Nazis). In the light of these models, it seems quite clear that those countries that relied most heavily on new foreign credits tried to resume payments as soon as possible. In our sample, this was the case especially for Belgium and (to a lesser degree) for Austria. As a consequence, Belgian government bonds already reached par in 1947, and Austrian bonds in 1951.

As is well known, Germany faced the destruction of much of its production capacity after 1945. Hyperinflation and rationing followed. While a currency reform was undertaken in 1948 to cope with the first problem, the latter could not be totally lifted until 1950. Until the currency reform in 1948, it was totally unclear whether Germany would pay off its (foreign) debt. As a consequence, the price of the German government bonds fell to as low as 15 per cent of par. It was only in 1953 that Germany signed the London, as well as the Swiss treaty, under which it began to service English and Swiss foreign debt in August 1953. Full servicing of all foreign debts was resumed in the third quarter of 1954.

In France, government debt had tripled between 1939 and 1945, while industrial production fell by 80 per cent. In order to cope with the resulting high inflation, the French government conducted a currency reform in 1946, accompanied by the introduction of heavy capital gains taxes. The result was a deep recession in 1947/48, which the French government tried to combat by heavy state interventions financed through new credits from the USA, as well as through the European Recovery Programme (ERP). The French government only resumed servicing its existing foreign debt at the end of 1949. As can be seen from Table 13.8, the actors in the financial markets nevertheless remained quite pessimistic about France's long term capacity to service its (foreign) debt until the end of 1955.

CONCLUDING REMARKS

Identifying break points in normalized values of capital market assets by econometric methods represents a so far little used avenue in historical research. The approach is useful for discussing two questions: 'Are the "facts" established in traditional historical research reflected in the capital market?' 'Can the identified breaks be reasonably related to historical "facts"?' On the basis of the empirical results for government bond values of four countries that were directly involved in World War II, we have argued that the answers to both questions reveal new insights. This approach is a complement to more traditional methods of historical research, but does not substitute for it in any way.

The approach could be extended in various directions. We have focused on the peaks of the impulses characterizing a break point, but the econometric method employed also allows us to look at the whole time distribution of the impulses. Thus, the length and form building up to the peak, as well as its aftermath, can be analysed. This, however, requires a more detailed analysis. Another extension would provide for a formal analysis of the relationship of the break points of the various countries. Another rather obvious extension would be to look at assets beyond government bonds, in particular stocks. Especially in wartime, trade in such assets may be limited to low quantities. This is the case for the stock exchange we consider in this study.

We conclude that the analysis of breaks in capital market during wartime provides a useful addition to cliometrics, which can be fruitfully extended in various directions.

SUGGESTIONS ON THE LITERATURE AND SOURCES

Historians' approach to the study of the past is for example discussed in
Handlin, Oscar et al. (1954), *The Harvard Guide to American History*, Cambridge: Harvard University Press.
Carr, Edward H. (1961), *What is History?*, London: Macmillan.
Marwick, Arthur (1970), *The Nature of History*, London: Macmillan.
Kozicki, Henry (ed.) (1993), *Developments in Modern Historiography*, New York: St Martin's Press.

The link between financial markets and historical events has been studied by
Willard, Kristen L., Timothy W. Guinnane and Harvey S. Rosen (1996), 'Turning Points in the Civil War: Views from the Greenback Market', *American Economic Review*, **86** (4), 1001–18.
Sobel, Russel S. (1998), 'Exchange Rate Evidence on the Effectiveness of United Nations Policy', *Public Choice*, **95**, 1–25.

For the 'New Economic History', see
North, Douglass C. (1977), 'The New Economic History after Twenty Years', *American Behavioral Scientist*, **21** (December), 187–200.
Goldin, Claudia (1995), 'Cliometrics and the Nobel', *Journal of Economic Perspectives*, **9** (Spring), 191–208.

The effects of marginal traders and the Hayek Hypotheses are discussed in
Smith, Vernon L. (1982), 'Markets as Economizers of Information: Experimental Examination of the "Hayek Hypothesis"', *Economic Inquiry*, **20** (2), 165–79.
Forsythe, Robert, Forrest Nelson, George R. Neumann and Jack Wright (1992), 'Anatomy of an Experimental Political Stock Market', *American Economic Review*, **82** (5), 1142–61.

The econometric estimation technique employed is based on
Perron, Pierre (1989), 'The Great Crash, the Oil Price Shock and the Unit Root Hypothesis', *Econometrica*, **57** (6), 1361–1401.
Banerjee, Anindya, Robin L. Lumsdaine and James H. Stock (1992), 'Recursive and Sequential Tests of the Unit Root and Trend Break Hypotheses: Theory and International Evidence', *Journal of Business and Economic Statistics*, **10** (3), 271–87.
Duffie, Darrell (1996), *Dynamic Asset Pricing Theory*, Princeton, NJ: Princeton University Press.
Campbell, John Y., Andrew W. Lo and Craig A. MacKinlay (1997), *The Econometrics of Financial Markets*, Princeton: Princeton University Press.

For the events during World War II see, for example,

Weinberg, Gerhard L. (1994), *A World at Arms: A Global History of World War II*, Cambridge: Cambridge University Press.

For Germany see, for example,
Bracher, Karl Dietrich (1964), *Die Auflösung der Weimarer Republik. Eine Studie zum Problem des Machtzerfalls in der Demokratie*, 4th edn, Villingen: Ring,

for Austria,
Henschy, Reg (1989), *Freedom at Midnight: Austria 1938–55: A Story of the Traumatic Years of Occupation*, Worcester: Billings and Son,

and for Switzerland
Schwab, Hubert (1948), *Der Schweizerische Effektenmarkt 1936–1946*, Zurich: University of Zurich.
Urner, Klaus (1990), *Die Schweiz muss noch geschluckt werden*, Zürich: Verlag Neue Zürcher Zeitung.
Jost, Hans-Ulrich (1998), *Politik und Wirtschaft im Krieg: die Schweiz, 1938–1948*, Zürich: Chronos.

Post-war developments are sketched in
Hardach, Gerd (1994), *Der Marshall-Plan: Auslandshilfe und Wiederaufbau in Westdeutschland 1948–1952*, München: dtv wissenschaft.
Parrish, Scott D. and Mikhail M. Narinsky (1994), *New Evidence on the Soviet Rejection of the Marshall Plan*, Washington, DC: Woodrow Wilson International Center for Scholars.

References

Adonis, Andrew and Stuart Jones (1991), 'Subsidiarity and the European Community's Constitutional Future', *Staatswissenschaft und Staatspraxis*, **2** (2), 179–96.

Akerlof, George A. (1970), 'The Market for "Lemons": Quality Uncertainty and the Market Mechanism', *Quarterly Journal of Economics*, **84**, 488–500.

Akerlof, George A. (1984), *An Economic Theorist's Book of Tales*, Cambridge: Cambridge University Press.

Argyle, Michael (1987), *The Psychology of Happiness*, London: Methuen.

Argyris, Chris (1964), *Integrating the Individual and the Organization*, New York: Wiley.

Arkes, Hal R. and Kenneth R. Hammond (eds) (1986), *Judgement and Decision Making: An Interdisciplinary Reader*, Cambridge: Cambridge University Press.

Arrow, Kenneth J., Robert S. Solow, Edward Leamer, Paul Portney, Ray Radner and Howard Schuman (1993), 'Report of the NOAA-Panel on Contingent Valuation', *Federal Register*, **58** (10), 4601–14.

Baker, Lynn A. and Robert E. Emery (1993), 'When Every Relationship Is Above Average. Perceptions and Expectations of Divorce at the Time of Marriage', *Law and Human Behavior*, **17**, 439–50.

Banerjee, Anindya, Robin L. Lumsdaine and James H. Stock (1992), 'Recursive and Sequential Tests of the Unit Root and Trend Break Hypotheses: Theory and International Evidence', *Journal of Business and Economic Statistics*, **10** (3), 271–87.

Barkema, Harry G. (1995), 'Do Job Executives Work Harder When They Are Monitored?', *Kyklos*, **48**, 19–42.

Bates, Robert H. (ed.) (1988a), *Toward a Political Economy of Development. A Rational Choice Perspective*, Berkeley: University of California Press.

Bates, Robert H. (1988b), 'Governments and Agricultural Markets in Africa', in Robert H. Bates (ed.), *Toward a Political Economy of Development. A Rational Choice Perspective*, Berkeley: University of California Press, pp. 80–130.

Baumol, William J. and Hilda Baumol (1994), 'On the Economics of Musical Composition in Mozart's Vienna', *Journal of Cultural Economics*, **18**, 171–98.

Becker, Gary S. (1971), *The Economics of Discrimination*, Chicago: Chicago University Press.

Becker, Gary S. (1976), *The Economic Approach to Human Behavior*, Chicago: Chicago University Press.

Becker, Gary S. (1981), *A Treatise on the Family*, Cambridge, MA: Harvard University Press.

Becker, Gary S. (1991), *A Treatise on the Family*, enlarged edn, Cambridge, MA: Harvard University Press.

Becker, Gary S. (1996), *Accounting for Tastes*, Cambridge, MA and London: Harvard University Press.

Bernholz, Peter (1988), 'Hyperinflation and Currency Reform in Bolivia: Studied from a General Perspective', *Journal of Theoretical and Institutional Economics*, **144** (5), 747–71.

Bernholz, Peter, Manfred E. Streit and Roland Vaubel (1998), *Political Competition, Innovation and Growth. A Historical Analysis*, New York: Springer.

Blankart, Charles B. (1992), 'Bewirken Referenden und Volksinitiativen einen Unterschied in der Politik?', *Staatswissenschaften und Staatspraxis*, **3**, 509–24.

Blaug, Mark (1980), *The Methodology of Economics. Or How Economists Explain*, Cambridge: Cambridge University Press.

Bohnet, Iris (1997), *Kooperation und Kommunikation. Eine ökonomische Analyse individueller Entscheidungen*, Tübingen: Mohr (Siebeck).

Bohnet, Iris, Bruno S. Frey and Steffen Huck (2000), 'More Order with Less Law: On Contract Enforcement, Trust and Crowding', *American Political Science Review* (forthcoming).

Bracher, Karl Dietrich (1964), *Die Auflösung der Weimarer Republik. Eine Studie zum Problem des Machtzerfalls in der Demokratie*, 4th edn, Villingen: Ring.

Brennan, Geoffrey and James M. Buchanan (1985), *The Reason of Rules. Constitutional Political Economy*, Cambridge: Cambridge University Press.

Breton, Albert (1996), *Competitive Governments. An Economic Theory of Politics and Public Choice Finance*, New York: Cambridge University Press.

Buchanan, James M. (1965), 'An Economic Theory of Clubs', *Economica*, **32** (February), 1–14.

Buchanan, James M. (1991a), *Constitutional Economics*, Oxford: Basil Blackwell.

Buchanan, James M. (1991b), 'An American Perspective on Europe's Constitutional Opportunity', *Cato Journal*, **10** (3), 619–29.

Buchanan, James M., Robert N. Tollison and Gordon Tullock (eds) (1980), *Toward a Theory of the Rent-seeking Society*, College Station, TX: Texas A&M University Press.

Buchanan, James M. and Gordon Tullock (1962), *The Calculus of Consent. Logical Foundations of Constitutional Democracy*, Ann Arbor: University of Michigan Press.

Budge, Ian (1996), *New Challenge of Direct Democracy*, Cambridge: Polity Press.

Burnheim, John (1985), *Is Democracy Possible?: The Alternative to Electoral Politics*, Cambridge: Polity Press.

Butler, David and Austin Ranney (eds) (1994), *Referendums Around the World. The Growing Use of Direct Democracy*, Washington, DC: AEI Press.

Cameron, Judy and W. David Pierce (1994), 'Reinforcement, Reward, and Intrinsic Motivation: A Meta-Analysis', *Review of Educational Research*, **64** (Fall), 363–423.

Campbell, John Y., Andrew W. Lo and Craig A. MacKinlay (1997), *The Econometrics of Financial Markets*, Princeton: Princeton University Press.

Carnes, S.A. et al. (1983), 'Incentives and Nuclear Waste Siting', *Energy Systems and Policy*, **7** (4), 324–51.

Carr, Edward H. (1961), *What is History?*, London: Macmillan.

Casella, Alessandra and Bruno S. Frey (1992), 'Federalism and Clubs: Towards an Economic Theory of Overlapping Political Jurisdictions', *European Economic Review*, **36**, 639–46.

Cassidy, John (1996), 'The Decline of Economics', *New Yorker* (2 December), 50–60.

Cate, Rodney M. and Sally A. Lloyd (1992), *Courtship*, London: Sage.

Centre for Economic Policy Research (CEPR) (1993), *Making Sense of Subsidiarity: How Much Centralization for Europe?*, London: CEPR.

Chesbrough, Henry W. and David J. Teece (1996), 'When Is Virtual Virtuous? Organizing for Innovation', *Harvard Business Review*, **74** (Jan./Feb.), 65–73.

Cialdini, Robert B. (1989), 'Social Motivations to Comply: Norms, Values and Principles', in Jeffrey A. Roth and John T. Scholz (eds), *Taxpayers Compliance*, Vol. 2, Philadelphia: University of Pennsylvania Press, pp. 200–79.

Cigno, Alessandro (1991), *Economics in the Family*, Oxford: Oxford University Press.

Cimbalo, Richard S., Virginia Faling and Patricia Mousaw (1976), 'The Course of Love: A Cross-sectional Design', *Psychological Reports*, **38**, 1292–4.

Clark, Margaret S. and Harry T. Reis (1988), 'Interpersonal Processes in Close Relationships', *Annual Review of Psychology*, **39**, 609–72.

Clower, Robert W. (1989), 'The State of Economics: Hopeless But Not

Serious?', in David Colander and A.W. Coats (eds), *The Spread of Economic Ideas*, Cambridge: Cambridge University Press.

Cohen, Lloyd (1987), 'Marriage, Divorce and Quasi Rents; or, "I gave him the best years of my life"', *Journal of Legal Studies*, **16** (June), 267–303.

Colander, David and Arjo Klamer (1987), 'The Making of an Economist', *Journal of Economic Perspectives*, **1** (2), 95–111.

Conner, Kathleen R. and Coimbatore K. Prahalad (1996), 'A Resource-based Theory of the Firm: Knowledge versus Opportunism', *Organization Science*, **7** (5), 477–501.

Cronin, Thomas E. (1989), *Direct Democracy. The Politics of Initiative, Referendum and Recall*, Cambridge, MA: Harvard University Press.

Csikszentmihalyi, Mihaly (1975), *Beyond Boredom and Anxiety*, San Francisco: Jossey-Bass.

Davis, James H., F. David Schoorman and Lex Donaldson (1997), 'Towards a Stewardship Theory of Management', *Academy of Management Review*, **22** (1), 20–47.

Dawes, Robyn M. (1988), *Rational Choice in an Uncertain World*, San Diego and New York: Harcourt Brace Jovanovich.

Dawes, Robyn M., Alphons J.C. van de Kragt and John M. Orbell (1988), 'Not Me or Thee but We: The Importance of Group Identity in Eliciting Cooperation in Dilemma Situations – Experimental Manipulations', *Acta Psychologica*, **68**, 83–97.

Dawes, Robyn M., Jeanne McTavish and Harriet Shaklee (1977), 'Behavior, Communication, and Assumptions about other People's Behavior in a Commons Dilemma Situation', *Journal of Personality and Social Psychology*, **35**, 1–11.

Deci, Edward L. (1971), 'Effects of Externally Mediated Rewards on Intrinsic Motivation', *Journal of Personality and Social Psychology*, **18** (1), 105–15.

Deci, Edward L. and Richard Flaste (1995), *Why We Do What We Do. The Dynamics of Personal Autonomy*, New York: Putnam.

Deci, Edward L., Richard Koestner and Richard M. Ryan (1999), 'A Meta-analytic Review of Experiments Examining the Effects of Extrinsic Rewards on Intrinsic Motivation', *Psychological Bulletin*, **125** (6), 627–68.

Deci, Edward L. and Richard M. Ryan (1985), *Intrinsic Motivation and Self-determination in Human Behavior*, New York: Plenum Press.

Di Tella, Rafael, Robert J. MacCulloch and Andrew J. Oswald (2001), 'Preferences over Inflation and Unemployment: Evidence from Surveys of Happiness', *American Economic Review*, forthcoming.

Diener, Ed and Shigehiro Oishi (2000), 'Money and Happiness: Income and Subjective Well-being Across Nations', in Ed Diener and Eunkook M. Suh (eds), *Subjective Well-being Across Cultures*, Cambridge, MA: MIT Press, forthcoming.

Diener, Ed, Eunkook M. Suh, Richard E. Lucas and Heidi L. Smith (1999), 'Subjective Well-being: Three Decades of Progress', *Psychological Bulletin*, **125** (2), 276–303.

Donaldson, Lex (1995), *American Anti-management Theories of Organization. A Critique of Paradigm Proliferation*, Cambridge, UK: Cambridge University Press.

Dreyer, Jacob S. and Andrew Schotter (1980), 'Power Relationships in the International Monetary Fund. The Consequences of Quota Changes', *Review of Economics and Statistics*, **62** (February), 97–106.

Drèze, Jacques (1993), 'Regions of Europe: A Feasible Status, to be Discussed', *Economic Policy*, **17**, 266–307.

Dryzek, John S. (1990), *Discursive Democracy: Politics, Policy and Political Science*, Cambridge: Cambridge University Press.

Duffie, Darrell (1996), *Dynamic Asset Pricing Theory*, Princeton, NJ: Princeton University Press.

Dunlap, Riley E. and Rodney K. Baxter (1988), *Public Reaction to Siting a High-level Nuclear Waste Repository at Hanford: A Survey of Local Area Residents*, Pullman: Washington State University.

Easterlin, Richard A. (1974), 'Does Economic Growth Improve the Human Lot? Some Empirical Evidence', in Paul A. David and Melvin W. Reder (eds), *Nations and Households in Economic Growth: Essays in Honour of Moses Abramowitz*, New York: Academic Press.

Easterlin, Richard A. (1995), 'Will Raising the Incomes of All Increase the Happiness of All?', *Journal of Economic Behavior and Organization*, **27**, 35–48.

Easterling, Douglas H. and Howard Kunreuter (1995), *The Dilemma of Siting a High-level Nuclear Waste Repository*, Boston: Kluwer.

Edwards, Sebastian (1989), *The IMF and the Developing Countries: A Critical Evaluation*, Carnegie-Rochester Conference Series on Public Policy.

Eichenberger, Reiner (1999), 'Dereguliert, liberalisiert und globalisiert die Politik. Ein politisch-ökonomischer Reformvorschlag', *Studia Philosophica*, **58**, 99–121.

Eichengreen, Barry and Richard Portes (1986), 'Debt and Default in the 1930s: Causes and Consequences', *European Economic Review*, **30** (3), 599–640.

Elster, Jon (1979), *Ulysses and the Sirens*, Cambridge: Cambridge University Press.

England, Paula and George Farkas (1986), *Households, Employment and Gender: A Social, Economic and Demographic View*, New York: Aldine de Gruyter.

European Constitutional Group (1993), *A Proposal for a European Constitution*, London: Policy Forum.

Fehr, Ernst and Georg Kirchsteiger (1994), 'Insider Power, Wage Discrimination, and Fairness', *Economic Journal*, **104**, 571–83.

Ferber, Marianne A. and Bonnie G. Birnbaum (1977), 'The New Home Economics: Retrospect and Prospects', *Journal of Consumer Research*, **4** (June), 19–29.

Forrester, Viviane (1997), *L'horreur économique*, Paris: Fayard.

Forsythe, Robert, Forrest Nelson, George R. Neumann and Jack Wright (1992), 'Anatomy of an Experimental Political Stock Market', *American Economic Review*, **82** (5), 1142–61.

Forte, Francesco and Giuseppe Eusepi (1990), 'La corte dei conti: Un "agente" alla ricerca del vero "principale"', *Giornale degli Economisti e Annali di Economia*, **49** (7–8), 315–29.

Foss, Nicholas J. (1996), 'Knowledge-based Approaches to the Theory of the Firm: Some Critical Comments', *Organization Science*, **7** (5), 470–76.

Frank, Robert H. (1985), *Choosing the Right Pond*, New York: Oxford University Press.

Frank, Robert H. (1988), *Passions with Reason. The Strategic Role of the Emotions*, New York: Norton.

Frank, Robert H. (1997), 'The Frame of Reference as a Public Good.', *Economic Journal*, **107** (445), 1832–47.

Frank, Robert H. (1999), *Luxury Fever. Why Money Fails to Satisfy in an Era of Excess*, New York: Free Press.

Frank, Robert H. and Philip J. Cook (1995), *The Winner-Take-All Society*, New York: Free Press.

Frey, Bruno S. (1983), *Democratic Economic Policy*, Oxford: Blackwell.

Frey, Bruno S. (1994a), 'Supreme Auditing Institutions: A Politico-Economic Analysis', *European Journal of Law and Economics*, **1**, 169–76.

Frey, Bruno S. (1994b), *International Political Economics*, Oxford: Blackwell.

Frey, Bruno S. (1997), *Not Just for the Money. An Economic Theory of Personal Motivation*, Cheltenham, UK and Lyme, US: Edward Elgar.

Frey, Bruno S. (1999), *Economics as a Science of Human Behaviour*, 2nd revised and extended edn, Boston and Dordrecht: Kluwer.

Frey, Bruno S. (2000), 'Was bewirkt die Volkswirtschaftslehre?', *Perspektiven der Wirtschaftspolitik*, **1** (1), 5–33.

Frey, Bruno S. and Iris Bohnet (1995), 'Institutions Affect Fairness: Experimental Investigations', *Journal of Institutional and Theoretical Economics*, **151** (June), 286–303.

Frey, Bruno S. and Reiner Eichenberger (1992), 'Behavioural Anomalies and Economics', in Bruno S. Frey, *Economics as a Science of Human Behaviour*, Boston and Dordrecht: Kluwer, pp. 171–95.

Frey, Bruno S. and Reiner Eichenberger (1999), *The New Democratic Federalism for Europe: Functional Overlapping and Competing Jurisdictions*, Cheltenham, UK and Northampton, US: Edward Elgar.

Frey, Bruno S. and Klaus Foppa (1986), 'Human Behavior: Possibilities Explain Action', *Journal of Economic Psychology*, **7**, 137–60.

Frey, Bruno S. and Beat Heggli (1999), 'An Ipsative Theory of Human Behaviour', in Bruno S. Frey, *Economics as a Science of Human Behaviour*, 2nd revised and extended edn, Boston and Dordrecht: Kluwer, pp. 195–211.

Frey, Bruno S. and Reto Jegen (2001), 'Motivation Crowding Theory: A Survey of Empirical Evidence', *Journal of Economic Surveys*, forthcoming.

Frey, Bruno S. and Friedrich Schneider (1986), 'Competing Models of International Lending Activity', *Journal of Development Economics*, **20**, 225–45.

Frey, Bruno S. and Friedrich Schneider (2001), 'Informal and Underground Economy', *International Encyclopedia of the Social and Behavioral Sciences*, forthcoming.

Frey, Bruno S. and Alois Stutzer (2000), 'Happiness, Economy and Institutions', *Economic Journal*, **110**, 918–938.

Furnham, Adrian and Alan Lewis (1986), *The Economic Mind. The Social Psychology of Economic Behaviour*, Baltimore and Brighton: Wheatsheaf Books, Harvester Press.

Gerrard, Michael B. (1994), *Whose Backyard, Whose Risk: Fear and Fairness in Toxic and Nuclear Waste Siting*, Cambridge, MA: MIT Press.

Gibbons, Robert (1998), 'Incentives in Organizations', *Journal of Economic Perspectives*, **12** (4), 115–32.

Goldin, Claudia (1995), 'Cliometrics and the Nobel', *Journal of Economic Perspectives*, **9** (Spring), 191–208.

Grant, Robert M. (1996), 'Toward a Knowledge-based Theory of the Firm', *Strategic Management Journal*, **17** (Winter Special Issue), 109–22.

Habermas, Jürgen (1987), *Die Theorie des kommunikativen Handelns*, Frankfurt a. M: Suhrkamp.

Habermas, Jürgen (1992), *Faktizität und Geltung: Beiträge zur Diskurstheorie des Rechts und des demokratischen Rechtsstaates*, Frankfurt a.M.: Suhrkamp.

Handlin, Oscar et al. (1954), *The Harvard Guide to American History*, Cambridge: Harvard University Press.

Hannan, Michael T. (1982), 'Families, Markets and Social Structures: An Essay on Becker's *A Treatise on the Family*', *Journal of Economic Literature*, **20** (March), 65–72.

Hardach, Gerd (1994), *Der Marshall-Plan: Auslandshilfe und Wiederaufbau in Westdeutschland 1948–1952*, München: dtv wissenschaft.

Harless, David W. (1989), 'More Laboratory Evidence on the Disparity between Willingness to Pay and Compensation Demanded', *Journal of Economic Behavior and Organization*, **11** (3), 359–79.

Hayek, Friedrich A. von (1960), *The Constitution of Liberty*, London: Routledge.

Heiner, Ronald A. (1983), 'The Origin of Predictable Behavior', *American Economic Review*, **73**, 560–95.

Hendrick, Susan S., Clyde Hendrick and Nancy L. Adler (1988), 'Romantic Relationships: Love, Satisfaction and Staying Together', *Journal of Personality and Social Psychology*, **54** (6), 980–8.

Henschy, Reg (1989), *Freedom at Midnight: Austria 1938–55: A Story of the Traumatic Years of Occupation*, Worcester: Billings and Son.

Herman, Fernand (Reporter) (1994), *Zweiter Bericht des Institutionellen Ausschusses über die Verfassung der Europäischen Union*, Sitzungsdokumente A3-0064/94, Europäisches Parlament.

Herzik, Eric (1993), *Nevada Statewide Telephone Poll Survey Data*, Reno: University of Nevada.

Hibbs, Douglas A. (1987), *The Political Economy of Industrial Democracies*, Cambridge, MA: Harvard University Press.

Hill, Charles T., Zick Rubin and Letitia Anne Peplau (1976), 'Breakups Before Marriage: The End of 103 Affairs', *Journal of Social Issues*, **32**, 257–68.

Hirschman, Albert O. (1970), *Exit, Voice and Loyalty*, Cambridge, MA: Harvard University Press.

Hirschman, Albert O. (1982a), *Shifting Involvements. Private Interests and Public Action*, Oxford: Martin Robertson.

Hirschman, Albert O. (1982b), 'Rival Interpretations of Market Society: Civilizing, Destructive, or Feeble?', *Journal of Economic Literature*, **20** (Dec.), 1463–84.

Hirshleifer, Jack (1985), 'The Expanding Domain of Economics', *American Economic Review*, **75** (May), 53–68.

Hogarth, Robin M. and Melvin W. Reder (eds) (1987), *Rational Choice*, Chicago: University of Chicago Press.

Homans, George C. (1961), *Social Behavior. Its Elementary Forms*, New York: Harcourt Brace Jovanovich.

Isaac, R. Mark and James M. Walker (1988), 'Communication and Free-riding Behavior: The Voluntary Contribution Mechanism', *Economic Inquiry*, **24**, 585–608.

Jones, Eric L. (1981), *The European Miracle*, Cambridge, UK: Cambridge University Press.

Jost, Hans-Ulrich (1998), *Politik und Wirtschaft im Krieg: die Schweiz, 1938–1948*, Zürich: Chronos.

Kahneman, Daniel, Ed Diener and Norbert Schwarz (1999), *Well-being: The Foundation of Hedonic Psychology*, New York: Russell Sage Foundation.

Kahneman, Daniel, Jack Knetsch, Richard Thaler (1986), 'Fairness as a Constraint on Profit Seeking: Entitlements in the Market', *American Economic Review*, **76** (Sept.), 728–41.

Kahneman, Daniel, Paul Slovic and Amos Tversky (eds) (1982), *Judgement under Uncertainty: Heuristics and Biases*, Cambridge: Cambridge University Press.

Kahneman, Daniel and Amos Tversky (1979), 'Prospect Theory: An Analysis of Decision Under Risk', *Econometrica*, **47** (2), 263–91.

Kahneman, Daniel and Amos Tversky (1984), 'Choices, Values, and Frames', *American Psychologist*, **39** (April), 341–50.

Kinder, Donald R. and D. Roderick Kiewit (1979), 'Economic Discontent and Political Behavior: The Role of Personal Grievances and Collective Judgements in Congressional Voting', *American Journal of Political Science*, **23** (3), 495–527.

Kirchgässner, Gebhard (1991), *Homo Oeconomicus: Das ökonomische Modell individuellen Verhaltens und seine Anwendung in den Wirtschafts- und Sozialwissenschaften*, Tübingen: Mohr (Siebeck).

Kirchgässner, Gebhard, Lars Feld and Marcel R. Savioz (1999), *Die direkte Demokratie: Modern, erfolgreich, entwicklungs- und exportfähig*, Basel et al.: Helbing and Lichtenhahn/ Vahlen/ Beck.

Kirchgässner, Gebhard and Werner W. Pommerehne (1996), 'Tax Harmonization and Tax Competition in the European Community: Lessons from Switzerland', *Journal of Public Economics*, **60**, 351–71.

Klöti, Ulrich et al. (1999), *Handbuch der Schweizer Politik*, Zürich: Verlag Neue Zürcher Zeitung.

Knetsch, Jack L. and J.A. Sinden (1984), 'The Persistence of Evaluation Disparities', *Quarterly Journal of Economics*, **102**, 691–5.

Kogut, Bruce and Udo Zahnder (1996), 'What Do Firms Do? Coordination, Identity, and Learning', *Organization Science*, **7**, 502–18.

Kozicki, Henry (ed.) (1993), *Developments in Modern Historiography*, New York: St Martin's Press.

Krueger, Anne O. (1992), *Economic Policy Reform in Developing Countries*, Oxford: Blackwell.

Kunreuter, Howard and Douglas Easterling (1990), 'Are Risk Benefit Tradeoffs Possible in Siting Hazardous Facilities?', *American Economic Review*, **68** (May), 64–9.

Kunreuter, Howard and Paul R. Kleindorfer (1986), 'A Sealed-bid Auction Mechanism for Siting Noxious Facilities', *American Economic Review*, **76** (May), 295–9.

Kuran, Timur (1995), *Private Truth, Public Lies: The Social Consequences of Preference Falsification*, Cambridge, MA: Harvard University Press.

Kurian, George (ed.) (1979), *Cross Cultural Perspectives of Mate-selection and Marriage*, Westport, CT and London: Greenwood Press.

Lane, Robert E. (1991), *The Market Experience*, Cambridge: Cambridge University Press.

Lane, Robert E. (2000), *The Loss of Happiness in Market Economies*, New Haven and London: Yale University Press.

Langer, Ellen J. (1975), 'The Illusion of Control', *Journal of Personality and Social Psychology*, **32**, 311–28.

Laumann, Edward O., John H. Gagnon, Robert T. Michael and Stuart Michaels (1994), *The Social Organization of Sexuality: Sexual Practices in the United States*, Chicago: The University of Chicago Press.

Lawler III, Edward E. (1990), *Strategic Pay: Aligning Organizational Strategies and Pay Systems*, San Francisco: Jossey-Bass.

Lazear, Edward (2000), 'Economic Imperialism', *Quarterly Journal of Economics*, **115** (Feb.), 99–146.

Lea, Stephen E.G., Roger M. Tarpy and Paul Webley (1987), *The Individual in the Economy. A Survey of Economic Psychology*, Cambridge: Cambridge University Press.

Ledyard, John O. (1995), 'Public Goods: A Survey of Experimental Research', in John Kagel and Alvin E. Roth (eds), *Handbook of Experimental Economics*, Princeton: Princeton University Press, pp. 111–94.

Leibenstein, Harvey (1976), *Beyond Economic Man. A New Foundation for Microeconomics*, Cambridge, MA: Harvard University Press.

Lepper, Mark R. and David Greene (eds) (1978), *The Hidden Costs of Reward: New Perspectives on Psychology of Human Motivation*, Hillsdale, NY: Erlbaum.

Leu, Robert E., Stefan Burri and Tom Priester (1997), *Lebensqualität und Armut in der Schweiz*, Bern: Haupt.

Levinger, George and O. Moles (eds) (1979), *Divorce and Separation: Context, Causes and Consequences*, New York: Basic Books.

Linder, Wolf (1999), *Schweizerische Demokratie: Institution, Prozesse, Perspektiven*, Bern/Stuttgart/Wien: Paul Haupt.

McGregor, Douglas (1960), *The Human Side of Enterprise*, New York: McGraw-Hill.

Machina, Mark J. (1987), 'Choice Under Uncertainty: Problems Solved and Unsolved', *Journal of Economic Perspectives*, **1** (1), 121–54.

Marwick, Arthur (1970), *The Nature of History*, London: Macmillan.

Mayer, Thomas (1993), *Truth versus Precision in Economics*, Aldershot, UK and Brookfield, US: Edward Elgar.

Michael, Robert T., John H. Gagnon, Edward O. Laumann and Gina Kolata (1994), *Sex in America. A Definitive Survey*, Boston: Little, Brown.

Milgrom, Paul and John Roberts (1992), *Economics, Organization and Management*, Englewood Cliffs, NJ: Prentice-Hall.

Morrison, Elizabeth Wolf and Sandra L. Robinson (1997), 'When Employees Feel Betrayed: A Model of How Psychological Contract Violation Develops', *Academy of Management Review*, **22** (1), 226–56.

Mortensen, Dale T. (1988), 'Matching: Finding a Partner for Life or Otherwise', *American Journal of Sociology*, **94**, 215–40.

Mueller, Dennis C. (1989), *Public Choice II*, 2nd edn, Cambridge: Cambridge University Press.

Mueller, Dennis C. (1995), *Constitutional Economics*, Cambridge: Cambridge University Press.

Mueller, Dennis C. (ed.) (1997), *Perspectives on Public Choice*, Cambridge: Cambridge University Press.

Nannestad, Peter and Martin Paldam (1997), 'The Grievance Asymmetry Revisited: A Micro Study of Economic Voting in Denmark, 1986–92', *European Journal of Political Economy*, **13** (1), 81–99.

Nannestad, Peter and Martin Paldam (1994), 'The VP-function: A Survey of the Literature on Vote and Popularity Functions after 25 Years', *Public Choice*, **79** (3–4), 213–45.

Nelson, Joan M. (1988), 'The Political Economy of Stabilization: Commitment, Capacity and Public Response', in Robert H. Bates (ed.), *Toward a Political Economy of Development. A Rational Choice Perspective*, Berkeley: University of California Press, pp. 80–130.

Nelson, Joan M. (ed.) (1989), *Fragile Coalitions: The Politics of Economic Adjustment*, New Brunswick: Transaction.

Nelson, Joan M. (1990), *Economic Crisis and Policy Choice*, Princeton: Princeton University Press.

Ng, Yew-Kwang (1997), 'A Case for Happiness, Cardinalism, and Interpersonal Comparability', *Economic Journal*, **107** (445), 1848–58.

Nonaka, Ikujiro and Hirotaka Takeuchi (1995), *The Knowledge-creating Company*, New York and Oxford: Oxford University Press.

North, Douglass C. (1977), 'The New Economic History after Twenty Years', *American Behavioral Scientist*, **21** (December), 187–200.

Oates, Wallace E. (1999), 'An Essay on Fiscal Federalism', *Journal of Economic Literature*, **37** (3), 1120–49.

O'Hare, Michael, Laurence Bacow and Debra Sanderson (1983), *Facility Siting and Public Opposition*, New York: Van Nostrand Reinhold.

Olson, Mancur (1965), *The Logic of Collective Action*, Cambridge, MA: Harvard University Press.

Olson, Mancur (1969), 'The Principle of "Fiscal Equivalence": The Division of Responsibilities among Different Levels of Government', *American Economic Review*, **59** (2), 479–87.

Olson, Mancur (1982), *The Rise and Decline of Nations: Economic Growth, Stagflation, and Social Rigidities*, New Haven, CT: Yale University Press.

Ostrom, Elinor (1990), *Governing the Commons: The Evolution of Institutions for Collective Action*, Cambridge: Cambridge University Press.

Ostrom, Elinor, Roy Gardner and James Walker (1994), *Rules, Games, and Common-pool Resources*, Ann Arbor: University of Michigan Press.

Ostrom, Elinor, Larry Schroeder and Susan Wynne (1993), *Institutional Incentives and Sustainable Development*, Boulder, CO: Westview Press.

O'Sullivan, Arthur (1993), 'Voluntary Auctions for Noxious Facilities: Incentives to Participate and the Efficiency of Siting Decisions', *Journal of Environmental Economics and Management*, **25**, 12–26.

Oswald, Andrew J. (1997), 'Happiness and Economic Performance', *Economic Journal*, **107** (445), 1815–31.

Pak, Hung Mo (1995), 'Effective Competition, Institutional Choice and Economic Development of Imperial China', *Kyklos*, **48**, 87–103.

Palda, Filip (1993), 'Can Repressive Regimes be Moderated through Foreign Aid?', *Public Choice*, **77** (3), 535–50.

Paldam, Martin (1987), 'Inflation and Political Instability in Eight Latin American Countries 1964–83', *Public Choice*, **52**, 143–68.

Paldam, Martin (1994), 'Political Business Cycles', in Dennis C. Mueller (ed.), *Handbook of Public Choice*, Oxford: Blackwell.

Parrish, Scott D. and Mikhail M. Narinsky (1994), *New Evidence on the Soviet Rejection of the Marshall Plan*, Washington, DC: Woodrow Wilson International Center for Scholars.

Perron, Pierre (1989), 'The Great Crash, the Oil Price Shock and the Unit Root Hypothesis', *Econometrica*, **57** (6), 1361–401.

Polanyi, Michael (1966), *The Tacit Dimension*, London: Routledge and Kegan Paul.

Pommerehne, Werner W., Friedrich Schneider, Guy Gilbert and Bruno S. Frey (1984), 'Concordia Discors: Or: What do Economists Think?', *Theory and Decision*, **16**, 251–308.

Pommerehne, Werner W. and Hannelore Weck-Hannemann (1996), 'Tax Rates, Tax Administration and Income Tax Evasion in Switzerland', *Public Choice*, **88** (1–2), 161–70.

Portney, Kent E. (1991), *Siting Hazardous Waste Treatment Facilities: The NIMBY Syndrome*, New York: Auburn House.

Posner, Richard A. (1988), *Law and Literature: A Misunderstood Relation*, Cambridge, MA: Harvard University Press.

Posner, Richard A. (1994), *Sex and Reason*, Cambridge, MA: Harvard University Press.

Prendergast, Canice (1999), 'The Provision of Incentives in Firms', *Journal of Economic Literature*, **37**, 7–63.

Quattrone, George A. and Amos Tversky (1988), 'Contrasting Rational and Psychological Analysis of Political Choice', *American Political Science Review*, **82** (3), 719–36.

Rabe, Barry G. (1994), *Beyond NIMBY: Hazardous Waste Siting in Canada and the United States*, Washington, DC: Brookings Institution.

Reder, Melvin W. (1999), *Economics. The Culture of a Controversial Science*, Chicago and London: University of Chicago Press.

Renn, Ortwin (1993), 'Public Participation in Decision Making: A Three-step Procedure', *Policy Sciences*, **26**, 189–214.

Richardson, James (1996), 'Vertical Integration and Rapid Response in Fashion Apparel', *Organization Science*, **7** (4), 400–12.

Romer, Thomas and Howard Rosenthal (1978), 'Political Resource Allocation, Controlled Agendas, and the Status Quo', *Public Choice*, **33** (4), 27–43.

Rousseau, Denise M. (1995), *Psychological Contracts in Organizations*, Thousand Oaks, CA: Sage.

Russo, Edward and Paul J.H. Schoemaker (1990), *Decision Traps: Ten Barriers to Brilliant Decision-making and How to Overcome Them*, New York: Simon and Schuster.

Sally, David (1995), 'Conversation and Cooperation in Social Dilemmas. A Meta-analysis of Experiments from 1958 to 1992', *Rationality and Society*, **7** (1), 58–92.

Samuelson, William and Richard Zeckhauser (1988), 'Status Quo Bias in Decision Making', *Journal of Risk and Uncertainty*, **1** (1), 1–53.

Schelling, Thomas C. (1980), 'The Intimate Contest for Self-command', *Public Interest*, **60** (Summer), 64–118.

Schelling, Thomas C. (1984), 'The Life You Save May Be Your Own', in Thomas C. Schelling (ed.), *Choice and Consequence. Perspectives of an Errant Economist*, Cambridge, MA and London: Harvard University Press, pp. 113–46.

Schlicht, Ekkehart (1998), *On Custom in the Economy*, Oxford: Clarendon Press.

Schneider, Friedrich (1985), *Der Einfluss der Interessengruppen auf die Wirtschaftspolitik: Eine empirische Untersuchung für die Schweiz*, Bern: Haupt.

Schneider, Friedrich (1996), 'The Design of a Minimal European Federal Union: Some Ideas Using the Public Choice Approach', in José Casas

Pardo and Friedrich Schneider (eds), *Current Issue in Public Choice*, Cheltenham, UK and Brookfield, US: Edward Elgar, pp. 203–22.

Schneider, Friedrich and Dominik Enste (2000), 'Increasing Shadow Economy All Over the World – Fiction or Reality?', *Journal of Economic Literature*, **38** (1), 77–114.

Schneider, Friedrich and Bruno S. Frey (1985), 'Economic and Political Determinants of Foreign Direct Investment', *World Politics*, **13**, 161–75.

Schneider, Friedrich and Bruno S. Frey (1988), 'Politico-economic Models of Macroeconomic Policy: A Review of the Empirical Evidence', in Thomas D. Willett (ed.), *The Political Economy of Money, Inflation and Unemployment*, Durham and London: Duke University Press, pp. 240–75.

Schoemaker, Paul J. (1982), 'The Expected Utility Model: Its Variants, Purposes, Evidence and Limitations', *Journal of Economic Literature*, **20** (June), 529–63.

Schwab, Hubert (1948), *Der Schweizerische Effektenmarkt 1936–1946*, Zurich: University of Zurich.

Scitovsky, Tibor (1976), *The Joyless Economy: An Inquiry into Human Satisfaction and Dissatisfaction*, Oxford: Oxford University Press.

Sen, Amartya K. (1970), *Collective Choice and Social Welfare*, San Francisco: Holden-Day; republished (1979), Amsterdam: North Holland.

Sen, Amartya K. (1977), 'Rational Fools: A Critique of the Behavioral Foundations of Economic Theory', *Philosophy and Public Affairs*, **6**, 317–44.

Sen, Amartya K. (1987), *On Ethics and Economics*, Oxford: Blackwell.

Shiller, Robert J. (1987), 'The Volantility of Stock Market Prices', *Science*, **235**, 33–7.

Simon, Herbert A. (1982), *Models of Bounded Rationality*, Cambridge, MA: MIT Press.

Simon, Julian L. (1998), *The Ultimate Resource*, 2nd edn, Princeton: Princeton University Press.

Smith, Vernon L. (1982), 'Markets as Economizers of Information: Experimental Examination of the "Hayek Hypothesis"', *Economic Inquiry*, **20** (2), 165–79.

Sobel, Russel S. (1998), 'Exchange Rate Evidence on the Effectiveness of United Nations Policy', *Public Choice*, **95**, 1–25.

Stern, Nicholas (1989), 'The Economics of Development: A Survey', *Economic Journal*, **99** (Sept.), 597–685.

Stutzer, Alois (1999), *Demokratieindizes für die Kantone der Schweiz*, Working Paper No. 23, Institute for Empirical Economic Research, University of Zurich.

Thaler, Richard H. (1992), *The Winner's Curse. Paradoxes and Anomalies of Economic Life*, New York: Free Press.

Thaler, Richard H. and H.M. Shefrin (1981), 'An Economic Theory of Self-control', *Journal of Political Economy*, **89** (April), 392–406.

Tiebout, Charles M. (1956), 'A Pure Theory of Local Expenditure', *Journal of Political Economy*, **64** (October), 416–24.

Tietz, Reinhard, Wulf Albers and Reinhard Selten (eds) (1986), *Bounded Rational Behavior in Experimental Games and Markets: Proceedings of the Fourth Conference on Experimental Economics*, Lecture Notes in Economics and Mathematical Systems series, New York, Berlin, London and Tokyo: Springer.

Tollison, Robert D. (1982), 'Rent Seeking: A Survey', *Kyklos*, **35** (4), 575–602.

Tullock, Gordon (1965), *The Politics of Bureaucracy*, Washington, DC: Public Affairs Press.

Tullock, Gordon (1967a), 'The Welfare Costs of Tariff, Monopolies and Theft', *Western European Journal*, **5** (June), 224–32.

Tullock, Gordon (1967b), *Towards a Mathematics of Politics*, Ann Arbor: University of Michigan Press.

Tullock, Gordon (1987), *Autocracy*, Dordrecht: Kluwer.

Tullock, Gordon (1994a), *New World of Economics: Explorations into the Human Experience*, New York: McGraw-Hill.

Tullock, Gordon (1994b), *On the Trail of Homo Economicus: Essays by Gordon Tullock*, Fairfax, VA: George Mason University Press.

Tullock, Gordon (1994c), *The New Federalist*, Vancouver: Fraser Institute.

Tversky, Amos (1972), 'Elimination by Aspects: A Theory of Choice', *Psychological Review*, **79**, 281–99.

Urner, Klaus (1990), *Die Schweiz muss noch geschluckt werden*, Zürich: Verlag Neue Zürcher Zeitung.

Van Dalen, Harry J. and Arjo Klamer (1997), 'Blood is Thicker than Water: Economists and the Tinbergen Legacy', in Peter A.G. van Bergeijk et al. (eds), *Economic Science and Practice: The Roles of Academic Economists and Policy-makers*, Cheltenham, UK and Lyme, US: Edward Elgar, pp. 60–91.

Vaubel, Roland (1995), *The Centralisation of Western Europe: The Common Market, Political Integration, and Democracy*, London: Institute of Economic Affairs.

Veenhoven, Ruut (1993), *Happiness in Nations: Subjective Appreciation of Life in 56 Nations 1946–1992*, Rotterdam: Erasmus University Press.

Vibert, Frank (1995), *Europe: A Constitution for the Millennium*, Aldershot: Dartmouth.

Von Armin, Hans Herbert (1997), *Fetter Bauch regiert nicht gern: Die politische Klasse – selbstbezogen und abgehoben*, München: Kindler.

Weber, Martin (1990), *Risikoentscheidungskalkül in der Finanzierungstheorie*, Stuttgart: C.E. Poeschel.

Weinberg, Gerhard L. (1994), *A World at Arms: A Global History of World War II*, Cambridge: Cambridge University Press.

Weingast, Barry R. (1993), 'Constitutions as Governance Structures: The Political Foundations of Secure Markets', *Journal of Institutional and Theoretical Economics (JITE)*, **149** (1), 286–311.

Weingast, Barry R. and Mark J. Moran (1983), 'Bureaucratic Discretion or Congressional Control? Regulatory Policymaking by the Federal Trade Commission', *Journal of Political Economy*, **91** (5), 765–800.

Weinstein, Neil D. (1980), 'Unrealistic Optimism About Future Life Events', *Journal of Personality and Social Psychology*, **39**, 806–20.

Willard, Kristen L., Timothy W. Guinnane and Harvey S. Rosen (1996), 'Turning Points in the Civil War: Views from the Greenback Market', *American Economic Review*, **86** (4), 1001–18.

Williamson, Oliver E. (1985), *The Economic Institutions of Capitalism. Firms, Markets, Relational Contradicting*, New York: Free Press.

Williamson, Oliver E. (1991), 'Comparative Economic Organization: The Analysis of Discrete Structural Alternatives', *Administrative Science Quarterly*, **36**, 269–96.

Williamson, Oliver E. (1996), 'Economic Organization: The Case for Candor', *Academy of Management Review*, **21**, 48–57.

Wintrobe, Ronald (1998), *The Political Economy of Dictatorship*, Cambridge: Cambridge University Press.

Index

Leibenstein, H. 53
Lewis, A. 5
lotteries 28
Lumsdaine, R.L. 196

MacCulloch, R.J. 145
managers, control of 64
markets, financial, effects of historical
    events 184–215
marriage 37–49
Marshall Plan Conference, effect on
    bond prices 210
Marwick, A. 187
McTavish, J. 105
Meade, J. 5
Milgrom, P. 89
Mill, J.S. 15
monetary compensation 61, 76–7, 80–85
monetary fines 62–3
monetary incentives 30, 60–2, 76–7,
    80–88
    see also bribery
Montesquieu 60, 149
moral costs of bribery 75–6, 82–3
motivation 14–15, 55–70, 88–98
    see also incentives
motivational transfer effect 67–8
Motorola 93

neo-classical theory of marriage 37–9,
    45
NIMBY problem (not in my backyard)
    73–4, 76, 111
nuclear waste disposal sites 73–4, 77–82

organization theory, motivation-based 89
organizational forms 93–7
Oswald, A.J. 145
other-regarding behaviour 103–12

paradoxical behaviour in marriage
    choices 37–49
pay-for-performance schemes 59–60,
    61–2, 88–9, 92
performance measurement, airline
    industry 63
Perron, P. 198
personal relationships
    increase motivation 91–2
    prevent free-riding 15

Pierce, W.D. 61
politicians' cartel 118–19, 120–28, 153
politics 10–11
    competition in 147–60
    effect on happiness 137–43
    European 147–60
    framing 27
    see also democracy; government
Portes, R. 213
price effect 53–4
price framing 27
price incentives *see* monetary incentives
price reforms 177–9
Prisoner's Dilemma game 104–7,
    113–14
Public Choice 10
public expenditure, effects of direct
    democracy 137–8
public spirit 76–85

Rational Choice Analysis 10
recession 175–6
reference point effect 26
referenda 118–32
regulatory control 63
Reis, H.T. 43
Relative Price Effect 53–4
rewards 55–65, 88–9, 92
Roberts, J. 89
Rosen, H.S. 196
Ryan, R.M. 61

Sally, D. 105
satisficing theory 41
Schelling, T.C. 52
Schlicht, E. 53
Scitovsky, T. 52
secession 150
Selten, R. 52
Sen, A.K. 52
Shaklee, H. 105
Shefrin, H.M. 52
Simon, H.A. 52
siting waste disposal facilities 73–4,
    77–82, 84
Sobel, R.S. 196
socialization 96
stabilization programmes 163–81
Stock, J.H. 196
subsidiarity 156, 157